Coursebook to accompany

MICROECONOMI

Private and Public Choice

Ninth Edition

RUSSELL S. SOBEL
West Virginia University

with the assistance of
KERI M. COWAN
West Virginia University

James D. Gwartney
FLORIDA STATE UNIVERSITY

Richard L. Stroup
MONTANA STATE UNIVERSITY

Russell S. Sobel
WEST VIRGINIA UNIVERSITY

THE DRYDEN PRESS
A DIVISION OF HARCOURT COLLEGE PUBLISHERS
Fort Worth   Philadelphia   San Diego   New York   Orlando   Austin   San Antonio
Toronto   Montreal   London   Sydney   Tokyo

Cover Image: © The Stock Market

ISBN: 0-03-025616-X

Address for Domestic Orders
The Dryden Press, 6277 Sea Harbor Drive, Orlando, FL 32887-6777
800-782-4479

Address for International Orders
International Customer Service
The Dryden Press, 6277 Sea Harbor Drive, Orlando, FL 32887-6777
407-345-3800
(fax) 407-345-4060
(e-mail) hbintl@harcourtbrace.com

Address for Editorial Correspondence
The Dryden Press, 301 Commerce Street, Suite 3700, Fort Worth, TX 76102

Web Site Address
http://www.harcourtcollege.com

Printed in the United States of America

9 0 1 2 3 4 5 6 7 8   202   9 8 7 6 5 4 3 2

The Dryden Press
Harcourt College Publishers

Preface

We are often asked why we call this book a *Coursebook* rather than a "study guide." We use this title because we feel the *Coursebook* goes well beyond the typical study guide in at least three ways:

1. *Critical Analysis.* We stress questions that require students to develop and use the economic way of thinking to come up with the answers, rather than having students passively choose between a group of prepared alternatives.

2. *Readings.* We include short, interesting readings by a broad spectrum of economists to provide a real-world context for applying the economic way of thinking to important issues.

3. *Explained Answers.* Except for the open-ended discussion questions, we include explanations of why a particular answer is correct and the alternatives incorrect.

In writing this *Coursebook,* we have attempted to strike a balance between economic reasoning and mechanics. Often a supplementary workbook is little more than a set of mechanical exercises. Such exercises lack substance and meaning for the student who has not yet acquired a firm foundation in the economic way of thinking. Our teaching experience has shown that stressing real-world situations, presenting actual data, providing selected short readings, and explaining why particular answers are correct—as we have done in the *Coursebook*—illuminate the power, and utility, of economic reasoning.

The *Coursebook* has been structured to maximize the student's comprehension of the concepts presented in each chapter of *Microeconomics: Private and Public Choice,* Ninth Edition. The first section of each chapter is composed of approximately fifteen true/false questions. Although this section has a realistic flavor, mechanics primarily are emphasized. When possible, students are tested on their ability to reject common economic fallacies or "Myths of Economics," as they are often referred to in the highlighted discussion boxes in the text. The second section of problems and projects generally contains about five problems that emphasize both mechanics and economic reasoning. The problems and projects are specifically designed to foster the economic way of thinking by guiding students through a series of smaller, logical steps when approaching each larger economic problem. The third section contains approximately twenty-five multiple-choice questions of the type familiar to most students. We have tried to maximize the usefulness of these questions in preparing students for tests by making these questions similar in wording, context, and logic to the ones available to instructors in the test bank that accompanies the book. They represent a fair mix of questions designed to test mechanics and economic thinking. Finally, each chapter contains approximately five discussion questions that are intended to provoke further speculation on economic issues.

The *Coursebook* also serves as a reader, presenting a "Perspectives in Economics" section in about half of the chapters. These articles are readable and engaging, will reinforce the classroom presentation of economic lessons, and will expand on important concepts discussed in the text. Following each selection are questions asking the student to evaluate the position of the author. Is the reasoning sound? Is it opinionated? Does empirical evidence support the author's contention? This feature of the *Coursebook* again highlights the usefulness of economics in our everyday lives.

Answers to virtually every question are provided in the "Answer Key" at the back of the *Coursebook*. The answers are followed by an explanation of why that particular answer is correct. Students who take the time to master these questions—and who understand the rationale behind each answer—should do very well in introductory economics classes.

Because of the change in authorship, this edition of the *Coursebook* contains more changes than usual. Approximately three-fourths of the questions in this ninth edition of the *Coursebook* are either entirely new or substantially revised from the previous edition. Careful attention was given to ensuring that the level of difficulty in the questions was at the appropriate level and that the questions accurately reflected the material covered in the text. The multiple-choice questions, previously divided into two sections, are now combined in a single section, and the number of articles has been reduced somewhat.

We would like to express our appreciation to Keri M. Cowan, an outstanding senior economics major from West Virginia University, whose careful and time-consuming effort have enabled such a substantial revision to the *Coursebook*. Others to whom we owe a debt of gratitude include A. H. Studenmund and Mary Hirschfeld of Occidental College for their contributions to previous editions of the *Coursebook*, Amy Ray of The Dryden Press for her dedication to all aspects of the Ninth Edition, and especially Terri and Reagan Sobel for their patience, support, and understanding.

Russell S. Sobel
James D. Gwartney
Richard L. Stroup

Harcourt Brace & Company

Contents

Making the Grade in Economics

Here are some hints that will help you to greatly improve your grade in economics.

Do your coursebook for each chapter. Students who use the coursebook generally average exam grades at least one letter grade higher than those who do not use it. The coursebook questions will likely be very similar to what will be on your exams. If you have trouble with the wording, or don't understand why the right answers are indeed right, get help. Have a friend, your instructor, or a tutor help you with the specific questions.

Learning this "economic way of thinking" is more important than being able to memorize definitions. However, being familiar with the key terms and the jargon of economics will help. These terms, with their definitions, can be found in the margins of your textbook.

When grading your answers, ask yourself, "Did I miss several questions all regarding the same idea?" The quickest way to fail an exam is to miss a key concept that accounts for several exam questions. The coursebook should enable you to find these problem spots *before* your exam, so you can correct them. Get additional help on these problem spots.

Use the coursebook to improve the effectiveness of your study time. Suppose you get all the questions on opportunity cost correct, while you miss several questions on scarcity. Additional study time should focus on learning what you missed, not on restudying what you know. The coursebook can help you figure out which is which.

Do not focus too much on the specific example. Economics is a set of ideas that can, and should, be applied consistently. The law of demand (from Chapter 3) states that as the price of a good rises, consumers will buy less of it. So what will happen if the price of *funerals* in your town rises, will the quantity of funerals purchased rise, fall or stay the same? Students often deduce that death is unavoidable, so the quantity of funerals purchased will stay the same. WRONG! The world is full of substitutes: You can buried in another town, or you could be cremated and have your ashes thrown over the ocean.

Because the specific example generally doesn't matter, a few key words generally determine the answer. Above, the key idea being tested is "a higher price causes . . ." find these key words in each question and ask what idea from the chapter is being tested. It isn't knowledge of the funeral home industry! That wasn't in the chapter.

Finally, remember what you already know from the real world. You have lived your entire life in an economy, and economic theory is meant to explain and give insights into the real world. Most students would know before ever taking economics that monopolies charge higher prices or that recessions are characterized by higher unemployment rates. Always double check the answer you get by applying economic theory against what you already know. Generally go with your first instinct on a question; students often read too much into questions when they overanalyze them.

CHAPTER 1

The Economic Approach

TRUE OR FALSE

T F

☐ ☐ 1. According to the economic guidepost that incentives matter, if there is an increase in the benefit derived from an activity, individuals will be more likely to choose that activity.

☐ ☐ 2. The opportunity cost of attending an economics class is the money spent on transportation (gasoline, parking, etc.) plus the cost of the books for the class.

☐ ☐ 3. Resources are inputs used to produce goods and services. They include human resources (such as labor), physical resources (such as capital), and natural resources (such as land).

☐ ☐ 4. The value of a good is objective; it is the same to everyone.

☐ ☐ 5. Economic activity often has secondary effects that are not initially observable.

☐ ☐ 6. Because public education is freely provided to students, it is by definition not a scarce or economic good.

☐ ☐ 7. One's time is scarce and thus must be rationed among alternative activities.

☐ ☐ 8. If you like pizza and steak equally well, economizing behavior suggests you will purchase whichever is more expensive.

☐ ☐ 9. A good is scarce if human desire for it exceeds the amount freely available from nature.

☐ ☐ 10. In economics, the term *ceteris paribus* means that everything is changing.

☐ ☐ 11. The following is a positive economic statement: "An increase in the minimum wage will increase unemployment among unskilled workers."

☐ ☐ 12. The following is a positive economic statement: "The government should increase its funding of welfare programs to help the poor."

☐ ☐ 13. The following is an example of marginal thinking: "I was going to buy a taco and a drink, but the value meal with two tacos and a drink costs only $.30 *more* and has one *additional* taco."

T F

☐ ☐ 14. Whenever two events frequently happen together, this necessarily implies that one causes the other.

☐ ☐ 15. Economics assumes people will generally make decisions with limited information because information is costly to obtain.

PROBLEMS AND PROJECTS

1. The text lists eight guideposts to the economic way of thinking. They are summarized below.
    Guidepost 1: The use of scarce resources to produce a good is always costly: "There is no such thing as a free lunch."
    Guidepost 2: Individuals choose purposefully; they will economize on the use of their resources.
    Guidepost 3: Incentives matter—choice is influenced in a predictable way by changes in economic incentives.
    Guidepost 4: Economic thinking is marginal thinking—decisions are made by comparing marginal costs and marginal benefits.
    Guidepost 5: Although information can help people make better choices, its acquisition is costly.
    Guidepost 6: Economic actions often generate secondary effects in addition to their immediate effects.
    Guidepost 7: The value of a good or service is subjective.
    Guidepost 8: The test of a theory is its ability to predict.

    Read each of the statements below and indicate in the blank space to the left of the statement the number of the guidepost that best accounts for the statement.
    ___ a. The luxury tax placed on expensive boats in 1990 was meant to increase the tax burden on the rich, but it ended up hurting many blue-collar manufacturing workers in the boat industry as they lost their jobs when boat sales fell substantially.
    ___ b. I will usually not stop to pick up a penny laying on the ground but will stop to pick up a dollar bill.
    ___ c. While I would really like to buy that $100 name-brand shirt, I will instead buy a less expensive, $30 shirt and save the $70 for something else.
    ___ d. The Food and Drug Administration should stop requiring all new drugs for AIDS be exhaustively tested for safety and effectiveness before approving their use. People who might have benefited from the drug are dying during the years required for the approval process.
    ___ e. I hate tomatoes, but my wife loves them. On the other hand, I love onions, and my wife hates them. When we go out to eat and order a salad, I give her my tomatoes and she gives me her onions.
    ___ f. Bill Gates spends hours each week caring for and growing grapes to make his own wine. That sure is some expensive wine!
    ___ g. Long ago people used to believe the earth was the center of the solar system, with the sun and the other planets orbiting around the earth. The

sun-centered solar system was originally considered a radical theory that finally gained acceptance because it better predicted the positions of the planets observed in the night sky.

_____ h. I love the beach, but because it is a six-hour drive, I don't go very often. However, each year when I visit my grandmother, I drive to the beach because she lives only one hour away.

2. Each of the following statements ignores or violates one of the eight guideposts to economic thinking (listed above in question 1). In each case, identify the guidepost and explain how it has been violated.

_____ a. Before voting in an election, each voter should learn everything possible about the issues and candidates involved.

_____ b. Reducing the prices of necessities would clearly benefit the poor. Therefore, it would help the poor if the government passed a law requiring landlords to reduce by half the rental rates for any tenant who makes less than $10,000 per year.

_____ c. Full scholarships make education free.

_____ d. Since I get the same satisfaction from reading a book, seeing a movie, or hearing a concert, there should be no reason for me to prefer one choice over the other.

_____ e. Because criminals are irrational, increasing the punishment associated with a crime will not affect the amount of the crime committed.

_____ f. Joe declares, "I'm not going to class today; I'd rather go to the beach." Sam responds, "But Joe, you are forgetting to consider the money you've already paid for tuition and books for the class."

_____ g. I'm trying to find a ticket for Saturday's sold-out game, but everyone I call wants at least $75 for their ticket. Don't these people understand that their tickets are only worth the $15 price they originally paid for them?

_____ h. Economics tries to explain the lower birth rate among educated women as being due to them having a higher opportunity cost of having children. This cannot be true because the decision to have a baby has nothing to do with economics.

3. The text discusses three common pitfalls to avoid in the economic way of thinking.
(1) Violation of the _ceteris paribus_ condition.
(2) Association is not causation.
(3) The fallacy of composition.
Indicate which pitfall applies to each of the following statements. Briefly explain each case.

_____ a. Since everyone buys a lottery ticket in hopes of winning a prize, the perfect lottery would pay back $1 to each player, making everyone a winner, instead of giving the money as only one big prize.

_____ b. The price of typewriters has fallen over the last 10 years, but less typewriters are sold today than 10 years ago. This rejects the economic theory that people buy more as the price falls.

_____ c. In the past, students who earn As in my class tend to be the ones who come up after class and ask questions. Perhaps I should require everyone to come up and ask questions to improve student grades.

Harcourt Brace & Company

4. [Note to students: The following problem relates to the addendum at the end of Chapter 1 on understanding graphs.] Exhibit 1 shows data on the relationship between gas consumption of a new Chevrolet and the number of miles traveled.

   a.   Graph the relationship between miles traveled and gas consumption in the space provided. Measure miles traveled on the horizontal axis (*x* axis) and gasoline consumption on the vertical axis (*y* axis). Label the graph clearly.

   b.   Is there a direct or inverse (that is, positive or negative) relationship between gasoline consumption and distance traveled?

   c.   What is the slope of the line? How is it related to the miles per gallon obtained in the Chevrolet (that is, how many miles can be traveled on a gallon of gas)?

EXHIBIT 1

TOTAL DISTANCE TRAVELED (MILES)	AMOUNT OF GASOLINE CONSUMED (GALLONS)
0	0
75	5
150	10
225	15
300	20
375	25
450	30

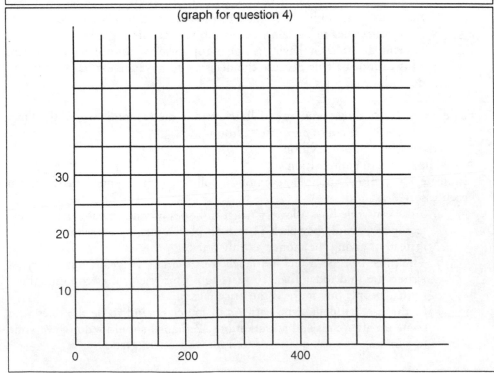

(graph for question 4)

Harcourt Brace & Company

5. [Note to students: The following problem relates to the addendum at the end of Chapter 1 on understanding graphs.] Exhibit 2 shows how the quantity of melons purchased by consumers depends on the price of melons and on average consumer income.

   a. In the space provided graph the relationship between price and quantity purchased if income is $10,000. Label this curve D_1.
   b. Are price and quantity purchased directly or inversely related to those with average incomes of $10,000 per year?
   c. Graph the relationship between price and quantity purchased if income is $15,000. Label this curve D_2.
   d. If price is fixed at 4 cents per pound, and consumer income rises from $10,000 to $15,000 per year, how much will quantity purchased change?

EXHIBIT 2

	QUANTITY PURCHASED (THOUSANDS OF TONS PER YEAR)	
PRICE	FOR AVERAGE INCOME OF	
(CENTS PER POUND)	$10,000/YEAR	$15,000/YEAR
1	900	1,100
2	800	1,000
3	700	900
4	600	800
5	500	700
6	400	600

(graph for question 5)

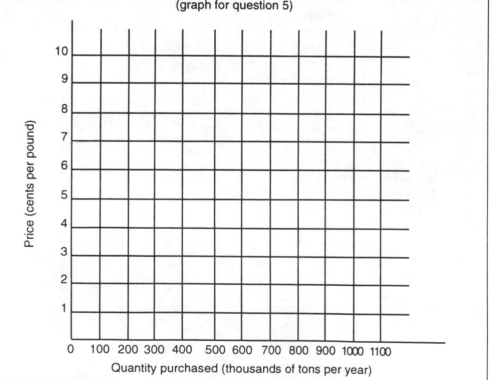

Harcourt Brace & Company

e. For a person with an income of $15,000 per year, if the price rises from 4 cents to 5 cents per pound, how much will quantity purchased change?

MULTIPLE CHOICE

1. Which of the following is true?
   a. Scarcity and poverty are basically the same thing.
   b. Poverty implies that some basic level of need has not been attained.
   c. Scarcity is the result of prices being set too high.
   d. All of the above are true.

2. Economics is the study of
   a. how individuals make choices because of scarcity.
   b. how to succeed in business.
   c. how to make money in the stock market.
   d. how the morals and values of people are formed.

3. When an economist states a good is scarce, she means that
   a. production cannot expand the availability of the good.
   b. it is rare.
   c. desire for the good exceeds the amount that is freely available from nature.
   d. people would want to purchase more of the good at any price.

4. When economists say an individual displays economizing behavior, they simply mean that the individual is
   a. making a lot of money.
   b. purchasing only those products that are cheap and of low quality.
   c. learning how to run a business more effectively.
   d. making choices to gain the maximum benefit at the least possible cost.

5. The national debt is too large. The government must stop spending so much money. This statement is
   a. a normative statement.
   b. a positive statement.
   c. a testable hypothesis.
   d. both b and c.

6. Which of the following is a guidepost to economic thinking?
   a. The value of a good can be objectively measured.
   b. Individuals should never make a decision without having complete information.
   c. Incentives matter.
   d. Goods are scarce for the poor but not for the rich.

7. Competitive behavior
   a. occurs as a reaction to scarcity.
   b. occurs only in a market system.
   c. occurs only when the government allocates goods and services.
   d. always generates waste.

8. In economics, the statement, "There is no such thing as a free lunch," refers to which of the following?
   a. Individuals must always pay personally for the lunch they consume.
   b. Production of a good requires the use of scarce resources regardless of whether it is supplied free to the consumers.
   c. Restaurant owners would never give away free lunches.
   d. All good theories are testable.

9. "If income were redistributed in favor of the poor, we would eliminate scarcity." The preceding statement is
   a. essentially correct.
   b. incorrect because shortages are always present.
   c. incorrect; it fails to recognize that poverty will be present as long as resources are scarce.
   d. incorrect; it confuses the elimination of poverty with elimination of the constraint imposed by scarcity.

10. Which of the following is *not* scarce?
    a. an individual's time
    b. air
    c. pencils
    d. automobiles

11. People make decisions at the margin. Thus, when deciding whether to purchase a second car, they would compare
    a. the total benefits expected from two cars with the costs of the two cars.
    b. the additional benefits expected from a second car with the total cost of the two cars.
    c. the dollar cost of the two cars with the potential income that the two cars will generate.
    d. the additional benefits of the second car with the additional costs of the second car.

12. The basic difference between macroeconomics and microeconomics is that
    a. macroeconomics looks at how people make choices, and microeconomics looks at why they make those choices.
    b. macroeconomics is concerned with economic policy, and microeconomics is concerned with economic theory.
    c. macroeconomics focuses on the aggregate economy, and microeconomics focuses on small components of that economy.
    d. macroeconomics is associated with the fallacy of composition, and microeconomics has little to do with the fallacy of composition.

13. The highest valued alternative that must be given up in order to choose an action is called its
    a. opportunity cost.
    b. utility.
    c. scarcity.
    d. *ceteris paribus.*

14. Which of the following actions is consistent with the basic economic postulate (the guidepost) that incentives matter?
    a. Consumers buy fewer potatoes when the price of potatoes increases.
    b. A politician votes against a pay raise for himself because most of his constituents are strongly opposed to it and would vote against him in the next election.
    c. Farmers produce less corn because corn prices have declined.
    d. All of the above.

15. If Susan bought nine gallons of gasoline at $1.50 per gallon, the car wash cost $1, but if she bought 10 gallons of gasoline, the car wash was free. Given that Susan is going to get the car wash, the marginal cost of the tenth gallon of gasoline is
    a. zero.
    b. $.50.
    c. $1.00.
    d. $1.50.

16. Positive economics differs from normative economics in that
    a. positive economics deals with how people react to changes in benefits, and normative economics deals with how people react to changes in costs.
    b. positive economic statements are testable, and normative statements are not.
    c. positive economic statements tell us what we should be doing, and normative economics tells us what we should have done.
    d. positive economic statements focus on the application of the theory, and normative economic statements are theoretical.

17. Which of the following represents a normative statement?
    a. Incentives matter.
    b. The temperature in this room is 120 degrees.
    c. It is too hot in this room.
    d. People will buy less butter at $1.50 per pound than they will at $1.00 per pound.

18. The economic way of thinking stresses that
    a. changes in personal costs and benefits will exert a predictable influence on the choices of human decision makers.
    b. only direct monetary costs matter in making decisions.
    c. if a good is provided free to an individual, its production will not consume valuable scarce resources.
    d. secondary effects are not important to consider when making decisions.

Harcourt Brace & Company

19. Which of the following is a positive economic statement?
    a. The federal minimum wage should be raised $6.50 per hour.
    b. The United States spends too much on national defense.
    c. Higher rates of investment lead to higher rates of economic growth.
    d. Economics is more interesting to study than history.

20. When economists use the term *ceteris paribus*, they indicate
    a. the causal relationship between two economic variables cannot be determined.
    b. the analysis is true for the individual but not for the economy as a whole.
    c. all other factors are assumed to be constant.
    d. their conclusions are based on normative economics rather than positive economic analysis.

21. In economics, the benefit (or satisfaction) that an individual gets from an activity is called
    a. scarcity.
    b. utility.
    c. opportunity cost.
    d. *ceteris paribus*.

DISCUSSION QUESTIONS

1. When a good is scarce, there is not enough of it freely available from nature to satisfy human desires for the good. Thus, some means of rationing the limited quantity among those who desire it is necessary. A market system allows prices to perform this rationing function. Prices simply rise until the number of people willing to buy is equal to the quantity available. Can you think of other rationing systems other than price? Contrast the secondary effects of the alternative rationing systems with price rationing.

2. List three things that are not scarce. List three things that are commonplace but still scarce. How did you decide whether an item was scarce or not?

3. "Economics is of limited relevance. Most people will not be directly involved in management or the production of material goods. They will neither put much money in the stock market. Understanding the economic approach will be of limited value to the typical student." Do you agree or disagree with this view? Be honest. Explain your reasoning.

4. "The minimum wage makes it more expensive for businesses to hire unskilled labor. As a result of the higher cost, businesses will hire fewer unskilled workers. Because unskilled workers find it harder to get jobs under a minimum wage, we should eliminate the minimum wage." Indicate the positive and normative aspects of these three statements.

5. "Under our plan, health care in the United States will now be free. No citizen will be denied medical care because of an inability to pay. The program will be funded by increasing the employer's tax on the wages of his employees."
   a. Will health care be free? If so, why? If not, who do you think will end up paying for it?
   b. Will the total amount of health care consumption rise or fall? Do you consider this change in health care consumption desirable or not? Explain.

PERSPECTIVES IN ECONOMICS

ECONOMICS IN ONE LESSON

by Henry Hazlitt

[Reprinted with permission from Henry Hazlitt, *Economics in One Lesson,* (New York: Crown, 1979) pp. 15–17 (abridged).]

Economics is haunted by more fallacies than any other study. This is no accident. The inherent difficulties of the subject would be great enough in any case, but they are multiplied a thousandfold by a factor that is insignificant in, say, physics, mathematics or medicine—the special pleading of selfish interests. While every group has certain economic interests identical with those of all groups, every group has also interests antagonistic to those of all other groups. While certain public policies would in the long run benefit everybody, other policies would benefit one group only at the expense of all other groups. The group that would benefit by such policies, having such a direct interest in them, will argue for them plausibly and persistently. It will hire the best buyable minds to devote their whole time to presenting its case. And it will finally either convince the general public that its case is sound, or so befuddle it that clear thinking on the subject becomes next to impossible.

In addition to these endless pleadings of self-interest, there is a second main factor that spawns new economic fallacies every day. This is the persistent tendency to see only the immediate effects of a given policy, or its effects only on a special group, and to neglect to inquire what the long-run effects of that policy will be not only on that special group but on all groups. It is the fallacy of overlooking secondary consequences.

In this lies the whole difference between good economics and bad. The bad economist sees only what immediately strikes the eye; the good economist also looks beyond. The bad economist sees only the direct consequences of a proposed course; the good economist looks also at the longer and indirect consequences. The bad economist sees only what the effect of a given policy has been or will be on one particular group; the good economist inquires also what the effect of the policy will be on all groups.

From this aspect, therefore, the whole of economics can be reduced to a single lesson, and that lesson can be reduced to a single sentence. The art of economics consists in looking not merely at the immediate but at the longer effects of any act or policy; it consists in tracing the consequences of that policy not merely for one group but for all groups.

DISCUSSION

1. Rephrase Hazlitt's lesson in your own words. Is it really possible to reduce the whole of economics to one sentence?

2. Which "Guideposts to Economic Thinking" corresponds to Hazlitt's lesson? Explain your choice(s).

3. Can you think of applications of Hazlitt's lesson in your own life? What are they?

Some Tools of the Economist

T F

☐ ☐ 1. The opportunity cost of washing your car is the discomfort and drudgery associated with the task.

☐ ☐ 2. Time is a component of opportunity cost.

☐ ☐ 3. For most students, the largest component of the cost of college is the opportunity cost of forgone earnings.

☐ ☐ 4. In each trade there is a winner and a loser; trade cannot make both parties better off.

☐ ☐ 5. The law of comparative advantage helps explain why fathers often have their 12-year-old sons mow the lawn even though the fathers could do it in less time.

☐ ☐ 6. Private property rights give owners a strong incentive to disregard the wishes of others when using or employing their property.

☐ ☐ 7. Property that is privately owned tends to be much better cared for and better conserved for the future, than property that is not privately owned.

☐ ☐ 8. Middlemen add to the buyer's cost without producing anything of value.

☐ ☐ 9. A country gains by importing products that are relatively expensive for them to produce, while exporting products that are relatively inexpensive for them to produce.

☐ ☐ 10. The principle of comparative advantage causes both individuals and nations to specialize in the production of those things for which they are the lowest opportunity cost producer.

☐ ☐ 11. All economies must make decisions about what to produce, how to produce it, and to whom to distribute the goods produced.

T F

☐ ☐ 12. Capitalism is the use of the political process and government planning to allocate goods and resources.

☐ ☐ 13. If an economy is operating efficiently, to produce more of one good it must produce less of another.

☐ ☐ 14. An increase in technology shifts the production possibilities curve inward.

PROBLEMS AND PROJECTS

1. Susan is a 30-year-old high-school graduate currently earning $20,000 at her job. She rents an apartment and pays for all of her own expenses (food, rent, transportation to and from work, etc.). She is considering quitting her job and enrolling in the local university to earn a college degree. The brochure for the local university gives the following table of the average cost of attending the university.

EXHIBIT 1

	PER YEAR	TOTAL FOR 4 YEARS
Tuition and fees	$2,191	$8,764
Books and supplies	$552	$2,208
Room and board	$4,434	$17,736
Transportation	$557	$2,228
Total	$7,734	$30,936

Using the economic tools of opportunity cost and the marginal way of thinking that you have learned in Chapters 1 and 2, evaluate Susan's cost of going to college relative to the table.
   a. What important component of her cost of going to college is omitted from the table? (Hint: Think of opportunity cost.)
   b. Are transportation and room and board (housing and food) really costs of going to college? Are they relevant costs in making her decision? (Hint: Use the marginal way of thinking.)
   c. Adjust the table according to your answers to a and b. What is her relevant 1-year and 4-year costs of going to college?
   d. What percent of this total cost is due to her forgone earnings?
   e. Because a person's earnings usually increase with age, can you think of a reason why people generally chose to go to college when they are younger instead of waiting?

2. The text lists the following four important factors and incentives created by private property rights.

Harcourt Brace & Company

(1) Private owners can gain from employing or using their property in ways that are beneficial to others, and they bear the opportunity cost of ignoring the wishes of others.

(2) The private owner has a strong incentive to care for and properly manage what he or she owns.

(3) The private owner has an incentive to conserve for the future if the item is expected to be worth more then.

(4) With private property rights, the property owner is accountable for damage to others through the misuse of the property. Private ownership links responsibility with the right of control.

Now read each of the statements below and indicate in the blank space to the left of the statement the number of the above feature or incentive of private property rights that best accounts for the statement.

____a. Before selling their home, most people fix it up and do needed repairs.

____b. You cause an automobile accident and must pay to repair the damage to the other automobile.

____c. When sharing an apartment with others, the common areas such as the living room and kitchen are usually not kept as clean as each person keeps their own room.

____d. John and Mary love to eat popcorn and watch movies on their VCR. However, they note that when they put the popcorn in one big bowl it gets eaten more quickly than if it is divided and each gets their own bowl of popcorn.

____e. Cows, pigs, and chicken are slaughtered in massive quantities each year for human benefit. Whales and African elephants are also killed for human benefit, but at much lower rates. However, whales and elephants are facing extinction while cows, pigs, and chicken are everywhere.

____f. People generally take better care of housing that they own than housing that they rent.

____g. Sam uses spray paint to paint his car pink and purple and puts bumper stickers all over the outside of the car. When he goes to sell it, he has trouble finding a buyer and ends up getting a much lower price than the average used value for his make and model car.

3. Bob needs to go from Atlanta to Miami. A bus ticket costs $200, and the bus takes 56 hours, while an airplane ticket costs $450 and takes 6 hours.
   a. What is the marginal cost of taking the plane? That is, how much *more* additional money does the plane ticket cost over the bus?
   b. What is the marginal benefit of taking the plane? That is, how many hours does he save over taking the bus?
   c. For 50 hours of Bob's time to be worth $250, how much must he value his time?
   d. If Bob's value of his time is $8 per hour, should he fly or take the bus?

4. Sam and Larry operate a furniture shop. They specialize in the production of tables and chairs. The data representing their respective production possibilities schedules are presented in Exhibit 2.

Harcourt Brace & Company

EXHIBIT 2

SAM'S WEEKLY PRODUCTION POSSIBILITIES		LARRY'S WEEKLY PRODUCTION POSSIBILITIES	
TABLES	CHAIRS	TABLES	CHAIRS
5	0	4	0
4	2	3	1
3	4	2	2
2	6	1	3
1	8	0	4
0	10		

a. Plot the data given in the exhibit for Larry in the graph to graphically show his production possibilities curve.

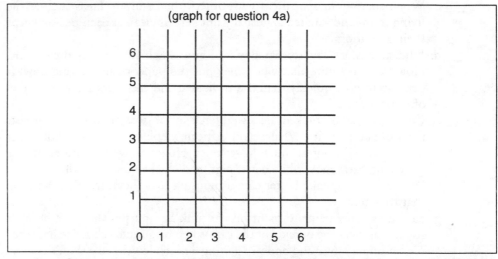

(graph for question 4a)

b. If Larry produces no tables, and instead devotes all of his time to producing chairs, how many chairs can he produce? If Larry produces one table, how many chairs can he produce with his remaining time? How many chairs did Larry have to give up to produce this one table?

c. If Sam produces no tables, and instead devotes all of his time to producing chairs, how many chairs can he produce? If Sam produces one table, how many chairs can he produce with his remaining time? How many chairs did Sam have to give up to produce this one table?

d. Who gives up the fewest chairs to produce one table (that is, who has the comparative advantage in producing tables, or equivalently, who is the lowest opportunity cost producer of tables)?

e. Using the same process as above in parts b through d, can you find both Larry's and Sam's opportunity cost of producing one *chair*? Who has the comparative advantage in producing chairs?

f. Sam currently produces 2 tables and 6 chairs, and Larry produces 1 table and 3 chairs. Total production is 3 tables and 9 chairs. Using your answers to parts d and e, allow Larry and Sam to specialize in the area of their comparative advantage and see how much they can produce in total if they specialize. Is it more or less total output than now?

5. The following questions relate to the data given in Exhibit 3 on the hours of work required to produce tons of coffee and tobacco in the U.S. and Brazil.

EXHIBIT 3		
	HOURS OF WORK REQUIRED PER TON OF	
	COFFEE	TOBACCO
United States	15	45
Brazil	25	50

   a. If it takes the U.S. 15 hours to produce a ton of coffee and 45 hours to produce a ton of tobacco, how many tons of coffee must the U.S. give up to produce one ton of tobacco? (Hint: How many tons of coffee could be produced in the same 45 hours?)
   b. How many tons of coffee must Brazil give up to produce one ton of tobacco?
   c. Which country has the lowest opportunity cost (in terms of forgone coffee) of producing tobacco?
   d. Which country has the lowest opportunity cost (in terms of forgone tobacco) of producing coffee?
   e. What implications does this have for trade between the U.S. and Brazil?

6. Exhibit 4 shows the production possibilities curve for growing wheat and corn.
   a. Are resources efficiently employed at point *A*? At point *B*? At point *D*?
   b. At point *A*, how much wheat is being produced? How much corn?

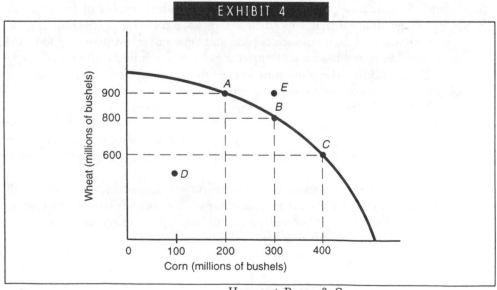

EXHIBIT 4

Harcourt Brace & Company

c. To increase corn production from *A* to *B*, how much wheat must be sacrificed? What is the opportunity cost of one bushel of corn when production moves from point *A* to *B*?

d. Can the country produce 900 million bushels of wheat and 300 million bushels of corn (the output shown at point *E*)?

7. The division of labor enhances the value that citizens contribute to an economy. Each of the five statements below is a potential answer to a question about the division of labor; read them before going on.

(1) According to the laws of physics, matter is neither created or destroyed, it is only rearranged. Manufacturing reshapes matter; distribution relocates it. Both activities, done wisely, rearrange matter in a way that increases its value.

(2) Deciding which activities to undertake and how to undertake them are risky and costly decisions.

(3) "You measure the worth of a ballplayer by how many fannies he puts in the seats." (George Steinbrenner, baseball team owner).

(4) For jobs that are not inherently pleasant, groups of workers left on their own may not accomplish much.

(5) Lots of activities generate value without being exchanged in the marketplace.

Now read each of the questions below and indicate in the blank space to the left of the question the number of the statement above that best answers the question.

____ a. How can a baseball player ever be worth over $6 million a year?

____ b. Why not buy direct more often and cut out the wasteful middleman?

____ c. Why do so many house spouses just "sit at home" instead of going out and getting a "real" job?

____ d. Why don't we encourage more labor-managed firms so we can eliminate unproductive jobs like shift leaders and supervisors?

____ e. Why does the compensation of presidents and owners of corporations often rise and fall with the profitability of their firms instead of being fixed like most salaries?

8. Exhibit 5 contains a production possibility curve, but instead of for two consumption goods as usual, it is specified in terms of a country's production of goods for current consumption (*C*) such as pizza and beer, and investment (*I*) goods such as new buildings and machines. Output is measured in millions of units.

$C^* = 3$ indicates the minimum level of the consumption good *C* that must be produced in order to avoid starving its citizens.

$I^* = 3$ indicates the amount of the investment good *I* necessary to replace capital equipment and resources that wear out each year. If investment falls short of I^*, the economy's production possibilities curve will shrink from its present position. If investment exceeds I^*, the economy's production possibilities curve will expand.

a. What will be the consumption/investment good production point(s) if the country wants to (1) grow as rapidly as possible without starving its citizens, or (2) wants to enjoy as much consumption as possible without reducing its future production capabilities?

Harcourt Brace & Company

EXHIBIT 5

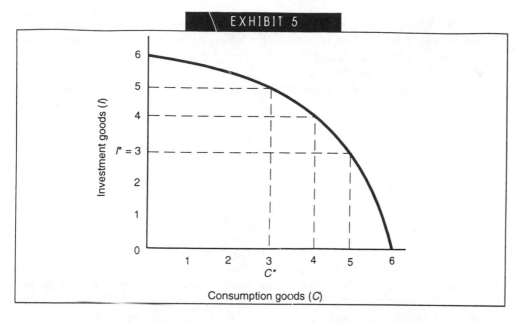

b. Circle the portion of the production possibilities curve that corresponds to all points that have both more *I* than is needed for replacement and more *C* than is required to avoid starvation.

MULTIPLE CHOICE

1. The opportunity cost to the United States of placing a man on the moon was
    a. the loss of government revenues that were allocated to the mission.
    b. the cost of all production involved in the space program.
    c. the loss of utility from the highest valued bundle of products that had to be foregone because of the moon mission.
    d. less than zero, since the long-run benefit of the project will be greater than the cost.

2. When Benjamin Franklin wrote, "Remember that time is money!" he understood
    a. the incentives created by property rights.
    b. the law of comparative advantage.
    c. the concept of opportunity cost.
    d. that watches cost money.

3. An airline ticket from Seattle to Miami costs $525. A bus ticket is $325. Traveling by plane will take 5 hours, compared with 25 hours by bus. Thus, the plane costs $200 more but saves 20 hours of time (Hint: Note how we are "thinking at the margin" here by looking at the changes). Other things constant, an individual will gain by choosing air travel if, and only if, each hour of her time is valued at more than
    a. $10 per hour.
    b. $13 per hour.
    c. $20 per hour.
    d. $105 per hour.

4. Which of the following best describes the implications of the law of comparative advantage? If each person sells goods for which he or she has the greatest comparative advantage in production and buys those for which his or her comparative advantage is least, the
   a. total output available to each person can be expanded by specialization and exchange.
   b. total output will fall.
   c. buyers of goods will gain at the expense of sellers.
   d. sellers of goods will gain at the expense of buyers.

5. Keri decided to sleep in today rather than attend her 9 A.M. economics class. According to economic analysis, her choice was
   a. irrational, because economic analysis suggests you should always attend classes that you have already paid for.
   b. irrational, because oversleeping is not in Keri's self-interest.
   c. rational if Keri has not missed any other classes.
   d. rational if Keri values sleep more highly than the benefit she expects to receive from attending the class.

6. Which of the following is *not* one of the basic economic questions that all economies must answer?
   a. What will be produced?
   b. To whom will the goods produced be allocated?
   c. How will goods be produced?
   d. Which government agency will set the prices of the goods produced?

7. The owners of private property will
   a. use their property for selfish ends, taking no account of the impact their behavior has on others.
   b. use their property in ways that others value because the market will generally reward them with profits (or a higher selling price) if they do so.
   c. find very little incentive to take care of the property or conserve it for the future.
   d. lose profits when they take the wishes of others into consideration.

8. Ken values his boat at $5,000, and Monica values it at $8,000. If Monica buys it from Ken for $7,000, which of the following is true?
   a. Ken gains $2,000 of value, and Monica gains $1,000 of value.
   b. Ken gains $7,000 of value, and Monica loses $7,000 of value.
   c. Ken gains $7,000 of value, and Monica gains $3,000 of value.
   d. Ken and Monica both gain $7,000 of value.

9. When collective decision making (the political process) is used to resolve economic questions regarding the allocation of resources,
   a. decentralized decision making is present.
   b. central planning and political bargaining will replace market forces.
   c. individual preferences are of no importance.
   d. economic equality will result.

Harcourt Brace & Company

10. The law of comparative advantage suggests that
    a. individuals, states, and nations can all benefit if they trade with others.
    b. free trade among nations is harmful to an economy.
    c. each economy should strive to be self-sufficient.
    d. each country should attempt to produce roughly equal amounts of all goods.

11. When resources are being used wastefully or inefficiently,
    a. the production possibilities curve shifts inward.
    b. the production possibilities curve shifts outward.
    c. the economy is operating at a point inside its production possibilities constraint.
    d. the economy is operating at a point outside its production possibilities constraint.

12. Which of the following is a transaction cost?
    a. price of a ticket to a concert
    b. price of food eaten before a concert
    c. time spent standing in line to buy the ticket
    d. price of a T-shirt at the concert

13. Middlemen, such as grocers, stockbrokers, and Realtors
    a. specialize in reducing transactions costs.
    b. provide nothing of value to either the buyer or the seller.
    c. have no effect on economic output in society.
    d. do not exist in capitalist economies.

14. Private property rights exist when property rights are
    a. exclusively controlled by the owner or owners.
    b. transferable to others.
    c. protected by legal enforcement.
    d. all of the above.

15. When an economy is operating efficiently, the production of more of one good will result in the production of less of some other good because
    a. consumers do not want more of both goods.
    b. resources are limited (scarce) and efficiency implies that all are already in use.
    c. the production possibilities curve shifts inward as more of one good is produced.
    d. technological improvement can only improve the production of a single good.

16. Which of the following would allow the production possibilities curve for an economy to shift outward?
    a. a better social organization of economic activity, such as conversion from socialism to capitalism
    b. a decrease in unemployment and/or a reduction in the number of factories that are not utilized
    c. more investment leading to better technology and more innovation
    d. all of the above

Harcourt Brace & Company

17. "If I didn't have a date tonight, I would save $10 and spend the evening playing tennis." The opportunity cost of the date is
    a. the other things that could be purchased with the $10.
    b. the other things that could be purchased with the $10 plus the forgone value of a night of tennis.
    c. dependent upon how pleasant a time one has on the date.
    d. the forgone value of a night of tennis.

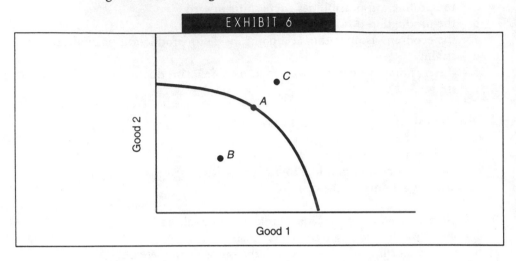

EXHIBIT 6

18. Use Exhibit 6 to answer the following question: In the above figure showing the production possibilities curve,
    a. A is efficient.
    b. B is inefficient.
    c. C is unattainable.
    d. all of the above are true.

19. Dr. Jones, a dentist, is choosing between driving and flying from Pittsburgh to New York City. If Jones drove, she would have to close her office four hours earlier than if she flew by airplane. Her expected income (after taxes) from her practice is $50 per hour. Assuming all other factors are equal, if Jones was a rational decision maker, she would drive if the price differential (air cost minus driving) was greater than
    a. $50.
    b. $100.
    c. $150.
    d. $200.

20. According to the law of comparative advantage,
    a. each producer should strive toward self sufficiency in order to maximize the total production of the economy.
    b. each product should be produced by the lowest opportunity cost producer in order to maximize output.
    c. one should never compare one's abilities with those of another.
    d. each product should be produced by the individual who can produce more of that product than any other individual.

Harcourt Brace & Company

21. "The economic wealth of this country was built primarily by some individuals profiting from a transaction, whereas others were harmed by that transaction." This statement indicates the person
    a. fails to comprehend the idea that all voluntary trades benefit both parties involved.
    b. fails to comprehend the fallacy of composition.
    c. fails to understand the significance of the production possibilities curve.
    d. uses the economic way of thinking. The statement is essentially correct.

22. Your favorite local bar increases its cover charge from $3 to $10. (I) You go speak to the manager and tell her how upset you are. (II) You decide to start going to a different bar instead.
    a. I is an example of the voice option; II is an example of the exit option.
    b. I is an example of the exit option; II is an example of the voice option.
    c. Both I and II are examples of the exit option.
    d. Both I and II are examples of the voice option.

23. Your local government increases its property tax rate from 3 percent to 10 percent. (I) You write letters to your local politicians and speak out at public meetings about how upset you are. (II) You decide to move to another city (or at least buy a home outside city limits).
    a. I is an example of the voice option; II is an example of the exit option.
    b. I is an example of the exit option; II is an example of the voice option.
    c. Both I and II are examples of the exit option.
    d. Both I and II are examples of the voice option.

DISCUSSION QUESTIONS

1. As an individual, you will ultimately take part in determining how your economy answers its three basic economic decisions. What will help you choose what *you* should produce, how *you* should produce it, and *for whom* you should produce it? Are these answers at all interrelated?

2. Consider the cost of this economics course to you.
    a. About how much money did you spend on tuition and books for this course? When did you incur these costs?
    b. What is the cost of actually attending the class once you've paid your tuition and purchased your books?
    c. Use your answer to part b to comment on the following quote: "I could earn $15 if I worked during today's economics class, but tuition averages out to $20 per lecture, so I can't afford to go. If only I went to a university where tuition is lower, I could skip class and earn the money." Do you agree or disagree? Explain your answer.

3. Explain why it is often efficient for faculty members with training in computer programming to hire student programmers to do their computer work.

Harcourt Brace & Company

4. Consider the following quote by a medical doctor who knows something about economics: "It doesn't make sense for me to care for my own lawn when my opportunity cost is $80 per hour."
    a. Do you agree with the doctor's view? Explain.
    b. Would you be surprised to find this doctor's lawn exquisitely maintained? Explain.

5. When the Khmer Rouge came to power in Cambodia in 1975, they sought to eliminate the evils of money. One part of their strategy was to eliminate those jobs that dealt primarily in money rather than the production of goods and services. In other words, they got rid of the "middlemen." What would happen to an economy that had no middlemen? What would happen to the standard of living of the average consumer? Explain.

PERSPECTIVES IN ECONOMICS

UNFAIR COMPETITION WITH THE SUN

By Frederic Bastiat

[From Frederic Bastiat, "Petition of the Manufacturers of Candles, Wax-Lights, Lamps, Candlesticks, Street Lamps, Snuffers, Extinguishers, and of the Producers of Oil, Tallow, Resin, Alcohol, and Generally, of Everything Connected with Lighting." To messieurs the members of the Chamber of Deputies.]

Gentlemen,—You are on the right road. You reject abstract theories, and have little consideration for cheapness and plenty. Your chief care is the interest of the producer. You desire to protect him from foreign competition, and reserve the *national market for national industry.*

We are suffering from the intolerable competition of a foreign rival, placed, it would seem, in a condition so far superior to ours for the production of light that he absolutely *inundates* our *national market* with it at a price fabulously reduced. The moment he shows himself our trade leaves us—all consumers apply to him; and a branch of native industry, having countless ramifications, is all at once rendered completely stagnant. This rival, who is no other than the sun, wages war to the knife against us, and we suspect that he has been raised up by *perfidious Albion* (a good policy as times go); inasmuch as he displays towards that haughty island a circumspection with which he dispenses in our case.

What we pray for is, that it may please you to pass a law ordering the shutting up of all windows, skylights, dormer-windows, outside and inside shutters, curtains, blinds, bull's-eyes, in a word, of all openings, holes, chinks, clefts, and fissures, by or through which the light of the sun has been in use to enter houses, to the prejudice of the meritorious manufactures with which we flatter ourselves we have accommodated our country—a country, which, in gratitude, ought not abandon us now to a strife so unequal.

We trust, Gentlemen, that you will not regard this our request as a satire, or refuse it without at least previously hearing the reasons which we have to urge in its support.

And, first, if you shut up as much as possible all access to natural light, and create a demand for artificial light, which of our French manufacturers will not be encouraged by it?

We foresee your objections, Gentlemen, but we know that you can oppose to us none but such as you have picked up from the effete works of the partisans of Free Trade. We defy you to utter a single word against us which will not instantly rebound against yourselves and your entire policy.

You will tell us that, if we gain by the protection which we seek, the country will lose by it, because the consumer must bear the loss.

We answer:

You have ceased to have any right to invoke the interest of the consumer for, whenever his interest is found opposed to that of the producer, you sacrifice the latter. You have done so for the purpose of encouraging workers and those who seek employment. For the same reason you should do so again.

You have yourselves obviated this objection. When you are told that the consumer is interested in the free importation of iron, coal, corn, textile fabrics—yes, you reply, but the producer is interested in their exclusion. Well, be it so; if consumers are interested in the free admission of natural light, the producers of artificial light are equally interested in its prohibition.

If you urge that the light of the sun is a gratuitous gift of nature, and that to reject such gifts is to reject wealth itself under pretense of encouraging the means of acquiring it, we would caution you against giving a death-blow to your own policy. Remember that hitherto you have always repelled foreign products, *because* they approximate more nearly than home products to the character of gratuitous gifts.

Nature and human labour cooperate in various proportions (depending on countries and climates) in the production of commodities. The part which nature executes is very gratuitous; it is the part executed by human labour which constitutes value, and is paid for.

If a Lisbon orange sells for half the price of a Paris orange, it is because natural, and consequently gratuitous, heat does for the one what artificial, and therefore expensive, heat must do for the other.

When an orange comes to us from Portugal we may conclude that it is furnished in part gratuitously, in part for an onerous consideration; in other words, it comes to us at *half-price* as compared with those of Paris.

Now, it is precisely the gratuitous *half* (pardon the word) which we contend should be excluded. You say, How can national labour sustain competition with foreign labour, when the former has all the work to do, and the latter only does one-half, the sun supplying the remainder. But if this *half*, being gratuitous, determines you to exclude competition, how should the *whole*, being gratuitous, induce you to admit competition? If you were consistent, you would, while excluding as hurtful to native industry what is half gratuitous, exclude a *fortiori* and with double zeal, that which is altogether gratuitous.

One more, when products such as coal, iron, corn, or textile fabrics are sent us from abroad, and we can acquire them with less labour than if we made them ourselves, the difference is a free gift conferred upon us. The gift is more or less considerable in proportion as the difference is more or less great. It amounts to a quarter, a half, or three-quarters of the value of the product, when the foreigner only asks us for three-fourths, a half or a quarter of the price we should otherwise pay. It is as perfect and complete as it can be, when the donor (like the sun is furnishing us with light) asks us for nothing. The question, and we ask it formally, is this: Do you desire for our country the benefit of gratuitous consumption, or the pretended advantages of onerous production?

Make your choice, but be logical; for as long as you exclude as you do, coal, iron, corn, foreign fabrics, in proportion as their price approximates to zero what inconsistency it would be to admit the light of the sun, the price of which is already at zero during the entire day!

DISCUSSION

1. What does the Bastiat reading have to do with this chapter? [*Hint:* The text states that the law of comparative advantage applies to nations as well as to individuals.] Does comparative advantage mean that *all* trade is good? Explain your answer.

2. Do you think that individuals or industries ever need protection from competition? If so, how would we decide whether an industry (like the lighting industry or the automobile industry) deserves to be protected from competition?

3. What economic arguments can you use to argue against the proposal?

CHAPTER 3

Supply, Demand, and the Market Process

TRUE OR FALSE

T F

☐ ☐ 1. Consumers will purchase fewer tacos at higher prices than at lower prices if other factors remain the same.

☐ ☐ 2. If the price of bananas increased, the demand for substitutes such as oranges and apples would increase.

☐ ☐ 3. The law of supply reflects the willingness of producers to expand output in response to an increase in the price of a product.

☐ ☐ 4. When consumer purchases of a good are highly responsive to a change in the price of a good, the demand for that good is said to be relatively inelastic.

☐ ☐ 5. An increase in demand for coffee would cause its price to rise and producers to expand output.

☐ ☐ 6. A reduction in the supply of beef would cause the price of beef to fall.

☐ ☐ 7. Hamburgers and hot dogs would be considered substitutes, while peanut butter and jelly would be considered compliments.

☐ ☐ 8. If Terri would be willing to pay up to $50 for a pair of jeans and finds them for $30, her purchase would give her $20 in consumer surplus.

☐ ☐ 9. If an increase in the price of pizza resulted in fewer pizzas being sold, this would be considered a reduction in quantity demanded, not a reduction in demand.

☐ ☐ 10. Three factors that will each cause the supply curve for Napa county wine to shift to the left include a drought in Napa county, higher wages for Napa county grape pickers, and lower prices for Napa county wine.

☐ ☐ 11. If an increase in the cost of lumber resulted in fewer new homes being produced, this would be considered a reduction in quantity supplied, not a reduction in supply.

☐ ☐ 12. An increase in the price of lumber used in the construction industry would cause housing prices to rise and the demand for housing to decline.

☐ ☐ 13. An increase in consumer income would cause the demand for new cars to increase.

☐ ☐ 14. Government regulation is the only way to coordinate economic activity in complex societies like the U.S. with millions of individuals buying and selling goods and services.

Harcourt Brace & Company

PROBLEMS AND PROJECTS

1. Exhibit 1 presents hypothetical supply and demand schedules for shoes in a local market area.
   a. Graph the initial demand curve (column 2) on the chart below.
   b. Graph the initial supply curve (column 3) on the chart below.
   c. What is the initial equilibrium price?
   d. The region experiences a boom and consumer income increases, causing an increase in demand. The new demand schedule is indicated in column 4. Graph the new demand curve in the chart.
   e. What is the new equilibrium price?

EXHIBIT 1

PRICE (1)	INITIAL QUANTITY DEMANDED (2)	QUANTITY SUPPLIED (3)	NEW QUANTITY DEMANDED (4)
$ 6	60	20	80
9	50	30	70
12	40	40	60
15	30	50	50
18	20	60	40
21	10	70	30

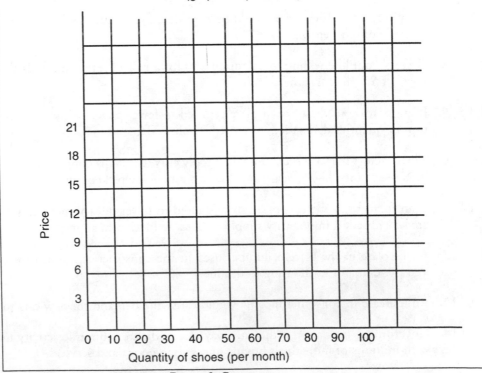

(graph for question 1)

Harcourt Brace & Company

f.   What has happened on the demand side of the market? Is it a change in demand or a change in quantity demanded?

g.   What has happened on the supply side of the market? Is it a change in supply or a change in quantity supplied?

2.   As indicated by Exhibit 2, the initial demand for hot dogs is D_1. The supply is S.

a.   What is the initial equilibrium price? Quantity sold?

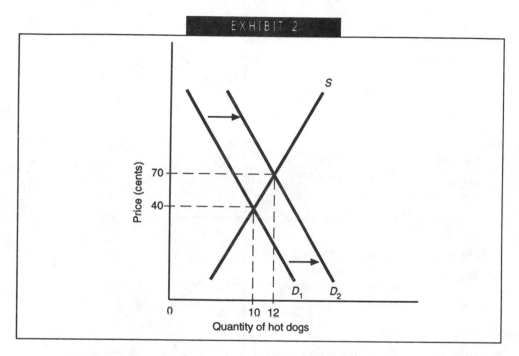

EXHIBIT 2

b.   Hamburgers are a substitute for hot dogs. Higher hamburger prices cause the demand for hot dogs to increase to D_2. What is the new equilibrium price? Quantity sold?

c.   Suppose instead of hamburger prices rising, hot dog *bun* prices have fallen instead. Would the impact of the lower hot dog bun prices on the market for hot dogs be the same?

3.   The pricing system sends out signals that influence the decisions of producers and consumers. Understanding the secondary effects of a change in market conditions is essential if one is to understand how a market system works. Suppose that the price of gasoline rose sharply, what do you think would happen to

a.   the demand for smaller, more fuel efficient cars relative to large cars?

b.   the demand for other leisure goods (such as home swimming pools), relative to cross-country driving vacations?

c.   employment in the tourism industry?

d.   the prices of consumer goods that require transportation?

e.   the demand for alternative energy sources (such as solar power) and the incentive to produce them?

f.   the incentive to find and develop new oil reserves to produce gasoline?

g.   the price of electricity, firewood, and other substitute fuels?

Harcourt Brace & Company

4. Use the diagrams below to indicate the changes in demand (D), supply (S), equilibrium price (P), and equilibrium quantity (Q) in response to the events described to the left of the diagrams. First show in the diagrams how supply and/or demand shift in response to the event, and then fill in the table to the right of the diagrams using a plus sign (+) to indicate an increase, a negative sign (–) to indicate a decrease, and 0 to indicate no change. As an example, the first question has been answered.

Market	Event	Diagrams	D	S	P	Q
a. Automobiles	The wages of autoworkers increases.		0	–	+	–
b. Oranges	Frost destroys half the Florida orange crop.		—	—	—	—
c. Butter	There is a decrease in the price of margarine (a subsitute for butter)		—	—	—	—
d. Lumber	Lower interest rates cause a housing construction boom.		—	—	—	—
e. Wine	A technological advance lowers the cost of growing grapes		—	—	—	—

5. Exhibit 3 illustrates two different demand curves with different slopes, D_1 and D_2.
    a. If the price rises from \$5 to \$15, by how much will consumer purchases fall if the demand curve is given by D_1?
    b. If the price rises from \$5 to \$15, by how much will consumer purchases fall if the demand curve is instead given by D_2?
    c. Which of the demand curves represents consumers being more responsive in their purchases to a change in the price of the good?
    d. Which of the demand curves would be considered relatively elastic? Which would be considered relatively inelastic?

Harcourt Brace & Company

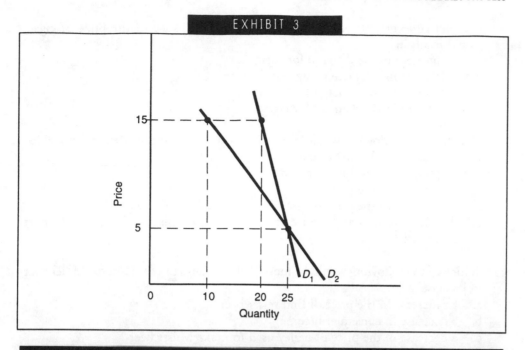

EXHIBIT 3

MULTIPLE CHOICE

1. If the price of tickets to the World Series were set below the equilibrium price,
   a. the quantity demanded would be smaller than the quantity supplied.
   b. the demand for World Series tickets would be highly responsive to the price.
   c. there would be no transactions between buyers and sellers of the tickets.
   d. the number of persons seeking to obtain tickets to World Series games would be greater than the number of tickets available.

2. Which of the following would cause the price of automobiles to rise?
   a. a decrease in the wages of autoworkers
   b. a reduction in the price of bus travel
   c. an increase in the price of gasoline
   d. an increase in consumer income

3. Which of the following would be the best example of consumer surplus?
   a. Jane pays $30 a month for phone service even though it is worth $70 to her.
   b. Sam refuses to pay $10 for a haircut because it is only worth $8 to him.
   c. Fred buys a car for $4,000, the maximum amount that he would be willing . to pay for it.
   d. When Sue purchases a candy bar for $.50, she uses a $20 bill to pay for it.

4. If cigars and cigarettes are substitute goods, an increase in the price of cigars would result in
   a. an increase in the demand for cigarettes.
   b. a decrease in the price of cigarettes.
   c. a decrease in the demand for cigarettes.
   d. a decrease in the demand for cigars.

5. Which of the following would most likely cause the current demand for video cassette recorders (VCRs) to fall?
   a. an increase in consumer income
   b. an increase in the price of VCRs
   c. an increase in the price of laser disc players, a substitute good
   d. the expectation that the price of VCRs will decrease sharply during the next six months

6. Which of the following would be most likely to cause the demand for Miller beer to increase?
   a. an increase in the price of Budweiser beer
   b. a decrease in consumer income
   c. a decrease in the price of barley used to make Miller beer
   d. a decrease in the price of Miller beer

7. (I) The height of the demand curve for a commodity indicates the maximum amount the consumer would be willing to pay for each unit of the good. (II) The height of the supply curve for a commodity indicates the minimum price the seller would accept for each unit of the good.
   a. I is true; II is false.
   b. I is false; II is true.
   c. Both I and II are false.
   d. Both I and II are true.

8. All things constant, a decrease in bus, train, and airplane fares will
   a. shift the demand curve for automobiles to the left.
   b. cause a movement along the demand curve for automobiles.
   c. shift the demand curve for automobiles to the right.
   d. have no impact on the demand curve for automobiles.

9. If coffee and cream are complements, a decrease in the price of coffee will cause
   a. the demand for cream to decrease.
   b. the demand for cream to increase.
   c. the demand for coffee to increase.
   d. no change in the demand for cream; only quantity demanded would be affected.

10. If the market price is above the equilibrium price, there will be a tendency for price to decrease, causing
    a. the quantity demanded to decrease and the quantity supplied to increase until they are equal.
    b. the quantity demanded to increase and the quantity supplied to decrease until they are equal.
    c. both quantity demanded and quantity supplied to decrease until they are equal.
    d. both quantity demanded and quantity supplied to increase until they are equal.

11. According to the law of supply, as the price of a good decreases
    a. buyers will buy more of the good.
    b. sellers will produce more of the good.
    c. buyers will buy less of the good.
    d. sellers will produce less of the good.

12. John advertises his used car for $3,000 in the newspaper. He would be willing to sell his used car for as low as $2,000. He is offered $2,600 for it from a buyer and accepts it. In this trade, John receives
    a. producer surplus of $3,000.
    b. producer surplus of $2,600.
    c. producer surplus of $600.
    d. consumer surplus of $400.

13. Economic efficiency requires that
    a. individuals take all actions within their power.
    b. only long-lasting, high-quality products be produced.
    c. income be distributed equally among individuals.
    d. all economic activity generating more benefits than costs to individuals in the economy be undertaken.

14. If the demand for beer increased, what would be the effect on the equilibrium price and quantity of beer?
    a. price increases, quantity decreases
    b. price decreases, quantity decreases
    c. price increases, quantity increases
    d. price decreases, quantity increases

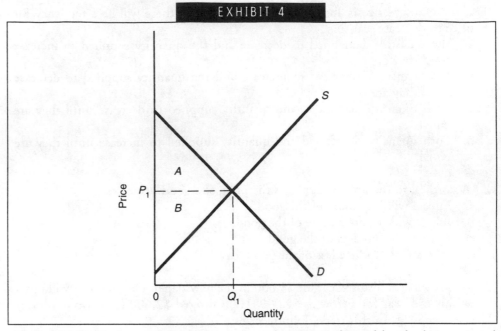

EXHIBIT 4

15. In Exhibit 4 above, there are two triangular areas indicated by the letters *A* and *B*. Which of the following is true?
    a.   *A* represents consumer surplus; *B* represents producer surplus.
    b.   *A* represents producer surplus; *B* represents consumer surplus.
    c.   Both areas *A* and *B* represent consumer surplus.
    d.   Both areas *A* and *B* represent producer surplus.

16. "Falling consumer income from the recent recession has hurt automakers in more ways than one. Not only have sales of new cars fallen, but car prices have fallen as well. As a result, the major automakers have announced cutbacks in production and layoffs of workers." Which of the following places these statements in the proper economic terminology within the context of the supply and demand model? [Note: It may help to graph this first.]
    a.   a decrease in demand and a decrease in supply
    b.   a decrease in demand and a decrease in quantity supplied
    c.   a decrease in quantity demanded and a decrease in quantity supplied
    d.   a decrease in quantity demanded and a decrease in supply.

17. "If gasoline were taxed, the price of gasoline would rise. Consequently, the demand for gasoline would fall, causing the price to fall to the original level." This statement
    a.   is essentially correct.
    b.   is incorrect-after the demand falls, the price would fall but to some level higher than the original level.
    c.   is incorrect-demand and quantity demanded are confused. The price increase would reduce quantity demanded, not demand.
    d.   is incorrect-after the demand falls, the price would fall but to some level lower than the original level.

Harcourt Brace & Company

18. Over the past twenty years both the quantity of health care provided and health care prices have been rising rapidly. Economic theory would suggest that the observed data could best be explained as
    a. an increase in supply, while demand remained relatively constant.
    b. a decrease in both supply and demand.
    c. an increase in demand, while supply remained relatively constant.
    d. a sharp increase in both supply and demand.

19. A decrease in the supply of a good will
    a. decrease the demand for the good.
    b. cause the price of the good to fall.
    c. lead to an increase in the price of the good.
    d. increase the quantity of the good bought and sold.

20. Which of the following would most likely decrease the price of beef?
    a. lower prices of grains used to produce cattle feed
    b. higher prices for chicken, a substitute for beef
    c. a cow disease that destroys millions of cattle (and makes their meat unfit for consumption) before they are ready for market
    d. an increase in consumer income

21. The price of gasoline increases. Purchasers of gasoline will probably
    a. reduce their purchases more in the long run than in the short run.
    b. reduce their purchases more in the short run than in the long run.
    c. reduce their purchases equally in both the short and long run.
    d. increase their purchases, since the higher gasoline price will increase supply.

22. When Adam Smith said economic activity was directed by an "invisible hand," he was referring to the fact that
    a. competitive markets motivate altruistic individuals to pursue productive activities that only serve their private interests.
    b. when economic activity is directed by competitive markets, the actions of self-interested individuals will generally serve the public interest.
    c. invisible forces will lead to economic chaos unless wise central planning directs economic activity.
    d. scarcity is largely the result of invisible forces that would be eliminated if individuals were free to pursue their own self-interests.

23. A hurricane damaged much of the housing in Miami. Shortly thereafter, the price of plywood rose significantly. The events suggest that
    a. a decrease in the supply of plywood caused the price of plywood to rise.
    b. an increase in the supply of plywood caused the price of plywood to rise.
    c. a decrease in the demand for plywood caused the price of plywood to rise.
    d. an increase in the demand for plywood caused the price of plywood to rise.

Harcourt Brace & Company

24. If the demand for a good increases, which of the following will generally occur in a market setting?
    a. The price of the good will decrease.
    b. The supply of the good will increase.
    c. The quantity supplied will increase.
    d. Producer profits will fall.

DISCUSSION QUESTIONS

1. In an effort to increase the number of students going to college, the federal government is considering legislation that would give a large tax credit to low-income families with college tuition payments. What impact would the legislation have on the
   a. number of students attempting to enroll in college?
   b. the price of tuition for other students?
   c. the salaries earned by college graduates?
   d. the wage rates in low-skilled occupations that only require a high school degree?
   e. the salaries earned by college professors?

2. Consider the following statement: "Campus parking permits and meters are inefficient and unfair. Campus parking should be free, with parking spaces allocated on a first-come, first-served basis."
   a. Is "free" parking that requires time to hunt for a space (or requires students to get into school earlier) really free?
   b. Is "free" parking more efficient than permit or meter parking? In other words, is rationing the spaces by price more or less efficient than rationing them by the cost of student time?
   c. With "free" parking, who, if anyone, gains? Who loses?
   d. Would you favor "free" parking on your campus? Why or why not?

3. Explain what is wrong with the following reasoning: "When meat prices rise due to a decrease in the supply of meat, the demand for meat decreases, so meat prices end up falling."
   a. Suppose a price is temporarily above its equilibrium level. How do you think producers figure out the price is in fact "too high"? Explain how a lower price causes both production and consumption adjustments to help correct the situation.
   b. Suppose a price is temporarily below its equilibrium level. How do you think producers figure out the price is in fact "too low"? Explain how a higher price causes both production and consumption adjustments to help correct the situation.

4. People often use the term "demand" when they actually mean "quantity demanded"; the same is true of "supply" and "quantity supplied."
   a. What causes a change in quantity demanded but not a change in demand?

Harcourt Brace & Company

b. With market determined prices, can the following statement be true: "The demand for oil is expected to exceed supply by 2050"?

c. How can you rephrase the statement of part b so that it makes economic sense?

5. Define both consumer and producer surplus, and give an example of each. Define economic efficiency, and show graphically how it relates to the consumer and producer surplus areas within a supply and demand graph.

6. There are some occasions when shortages or surpluses appear. For example, there is routinely a shortage of tickets to "hot" concerts or sporting events-people who want the tickets at the listed price are unable to get them. Can you think of any other situations you have seen where the market had either a shortage or a surplus (in other words, out of equilibrium)? Was the situation temporary? What caused the problem, was the price set too high or too low?

PERSPECTIVES IN ECONOMICS

THE USE OF KNOWLEDGE IN SOCIETY

by Friedrich A. Hayek

[Abridged from "The Use of Knowledge in Society," *American Economic Review,* volume 35, number 4, September 1945, pp. 519–530. Reprinted with permission.]

What is the problem we wish to solve when we try to construct a rational economic order?

On certain familiar assumptions the answer is simple enough. *If* we possess all the relevant information, *if* we can start out from a given system of preferences and *if* we command complete knowledge of available means, the problem which remains is purely one of logic.

This, however, is emphatically *not* the economic problem which society faces. The reason for this is that the "data" from which the economic calculus starts are never for the whole society "given" to a single mind which could work out the implications, and can never be so given.

The peculiar character of the problem of a rational economic order is determined precisely by the fact that the knowledge of the circumstances of which we must make use never exists in concentrated or integrated form, but solely as the dispersed bits of incomplete and frequently contradictory knowledge which all the separate individuals possess. The economic problem of society is thus not merely a problem of how to allocate "given" resources—if "given" is taken to mean given to a single mind which deliberately soles the problem set by these "data." It is rather a problem of how to secure the best use of resources known to any of the members of society, for ends whose relative importance only these individuals know. Or, to put it briefly, it is a problem of the utilization of knowledge not given to anyone in its totality.

If we can agree that the economic problem of society is mainly one of rapid adaptation to changes in the particular circumstances of time and place, it would seem to follow that the ultimate decisions must be left to the people who are familiar with these circumstances, who know directly of the relevant changes and of the resources immediately available to meet them. We cannot expect that this problem will be solved by first communicating all this knowledge to a central board which, after integrating *all* knowledge, issues its orders. We must solve it by some form of decentralization. But this answers only part of our problem. We need decentralization because only thus can we ensure that the knowledge of the particular circumstances of time and place will be promptly used. But the "man on the spot" cannot decide solely on the basis of his limited but intimate knowledge of the facts of his immediate surroundings. There still remains the problem of communicating to him such further information as he needs to fit his decisions into the whole pattern of changes of the larger economic system.

There is hardly anything that happens anywhere in the world that *might* not have an effect on the decision he ought to make. Be he need not know of these events as such, not of *all* their effects. It does not matter for him *why* at the particular moment more screws of one size than of another are wanted, *why* paper bags are more readily available than canvas bags, or *why* skilled labor, or particular machine tools, have for the moment become more difficult to acquire. All that is significant for him is *how much more or less* difficult to procure they have become compared with other things with which he is also concerned, or how much more or less urgently wanted are the alternative things he produces or uses. It is always a question of the relative importance of the particular things with which he is concerned, and the causes which alter their relative importance are of no interest to him beyond the effect on those concrete things of his own environment.

Fundamentally, in a system where the knowledge of the relevant facts is dispersed among many people, prices can act to coordinate the separate actions of different people in the same way as subjective values help the individual to coordinate the parts of his plan. It is worth contemplating for a moment a very simple and commonplace instance of the action of the price system to see what precisely it accomplishes. Assume that somewhere in the world a new opportunity for the use of some raw material, say tin, has arisen, or that one of the sources of supply of tin has been eliminated. It does not matter for our purpose—and it is very significant that it does not matter—which of these two caus-

Harcourt Brace & Company

es has made tin more scarce. All that the users of tin need to know is that some of the tin they used to consume is now more profitably employed elsewhere, and that in consequence they must economize tin. There is no need for the great majority of them even to know where the more urgent need has arisen, or in favor of what other needs they ought to husband the supply. If only some of them know directly of the new demand, and switch resources over to it, and if the people who are aware of the new gap thus created in turn fill it from still other sources, the effect will rapidly spread throughout the whole economic system and influence not only all the uses of tin, but also those of its substitutes and the substitutes of these substitutes, the supply of all the things made of tin, and their substitutes, and so on; and all this without the great majority of those instrumental in bringing about these substitutions knowing anything at all about the original cause of these changes. The whole acts as one market, not because any of its members survey the whole field, but because their limited individual fields of vision sufficiently overlap so that through many intermediaries the relevant information is communicated to all.

We must look at the price system as such a mechanism for communicating information if we want to understand its real function. The most significant fact about this system is the economy of knowledge with which it operates, or how little the individual participants need to know in order to be able to take the right action. In abbreviated form, by a kind of symbol, only the most essential information is passed on, and passed on only to those concerned. It is more than a metaphor to describe the price system as a kind of machinery for registering change, or a system of telecommunications which enables individual producers to watch merely the movement of a few pointers, as an engineer might watch the hands of a few dials, in order to adjust their activities to changes of which they may never know more than is reflected in the price movement.

Of course, these adjustments are probably never "perfect" in the sense in which the economist conceives of them in his equilibrium analysis. But I fear that our theoretical habits of approaching the problem with the assumption of more or less perfect knowledge on the part of almost everyone has made us somewhat blind to the true function of the price mechanism and led us to apply rather misleading standards in judging its efficiency. The marvel is that in a case like that of a scarcity of one raw material, without an order being issued, without more than perhaps a handful of people knowing the cause, tens of thousands of people whose identity could not be ascertained by months of investigation, are made to use the material or its products more sparingly; *i.e.,*

they move in the right direction. This is enough of a marvel even if, in a constantly changing world, not all will hit it off so perfectly that their profit rates will always be maintained at the same constant or "normal" level.

I have deliberately used the word "marvel" to shock the reader out of the complacency with which we often take the working of this mechanism for granted. I am convinced that if it were the result of deliberate human design, and if the people guided by the price changes understood that their decisions have significance far beyond their immediate aim, this mechanism would have been acclaimed as one of the greatest triumphs of the human mind. Its misfortune is the double one that it is not the product of human design and that the people guided by it usually do not know why they are made to do what they do. But those who clamor for "conscious direction"—and who cannot believe that anything which has evolved without design (and even without our understanding it) should solve problems which we should not be able to solve consciously—should remember this: The problem is precisely how to extend the span of our utilization of resources beyond the span of the control of any one mind; and, therefore, how to dispense with the need of conscious control and how to provide inducements which will make the individuals do the desirable things without anyone having to tell them what to do.

The price system is just one of those formations which man has learned to use (though he is still very far from having learned to make the best use of it) after he had stumbled upon it without understanding it. Through it not only a division of labor but also a coordinated utilization of resources based on an equally divided knowledge has become possible. The people who like to deride any suggestion that this may be so usually distort the argument by insinuating that it asserts that by some miracle just that sort of system has spontaneously grown up which is best suited to modern civilization. It is the other way round: man has been able to develop that division of labor on which our civilization is based because he happened to stumble upon a method which made it possible. Had he not done so he might still have developed some other, altogether different, type of civilization, something like the "state" of the termite ants, or some other altogether unimaginable type. All that we can say is that nobody has yet succeeded in designing an alternative system in which certain features of the existing one can be preserved which are dear even to those who most violently assail it-such as particularly the extent to which the individual can choose his pursuits and consequently freely use his own knowledge and skill.

DISCUSSION

1. What does the Hayek reading have to do with this chapter? How does it relate to Adam Smith's invisible hand principle?

2. Are prices an effective mechanism to communicate information? Do they save people time in having to acquire information about events to adjust their behavior?

3. Do the signals sent by price changes cause people to adjust their behavior in ways that are consistent with what is best for society in the face of the new events?

CHAPTER 4

Supply and Demand: Applications and Extensions

TRUE OR FALSE

T F

☐ ☐ 1. Wage rates, interest rates, and exchange rates are all market prices determined by the relative supply and demand in those markets.

☐ ☐ 2. If the demand for housing increased, the demand for resources used to produce housing (such as lumber) would fall.

☐ ☐ 3. A sudden increase in the willingness of individuals to save would cause the market interest rate to rise.

☐ ☐ 4. If the current exchange rate is one dollar equals three Mexican pesos, the cost of purchasing a sixty peso product in dollars is $20.

☐ ☐ 5. An increase in foreign demand for products made in the U.S. would cause the dollar to appreciate.

☐ ☐ 6. A depreciation of the U.S. dollar would make U.S. products more expensive to foreigners, thus causing U.S. exports to decline.

☐ ☐ 7. If the government imposed a price ceiling of $1 on compact discs, there would be a surplus of compact discs.

☐ ☐ 8. Shortages arise when prices are legally set above the equilibrium level.

☐ ☐ 9. The minimum wage increases unemployment among unskilled workers.

☐ ☐ 10. As illegal drug markets illustrate, the lack of contract and private property right enforcement causes harmful secondary effects that keep these black markets from operating as smoothly as legal markets.

☐ ☐ 11. The individuals on whom a tax is imposed are always the ones who end up bearing the burden of the tax.

☐ ☐ 12. The actual burden of a tax does not depend on the original legal (or statutory) assignment of the tax, but it does depend upon the elasticities of demand and supply.

☐ ☐ 13. Because taxes reduce the number of mutually beneficial trades in a market, they create an excess burden (or deadweight loss) in addition to the direct revenue burden of the tax.

T F

☐ ☐ 14. A proportional tax is one in which everyone pays the same dollar amount of taxes regardless of income.

☐ ☐ 15. When marginal tax rates are very high, the Laffer curve suggests that lowering tax rates will result in an *increase* in tax revenue.

PROBLEMS AND PROJECTS

1. Using the supplied diagrams, show how the indicated events would affect these markets.
    a. Exhibit 1A shows the job market for accountants. Using Exhibit 1A (i) show how an increase in the number of students majoring in accounting would affect the wage rate and employment of accountants. Using Exhibit 1A (ii) show how a tax reform that vastly increased the simplicity of the tax code would affect the wage rate and employment of accountants.

EXHIBIT 1A

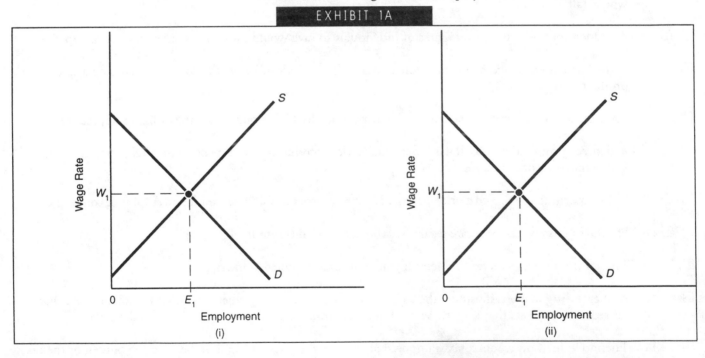

b. Exhibit 1B shows the market for loanable funds. Using Exhibit 1B (i) show how a decrease in the number of persons seeking new automobile loans would affect the interest rate and quantity of loans. Using Exhibit 1B (ii) show how an increase in the desire of households to save their income would affect the interest rate and quantity of loans.

EXHIBIT 1B

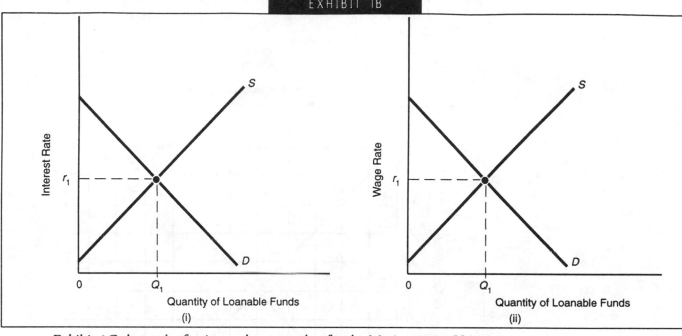

Quantity of Loanable Funds (i)

Quantity of Loanable Funds (ii)

c. Exhibit 1C shows the foreign exchange market for the Mexican peso. Using Exhibit 1C (i) show how an increase in the desire of Americans to go on vacation to Mexico would affect the value of the peso and the quantity

EXHIBIT 1C

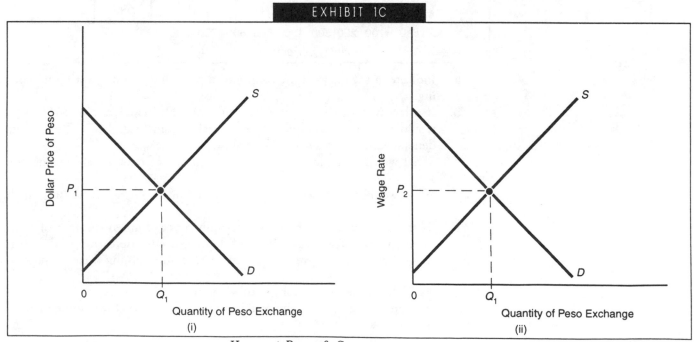

Quantity of Peso Exchange (i)

Quantity of Peso Exchange (ii)

Harcourt Brace & Company

exchanged. In Exhibit 1C (i), has the peso appreciated or depreciated relative to the U.S. dollar? Using Exhibit 1C (ii) show how an increase in the desire of Mexicans to purchase foreign-made goods (for instance, U.S. automobiles) would affect the value of the peso and the quantity exchanged. In Exhibit 1C (ii), has the peso appreciated or depreciated relative to the U.S. dollar?

2. Exhibit 2 shows the market for rental housing in a college town.

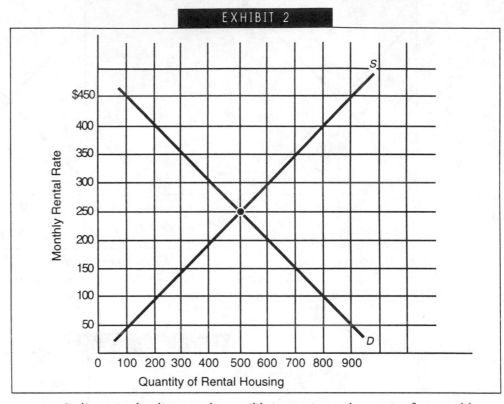

EXHIBIT 2

a. Indicate in the diagram the equilibrium price and quantity for rental housing.
b. If a law is passed setting a maximum monthly rental rate at $100, what would happen to the quantity of rental housing supplied? The quantity demanded? Is there a surplus or a shortage?
c. What would you expect to happen to the rate of new rental housing construction in the future?
d. What would you expect to happen to the quality of rental housing in the area?
e. With so many renters hunting after only a very limited number of apartments, what criterion do you think landlords will use to ration the apartments now that they are forbidden by law from rationing them by price?

3. Exhibit 3 shows the market for unskilled labor.
a. Indicate in the diagram the equilibrium wage and level of employment for unskilled labor.

Harcourt Brace & Company

EXHIBIT 3

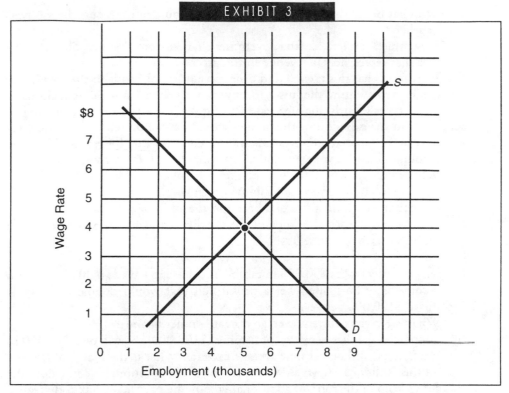

b. Suppose a minimum wage of $6 per hour is enacted for unskilled labor. What would happen to the number of workers searching for jobs in this market (that is, the quantity of labor supplied)? What would happen to the number of job openings available at this higher wage rate (that is, the quantity of labor demanded)?

c. Does the imposition of the minimum wage create a shortage or a surplus of labor?

d. Are the workers who are able to retain their jobs at this higher wage better off or worse off?

e. Are the workers who are now no longer able to find jobs at this higher wage better off or worse off?

4. Exhibit 4 shows how a $1 per beer tax, statutorily imposed on beer sellers, affects the market for beer. Use the exhibit to answer the following questions.

a. What was the original price of beer prior to the imposition of the tax?

b. What is the new price that a consumer must pay for a beer after the imposition of the tax on sellers? How much has the price to consumers risen?

c. After selling a beer at the new market price, the seller must send the government $1 in tax for the beer. What is the new net (after-tax) price the seller receives from selling a beer? How much has the price a seller receives fallen?

EXHIBIT 4

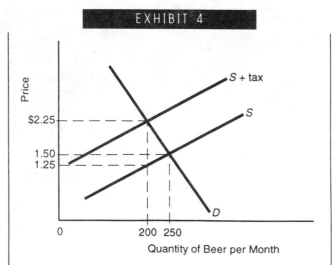

Harcourt Brace & Company

d. Who has borne the larger share of the actual burden of the tax, beer buyers or sellers?

e. How much revenue has the government raised from this tax? Shade in the area that represents tax revenue in the exhibit.

f. How much has this tax reduced beer consumption? Shade in the area in the exhibit representing the losses to buyers and sellers from the reductions in these trades (that is, the area representing the deadweight loss of the tax).

g. Show in the exhibit how the market would have appeared had an equal tax have been imposed on buyers instead of sellers (so that there would be a tax amount added on your purchase, just as is the regular consumer sales tax). What would have been the new market price of beer? How much would sellers have received per beer sold? How much would consumers pay for a beer considering both the price of a beer and the additional $1 tax?

h. How would the actual burden of the tax differed had the tax been imposed on buyers rather than sellers?

5. Reagan currently makes $50,000 in taxable income and pays $10,000 in taxes on her income. Her boss offers her a promotion that would double her taxable income to $100,000 per year.

a. What is Reagan's current average tax rate on her income?

b. Suppose that at her new level of income ($100,000) she will owe $15,000 in taxes. What will be her new average tax rate? What is the marginal tax rate on this additional income? What percent of her additional income does she get to keep in the form of additional take-home pay? Is this tax code regressive, proportional, or progressive?

c. Explain how in part b above the tax is regressive even though she is now paying more taxes than before ($15,000 in taxes as opposed to her old taxes of $10,000).

d. Instead, now suppose that at her new level of income ($100,000) she will owe $20,000 in taxes. What will be her new average tax rate? What is the marginal tax rate on this additional income? What percent of her additional income does she get to keep in the form of additional take-home pay? Is this tax code regressive, proportional, or progressive?

e. Instead, now suppose that at her new level of income ($100,000) she will owe $35,000 in taxes. What will be her new average tax rate? What is the marginal tax rate on this additional income? What percent of her additional income does she get to keep in the form of additional take-home pay? Is this tax code regressive, proportional, or progressive?

f. Instead, now suppose that at her new level of income ($100,000) she will owe $60,000 in taxes. What will be her new average tax rate? What is the marginal tax rate on this additional income? What percent of her additional income does she get to keep in the form of additional take-home pay? Is this tax code regressive, proportional, or progressive? Under this final case, would you suggest she take the promotion if it required additional responsibilities and longer work hours?

6. When a tax is imposed on a product, the price rises and consumers cut back on their purchases of the product. Exhibit 5 shows this relationship for a tax on candy bars.

Harcourt Brace & Company

EXHIBIT 5

TAX PER CANDY BAR	QUANTITY OF CANDY BARS SOLD	TAX REVENUE
$0	600	$ _____
1	500	_____
2	400	_____
3	300	_____
4	200	_____
5	100	_____
6	0	_____

a. For each tax rate, calculate the total tax revenue raised by the tax and put your numbers in the spaces provided in the table.

b. Now, using your answers from part a, plot the relationship between the tax rate and tax revenue in the space provided. Connect the data points with a curved line, this is the Laffer curve for the candy bar tax.

c. If the government's objective was to maximize the revenue from this tax, what tax rate should be chosen?

d. If the current tax rate on candy bars was $5, what would you suggest the government do if it wanted to increase its revenue, lower or raise the candy bar tax?

MULTIPLE CHOICE

1. An increase in the demand for a product will cause output to
   a. increase and both the demand for and prices of the resources used to produce the product to increase.
   b. increase and both the demand for and prices of the resources used to produce the product to decrease.
   c. decrease; the demand for the resources used to produce the product will remain constant.
   d. decrease; the price of resources used to produce the product will decrease.

2. Suppose business decision makers become more optimistic about future economic conditions and desire additional funds to expand their plant capacity. What is the likely effect on the loanable funds market?
   a. The demand for loanable funds will rise and the interest rate will rise.
   b. The demand for loanable funds will fall and the interest rate will fall.
   c. The supply for loanable funds will rise and the interest rate will fall.
   d. The supply for loanable funds will fall and the interest rate will rise.

3. An increase in the dollar price of the Mexican peso (an appreciation of the peso) would cause
   a. Mexico's imports to increase and exports to decline.
   b. Mexico's exports to increase and imports to decline.
   c. both Mexico's imports and exports to decline.
   d. both Mexico's imports and exports to rise.

4. During the imposition of price controls in the 1970s, long gasoline lines were common. In the absence of price controls, markets would have eliminated such excess demand by
   a. allowing the price to rise, so gas was rationed to those willing to pay the most for it.
   b. increasing the gap between supply and demand.
   c. allowing price to decline, so the poor could afford to buy more gas.
   d. mandating a 50-mile-per-hour speed limit to reduce consumption.

5. If an increase in the government-imposed minimum wage pushes the price (wage) of unskilled labor above market equilibrium, which of the following will most likely occur in the unskilled labor market?
   a. an increase in demand for unskilled labor
   b. a decrease in the supply of unskilled labor
   c. a shortage of unskilled labor
   d. a surplus of unskilled labor

6. With a price ceiling above the equilibrium price,
   a. quantity demanded would exceed quantity supplied.
   b. quantity supplied would exceed quantity demanded.
   c. the market would be in equilibrium.
   d. the equilibrium price would be expected to fall over time.

7. Rent controls generally fix the price of rental housing below market equilibrium. Economic analysis suggests these controls
   a. are effective in helping the poor find housing.
   b. improve the quality of housing available to consumers.
   c. create a surplus of rental housing.
   d. reduce the future supply of rental housing.

8. Because illegal drug markets operate outside the legal system,
   a. the quality of these drugs has increased.
   b. the sellers of illegal drugs earn less money.
   c. there is less violence in these markets than if they were legal.
   d. none of the above.

Harcourt Brace & Company

9. Currently, federal and state gasoline taxes (imposed statutorily on the sellers of gasoline) amount to about $.45 per gallon. Suppose the current price of gasoline is $1.20 per gallon, and that if the tax was not in place, the price would be only $.80.
   a. The full incidence of the tax is falling on consumers.
   b. The full incidence of the tax is falling on suppliers.
   c. A $.05 burden is being borne by sellers and $.40 by consumers.
   d. A $.05 burden is being borne by consumers and $.40 by sellers.

10. The deadweight loss resulting from levying a tax on an economic activity is
   a. the tax revenue directed to the government as the result of the tax.
   b. the loss of potential gains from trade from activities foregone because of the tax.
   c. the increase in the price of an activity as the result of the tax levied on it.
   d. the marginal benefits derived from the expansion in government activities made possible by the increase in tax revenues.

11. Suppose there is an increase in the excise tax imposed on cigarettes, a good for which the demand is relatively inelastic. The short-run burden of the tax increase will be borne primarily by
   a. consumers, because the increase in market price will be large relative to the increase in the excise tax.
   b. firms, because the increase in market price will be large relative to the increase in the excise tax.
   c. consumers, because the increase in market price will be small relative to the increase in the excise tax.
   d. firms, because the increase in market price will be small relative to the increase in the excise tax.

12. An income tax is regressive if
   a. the tax liability of high-income recipients exceeds the tax liability of those with low incomes.
   b. the tax liability of high-income recipients is less than the tax liability of those with low incomes.
   c. high-income recipients pay a higher percentage of their incomes in taxes than those with low incomes.
   d. high-income recipients pay a lower percentage of their incomes in taxes than those whose incomes are low.

13. Use the table below to choose the correct answer.

INCOME	TAX LIABILITY
$10,000	$1,000
20,000	2,000
30,000	3,000
40,000	4,000

For the income range illustrated, the tax shown here is
   a. regressive.
   b. proportional.
   c. progressive.
   d. progressive up to $30,000 but regressive beyond that.

Harcourt Brace & Company

14. In the mid-1940s, the marginal income tax rate in the top income tax bracket was 94 percent. In the 1960s, the top rate was lowered to 70 percent, and in the 1980s, the top rate was again lowered to 28 percent. The data show that as a result of these tax rate reductions, tax revenue (particularly from the rich) increased. This is consistent with the idea illustrated with the
    a. Laffer curve.
    b. production possibilities curve.
    c. supply of loanable funds curve.
    d. demand for unskilled labor curve.

15. The Laffer curve illustrates the principle that
    a. when tax rates are quite high, reducing tax rates will increase tax revenue.
    b. when tax rates are quite low, reducing tax rates will increase tax revenue.
    c. when tax rates are quite high, reducing tax rates will decrease tax revenue.
    d. increasing tax rates always increases tax revenue.

16. If Joan pays $5,000 in taxes when she earns $20,000 and must pay $12,000 in taxes when she earns $30,000, she faces a marginal tax rate in this income range of
    a. 25 percent.
    b. 30 percent.
    c. 40 percent.
    d. 70 percent.

17. A legal minimum wage is an example of
    a. the invisible hand principle.
    b. a price floor.
    c. a price ceiling.
    d. a fringe benefit.

18. Both price floors and price ceilings, when effective, lead to
    a. shortages.
    b. surpluses.
    c. an increase in the quantity traded.
    d. a reduction in the quantity traded.

19. If there was an increase in the excise tax on beer, what would be the effect on the equilibrium price and quantity of beer?
    a. price increases, quantity decreases
    b. price decreases, quantity decreases
    c. price increases, quantity increases
    d. price decreases, quantity increases

20. The more elastic the supply of a product, the more likely it is that the burden of a tax will
    a. fall on sellers.
    b. fall on buyers.
    c. fall equally on both buyers and sellers.
    d. be borne by the public sector, and not by market participants.

Harcourt Brace & Company

DISCUSSION QUESTIONS

1. Many uninformed people believe that the reductions in the income tax rates during the 1980s were the cause of the large budget deficits during that period. However, data show that the effect of the tax rate reductions was to increase tax revenue, not lower it.

   a. Use the Laffer curve to illustrate how a reduction in tax rates can increase tax revenue.

   b. Explain in words how it is possible to obtain more revenue when tax rates are lowered. (Hint: What must happen to the tax base?)

   c. Had the tax rate reductions not have been enacted, would the budget problems have been worse or better?

   d. Since the 1980s, the top marginal tax rate has been increased from 28 percent up to 39.6 percent. We know that the 1980s reductions from 70 to 28 percent increased revenue. The rate of 28 percent could have either been on the lower portion of the Laffer curve, right at the maximum, or it still could have been on the upper portion of the curve. Show what these three possibilities imply about the likely effects of the recent tax rate increases.

2. Evaluate the following statements. "Currently there are 100,000 six-packs of soda sold per year in our state. We are going to impose a $10 tax on each six-pack and require that the seller of the soda pays the tax. In this way we will raise $1,000,000 for the state budget, and none of the burden will be borne by our state consumers."

   a. Will the tax raise $1,000,000 in revenue? Explain.

   b. How much revenue would you expect the state to get from this tax?

   c. Is it true that consumers will bear none of the burden of this tax because it is legally imposed on the sellers? Show using a graph.

3. Consider the health care industry. We could allow the market to allocate health care through the price mechanism *(rationing by price)*, or we could have the government set the price of health care at a low level so that it would be "affordable" for all citizens. Assume that when the government sets a low price for health care, health care services are allocated on a first-come, first-served basis *(rationing by waiting)*.

   a. What type of waste occurs with rationing by waiting?

   b. Suppose there is a surge in demand for health care services. Which rationing system provides health care providers with better information and incentives? Explain.

   c. Health care involves a variety of services including preventive care (checkups and diagnostic procedures), treatment of illness and injuries, expensive and/or experimental procedures to care for the critically ill and injured, and plastic surgery or other elective procedures. What mix of these services would you expect to see in a system rationed by price? What mix of health care services would you expect to see in a system rationed by waiting? [Hint: Who would get more health care in a system rationed by price? By waiting?]

d.   What other rationing schemes are possible? What effects would they have on the efficiency of health care delivery? What effects would they have on the mix of health care services provided?

e.   Why should health care be rationed at all? Why not provide unlimited health care to everyone?

4.   In an effort to control rising prices during the 1970s, many governments adopted price controls, fixing prices (and wages) for extended periods of time and thereby causing shortages of some goods and surpluses of others. Respond to the following statement: "Shortages are a disadvantage of price controls, but surpluses are an offsetting advantage."

5.   Market prices coordinate economic activity by providing the proper incentives and bringing into harmony the desires of buyers and sellers. Explain how market prices coordinate the following.
a.   the actions of those wanting to save with those wanting to borrow.
b.   the relationship between a country's imports and exports.
c.   the markets for labor in terms of job seekers and employment offerings.
d.   the desires of the buyers and sellers of a product of your choosing.

PERSPECTIVES IN ECONOMICS

THE DRUG PROBLEM

by Randall G. Holcombe

[Abridged from "The Drug Problem," Chapter 10 in Randall G. Holcombe, *Public Policy and the Quality of Life.* (Westport, CT: Greenwood Press, 1995). Reprinted with permission.]

The public policy response to the drug problem has been to make recreational drug use illegal and then to enforce drug laws by arresting both users and sellers, even going overseas to nations supplying the underground drug markets to try to stop the supply at the source. The war on drugs is now decades old, and there is no evidence that the war is being won, or can be won.

As the very limited success of the war on drugs shows, drug use will continue to be extensive although drugs are illegal. Along with the law enforcement campaign against underground drug markets has come a public relations campaign to dissuade people from drug use. The public relations campaign appears more successful than the law enforcement campaign, and public relations campaigns can help to curtail the use of both illegal drugs and legal drugs such as alcohol and tobacco. This shows that there are alternative strategies to legal prohibition for those who want to use the government to reduce drug use. The costs of continuing to make recreational drug use illegal are many. The war on drugs is taking its toll on the individual rights our Constitution was designed to protect. Many of the negative consequences if illegal drug use stem from the fact that illegal drugs are illegal rather than that they are drugs. Because of the history of the legal prohibition on recreational drug use, it is reasonable to consider alternatives to help solve many of the problems that are a part of the drug problem.

The creation of illegal markets for recreational drugs has the obvious effect of making prices higher than they would be with legal markets. Higher prices contribute to property crime because high prices can push users into criminal activity to finance their drug purchases. The news often portrays drug users as criminals who steal to support their habit but rarely shows stories of alcoholics who steal to support their addictions. One reason is that alcohol prices are not forced upward artificially by legal prohibition.

Before considering some of the pros and cons of legalization, consider the question of whether it would ever be possible to win the war on drugs. One of the problems often cited in fighting the war on drugs is that users tend to be relatively insensitive to the price of drugs. If drugs become more costly, users will engage in various types of theft to acquire them. In the terminology of economists, the demand for recreational drugs is relatively inelastic, so that even a relatively large increase in the price will result in only a small decrease in the quantity of drugs demanded by users.

If users in the recreational drug market do not want to alter their consumption habits very much in response to price changes, consider the results of winning some battles in the war on drugs. Surely, sellers in the black market for drugs will charge whatever the market will bear, and if government efforts succeed in removing a small percentage of the supply of drugs from the market, competition among buyers for drugs will push prices up by a greater percentage than the decline in quantity, with the result that the drug market will take in more total money by selling fewer drugs.

Trade in illegal markets creates huge profits that entice people into the market. Legalization would take the glamour out of drug dealing, it would eliminate the problems produced by the profitability of dealing, and it would be more likely to keep children out of the drug market.

Another disadvantage to users of trading in illegal markets is that there is no legal protection for the transaction. This means, at a

Harcourt Brace & Company

minimum, that there is no recourse in case of a faulty product but also means that a buyer risks being the victim of other crimes in an attempt to purchase drugs. Users might be reluctant to tell the police that they were robbed by someone from whom they were trying to buy drugs.

One major disadvantage to drug users of trading in illegal markets is that their activities make them criminals. There are several negative side effects. First, there is a stigma attached to drug use simply because it is illegal. One need only remember the 1980s to recall that Judge Douglas Ginsberg's nomination to the Supreme Court was torpedoed because he had used marijuana. There was no evidence that it had affected his legal activities or his judgment in any other way. Simply the stigma attached to marijuana use was enough to keep him off the Supreme Court. If, instead, he had admitted to trying bourbon there would have been no issue raised.

This stigma will also make users more reluctant to seek treatment. People must admit not only that they cannot seem to get off drugs but also that they have been violating the law. Legalization would make it easier for people to seek treatment for drug problems if they desired it.

Another negative aspect of the profits generated by drug prohibition is they create an opportunity for corrupting law enforcement officers. Law enforcement is not a notably high-paid profession, and drug profits can be spent to pay law enforcement officers for protection or to look the other way while drug dealers transact their business.

Corruption of law enforcement officers is most serious with victimless crimes, such as drug sales, prostitution, gambling, and the like. Crimes with victims, like assault and burglary, have individuals who want to cooperate with law enforcement officers and who have an incentive to monitor the law enforcement system to see that justice is done. With victimless crimes nobody directly involved in the activity wants law enforcement. If an individual who commits an assault is able to buy his way out of an arrest, the assault victim will want to call that corruption to the attention of someone higher up in the political chain of command. The potential problems would be severe enough that there would be a high likelihood that the corrupt law enforcement officer would not benefit from the corrupt activity. With victimless crimes, nobody directly involved in the crime has an incentive to complain about corrupt activity. Therefore, corruption is more likely.

Corruption may not be the major problem related to the legal enforcement of drug crimes. Incentives in the legal system may lead law enforcement officers to pursue drug crimes at the expense of other types of crime, with the result that other crimes increase. The most obvious incentive is that often property confiscated by law enforcement officers through drug arrests remains with the law enforcement agency. Law enforcement officers will have more incentive to pursue these types of crimes if the budgets of their agencies can be directly enhanced as a result.

The incentives are structured so law enforcement officers can benefit from putting more law enforcement effort into drug crimes and less effort into property crimes. As a result of reduced effort fighting property crimes robbery and burglary will become less risky, and crime rates in those areas will increase.

Dealing in illegal drugs is a very profitable business for the dealers, but it is a business that has no access to legal protection. Whereas the legal system is, for the most part, designed to protect property and to defend the rights of individuals to engage in voluntary exchange and retain ownership over what they receive through market transactions, in the drug market, the legal system is worse than neutral toward protecting participants, Rather than just no offering those transactions any protection, the legal system actively seeks to confiscate any money and goods exchanged in the market. Because the government's legal system is openly hostile to drug markets those who participate in those markets must take steps to actively protect themselves.

Non-users suffer considerably because drugs are bought and sold on black markets, which offers no legal protection to those who deal in them. There is big money to be made dealing in drugs, and, without legal protection, those dealing in the markets must find ways to protect themselves. This is what leads to the gang warfare, the drive-by shootings, and the unsafe neighborhoods filled with criminal activity.

The consequences of the illegal profits in drug markets are overwhelmingly negative. The location of drug markets tends to be in poorer neighborhoods and in inner cities. The resulting crime harms those who do not participate in the markets but have a limited ability to move from the area. However, in poor neighborhoods, there is also the negative side effect of the incentives established by drug markets. In areas where unemployment may be high and employed people work for relatively low wages, much more money can be made by dealing in drugs than working in legal markets. The people with the new cars and the people with the gold chains will likely be those involved in the drug market. This entices others to enter the market and makes those who deal in drugs neighborhood role models. Why work for low wages, if one can find a job at all, when by working for dug dealers one can make more money?

If recreational drugs were legal, there would be no high profits to lure individuals into the market. There would still be drug users, to be sure, but those individuals would tend to be the losers-the equivalent of the skid row alcoholic-rather than the people to envy. Without the illegal profits, those involved in drugs would no longer look like role models to individuals in drug-infested neighborhoods. This is one argument for legalization. If all drugs were legalized, the drug culture would not look nearly as attractive because it would be stripped of its excess profits caused by government efforts to reduce supply.

If drugs were legalized, their quality would be controlled better because they would be sold in commercial markets. Firms would have an incentive to develop reputations for quality, and drugs would be packaged in standardized doses, which would reduce the incidence of accidental overdoses. Because drugs would be sold under brand names, sellers would have an incentive to distinguish their products and to be concerned about the health of their customers.

If drugs were legalized, there would not be the same incentives to produce drugs in concentrated doses. Transportation is more costly for illegal drugs because they must be concealed from law enforcement officers. Drugs that can contain more doses in a given volume will be more valuable, and one of the motivations of designer drugs is to allow easier transportation through more concentrated doses. Using alcohol as an example, high-proof liquor was more often produced than beer with low alcohol content during prohibition. Legalization would result in drugs that are not as strong.

If drugs were legalized, there would be an incentive for research and development in the recreational drug industry to produce designer drugs that cause better feelings but with fewer harmful side effects. The designer drug industry today shows the possibilities for research and development in recreational drugs, but, as just noted, the incentives today are to produce more concentrated drugs rather than less harmful drugs. This push toward less harmful designer drugs would be amplified if drug manufacturers were allowed to advertise their products.

Finally, if drugs were legalized, manufacturers would have an incentive to innovate because they could take advantage of patent protection and other legal protections that would go to producers in any legal industry. As it is, the incentives do not exist because drugs are illegal.

Legalization would bring the same benefits to users and non-users. Violence and unpredictable behavior from drug use should be reduced because of better information about drugs, quality control, increased variety, and the tendency for drugs to be packaged in less potent forms. Accidental deaths should fall, which would reduce costs to those with drug users in the family. Thus, the effects of drug use should be less burdensome to non-users if drugs were legalized.

Earlier, it was argued that the demand for recreational drugs is relatively inelastic meaning that a reduction in the price would not cause large increases in consumption. This suggests that legalization would have relatively little effect on drug use taking only the money price into account. For some people, however, the violation of drug laws might appear as a powerful and prohibitive deterrent because legalization would entice people who never had a desire to do so to try recreational drugs.

An important argument in favor of legalization, regardless of how many new users would be created, is that in a free society people should have the right to behave as they choose as long as their behavior does not harm others. People engage in many activities that are hazardous to their health, but society does not ban skydiving or motorcycle riding. One of the casualties of the war on drugs has been individual rights.

This discussion of drug policy considers a controversial issue but one that is worthwhile considering within the context of an examination of public policy and the quality of life. For one thing, a general framework should be able to deal with controversial issues, but a larger reason is that the issue of drug policy directly confronts the issue of the degree to which individual freedom contributes to the quality of life. Freedom is important enough to the quality of life to want to defend it as a goal of its own, but the protection of individual freedoms also indirectly enhances the quality of life. Freedom allows people to pursue their own interests as they understand them, and it allows them to profit form activities that benefit others. The protection of individual rights is necessary for a market system to operate, and the market system has proven itself to be an indispensable component in enhancing the welfare of a nation's citizens.

DISCUSSION

1. Using a demand and supply diagram, show how drug enforcement policies aimed at reducing the supply of drugs affect the price of drugs and the quantity traded. How do the effects on price and quantity compare with policies aimed at reducing demand (such as education and "Just say no" campaigns)?

2. Do you think the demand for illegal drugs is fairly inelastic? What does this imply about the ability to reduce consumption by supply side policies that increase the price of drugs?

3. Police departments have a fixed amount of resources that must be allocated across different crimes and laws that must be enforced. Use a production possibilities curve to show how increased enforcement of drug laws reduces the enforcement of other laws. What effect does this have on the amount of these other crimes committed?

4. If drugs were made legal, what do you think would happen to the following?
   a. the quantity of drugs consumed
   b. the profits of drug sellers
   c. the amount of gang violence
   d. the presence of street corner drug dealers (Hint: Could they compete with Wal-Mart?)
   e. the quality of drugs in terms of side-effects and tainted products
   f. the number of users willing to admit their problem and get help

5. During prohibition in the 1920s, alcohol was made illegal. As a result, gangsters controlled the alcohol trade, the murder rate rose substantially, high-potency moonshine was created, and deaths from tainted alcohol rose. Compare and contrast each of these with (1) the current market and usage of alcohol now that it is legal again (Are these problems gone or at least reduced?), and (2) with the current market and usage of illegal drugs.

CHAPTER 5

The Economic Role of Government

TRUE OR FALSE

T F

☐ ☐ 1. The total social cost of an action includes the costs to the voluntary participants and any costs imposed on third parties.

☐ ☐ 2. When production of a good results in externalities that impose a cost on others, the output level of the good often exceeds the socially ideal amount.

☐ ☐ 3. It is often difficult to exclude nonpaying customers from receiving the benefits of a public good.

☐ ☐ 4. Anything provided by the government (the public sector) is called a public good.

☐ ☐ 5. When an activity generates external costs, government intervention in the form of establishing private property rights or imposing a tax that would reduce the level of the activity could improve economic efficiency.

☐ ☐ 6. National defense is an example of a public good.

☐ ☐ 7. Poor information on the part of buyers is very seldom a factor in real-world markets.

☐ ☐ 8. Spillover, or third-party effects, are the same thing as externalities.

☐ ☐ 9. Getting accurate information is often difficult for consumers, but sellers offering good products have an incentive to provide this information to consumers.

☐ ☐ 10. *Consumer Reports* is an example of a government solution to the problems for the market created by information costs.

☐ ☐ 11. Externalities are the result of poorly defined or poorly enforced private property rights.

☐ ☐ 12. Externalities can be either negative (costs) or positive (benefits).

☐ ☐ 13. The free-rider problem occurs when it is easy to exclude nonpaying customers.

☐ ☐ 14. The market and public sector are similar in that individuals must pay exactly for the benefits they receive.

☐ ☐ 15. Scarcity is not present in the public sector because the government pays for all goods and services it provides free to citizens.

PROBLEMS AND PROJECTS

1. Public goods are goods that are both (1) joint-in-consumption and (2) nonex-cludable. For each of the goods listed below, indicate whether it meets each of these criterion with a "yes" or a "no" in the space provided. In the final column indicate whether the good is a public good or a private good based upon your answers.

GOOD	JOINT-IN-CONSUMPTION	NONEXCLUDABLE	PUBLIC GOOD OR PRIVATE GOOD
a. National defense	_____	_____	_____
b. A rock concert	_____	_____	_____
c. Mail and package delivery	_____	_____	_____
d. A cup of coffee	_____	_____	_____
e. A radio broadcast	_____	_____	_____
f. A movie at a theatre	_____	_____	_____
g. A taco	_____	_____	_____
h. A toll road	_____	_____	_____

2. Exhibit 1 shows the supply and demand schedules for pulp paper in Academia, a hypothetical country.
   a. Diagram the supply and demand curves and show the equilibrium price and quantity for pulp paper in Academia.

EXHIBIT 1

	QUANTITY (TON/YEAR)	
PRICE (PER TON)	DEMANDED	SUPPLIED
$150	1,000	7,000
140	2,000	6,000
130	3,000	5,000
120	4,000	4,000
110	5,000	3,000
100	6,000	2,000

Price

170

160

150

140

130

120

110

100

0   1,000 2,000 3,000 4,000 5,000 6,000 7,000   Quantity

Harcourt Brace & Company

b. Suppose the production of pulp paper results in external pollution costs of $20 per ton produced. In your diagram show a supply curve that includes these external costs. What are the socially ideal (efficient) price and quantity for pulp paper? Show these in your diagram.

c. Explain in your own words why the private market equilibrium you found in part a is inefficient.

d. Suppose the government levies a tax of $20 per ton on producers of pulp paper. How will this affect the market? How will the outcome compare with efficiency?

3. Exhibit 2 below depicts the market for baseball teams, with the total number of teams on the horizontal axis and the price of each team (in millions of dollars) on the vertical axis.

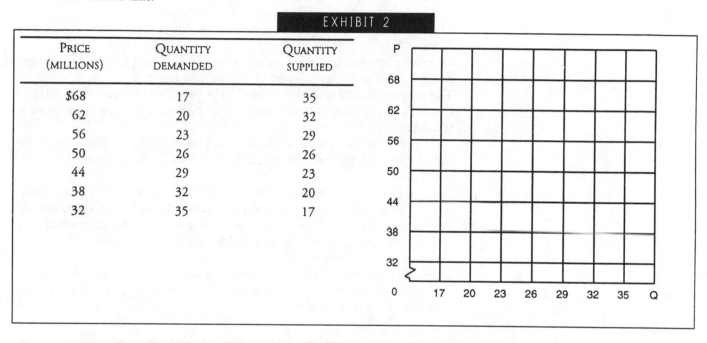

EXHIBIT 2

PRICE (MILLIONS)	QUANTITY DEMANDED	QUANTITY SUPPLIED
$68	17	35
62	20	32
56	23	29
50	26	26
44	29	23
38	32	20
32	35	17

a. Diagram the supply and demand curves and determine the values of the free market equilibrium price and quantity.

b. Some have argued that a baseball team generates external benefits for a city by increasing the city's morale and pride and by bringing in extra tourist revenue. Suppose the value of these external benefits turns out to be $24 million per team. Use your diagram from part a to depict these externalities. What is the efficient total number of baseball teams?

c. What type of policy could a city government use to attract a baseball team?

d. Suppose there really are no external benefits associated with baseball teams but that city governments subsidize them anyway. Will the resulting outcome be consistent with economic efficiency? Explain.

Harcourt Brace & Company

4. The book presents the following two conditions are necessary for economic efficiency:

    Rule 1: Undertaking an economic action will be efficient if it produces more benefits than costs for the individuals in the economy.

    Rule 2: Undertaking an economic action will be inefficient if it produces more costs than benefits to the individuals.

    Using these criterion, for each of the following cases, decide whether the action is efficient or inefficient and which rule applies.
    a. Buying a pair of jeans for $25 that you value at $30
    b. Building a new public park that generates $100 million in benefits to the public, but costs $150 million in tax revenue to build
    c. Making a $1,500 repair to your home that will allow you to sell it for $2,000 more
    d. Operating a recycling program that costs $50 million per year and creates benefits (such as energy savings) of $20 million per year
    e. The production of a good that yields $20 in benefits to a consumer, costs the firm $15 to produce, and generates $10 in external pollution costs when it is produced
    f. The production of a good that yields $20 in benefits to a consumer, costs the firm $5 to produce, and generates $10 in external pollution costs when it is produced
    g. Imposing a tax that costs the government $10 million to enforce and administer to correct an externality that was generating $5 million in external costs
    h. Purchasing an issue of *Consumer Reports* magazine for $3 that contains a review of writing pens to help you decide whether to purchase a Bic pen or a Papermate pen, both of which cost 50 cents
    i. Purchasing an issue of *Consumer Reports* magazine for $3 that contains a review of new automobiles to help you decide whether to purchase a Ford Explorer or a Jeep Cherokee

MULTIPLE CHOICE

1. Which one of the following would *reduce* the efficiency of the market process?
    a. promoting competitive markets
    b. protecting persons from fraud and theft
    c. providing a stable monetary environment
    d. protecting consumers by imposing legally mandated price ceilings

2. It is difficult for the market process to provide public goods because
    a. private firms generally cannot undertake large-scale projects.
    b. it will be difficult to get potential consumers to pay for such goods since there is not a direct link between payment for and receipt of the good.
    c. consumers do not really want public goods, even though such goods are best for them.
    d. individuals are generally made worse off by the production of public goods.

3. Which of the following is true about the market and public sectors?
   a. Competitive behavior is present in both sectors.
   b. The public sector utilizes the price mechanism more than the private sector.
   c. In both sectors, individuals always pay for the goods and services they consume.
   d. There is more free choice for individual consumers in the public sector than in the private sector.

4. Despite many differences, the market and public sectors are *similar* in which one of the following respects?
   a. In both sectors, income (or power) is distributed on the basis of the same criterion.
   b. Consumers in the market sector and voters in the public sector are equally well informed.
   c. Voluntary exchange, rather than compulsion, is characteristic of both sectors.
   d. It will be costly to use scarce goods, whether through the private or the public sector.

5. Which of the following activities is *least* likely to give rise to external costs or benefits?
   a. spraying to control mosquitos in your backyard
   b. driving one's car during rush hour
   c. inoculating your children during a flu epidemic
   d. buying a hamburger and eating it for lunch

6. Driving your automobile in Los Angeles during the rush hour causes externalities because
   a. it adds congestion and pollution from auto exhaust, reducing the welfare of others.
   b. gasoline is scarce and you must pay for it.
   c. gasoline is a public good.
   d. your actions will benefit others even though you will be unable to charge them for the service.

7. Criteria of ideal economic efficiency requires that (I) all actions generating more social benefit than cost be undertaken and (II) no actions generating more social cost than social benefit be undertaken.
   a. Both I and II are true.
   b. Both I and II are false.
   c. I is true; II is false.
   d. II is true; I is false.

8. Which of the following "goods" is the best example of a pure public good?
   a. highways
   b. national defense
   c. mail delivery
   d. welfare programs

9. In the absence of government intervention, goods with external costs tend to be
   a. overproduced.
   b. underproduced.
   c. efficiently produced.
   d. offset by goods generating external benefits.

10. The *absence* of well-defined and enforceable private property rights often
    a. causes people to work together for the common good.
    b. improves society because it avoids the selfish actions of private property owners.
    c. causes difficulties for society due to externalities.
    d. brings about efficiency by providing incentives to conserve resources.

11. The major distinction between private and public goods is that
    a. private goods are goods produced by private firms while public goods are goods produced by government—the public sector.
    b. unlike private goods, public goods are nonexcludable—it is difficult or impossible to prevent nonpaying customers from receiving the good.
    c. unlike private goods, public goods are joint-in-consumption—the consumption of a unit by one person does not detract from the amount available to others.
    d. both b and c are correct.

12. New products provide a classic case of the consumer information problem. However, in some cases consumers partially solve the problem by trusting the "brand name" of the producer of the new product. Since firms spend millions of dollars advertising and maintaining their brand names, the likelihood of a "brand name" firm's intentionally selling a dangerous or shoddy new product is
    a. high because big firms are always after a quick dollar.
    b. high because their brand name is a communal property right.
    c. low because big firms do not make mistakes.
    d. low because the firm with a brand name has a lot to lose if word spreads about bad consumer experiences.

13. Which of the following is legally permitted to use coercive force to modify the actions of adults against their will?
    a. banks
    b. corporations
    c. governments
    d. all of the above

14. Which of the following correctly describes an **external benefit** resulting from an individual's purchase of a winter flu shot?
    a. The flu shot is cheaper than the cost of treatment when you get the flu.
    b. The income of doctors increases when you get the flu shot.
    c. The flu shot reduces the likelihood of others catching the flu.
    d. The flu shot reduces the likelihood you will miss work as the result of sickness; therefore, you will earn more income.

Harcourt Brace & Company

15. Which of the following would be a protective function of government?
    a. providing national defense
    b. welfare programs and income redistribution
    c. mail delivery
    d. all of the above

16. Consider two goods—one that generates external benefits and another that generates external costs. A competitive market economy would tend to produce
    a. too much of both goods.
    b. too little of both goods.
    c. too much of the good that generates external benefits and too little of the good that generates external cost.
    d. too little of the good that generates external benefits and too much of the good that generates the external cost.

17. Externalities are due to which of the following?
    a. poorly defined or enforced private property rights
    b. individuals not caring sufficiently about the welfare of others
    c. the choice of a capitalist, rather than socialist, economy
    d. poor information on the part of buyers and sellers

18. The problem created when it is difficult to exclude nonpaying customers is called the
    a. consumption-payment link problem.
    b. free-rider problem.
    c. public sector dilemma.
    d. asymmetric information problem.

19. General agreement exists that the legitimate economic functions of government include
    a. protection against invasions from a foreign power.
    b. provision of goods that cannot easily be provided through markets.
    c. the maintenance of a framework of rules within which people can interact peacefully with one another.
    d. all of the above.

DISCUSSION QUESTIONS

1. Provide a specific example for each of the reasons why unregulated markets might fail to be efficient. For each case explain how government intervention might promote efficiency.

2. List as many goods as you can think of that have substantial public good characteristics that are provided by the private sector. Try weather forecasts and radio broadcasts for starters. Pick two of these goods and answer the following questions: How does the market cope with the public goods aspect of the good? Does

the market produce enough of the good? Would government provision of the good be more efficient?

3. For decades, smokers were free to smoke almost everywhere—at work, at parties, on airplanes, and in restaurants. Today, smokers face increasing restrictions about where they can smoke. Some of these restrictions are the result of government policy, but many have arisen without legislation and are simply imposed by private companies (such as airlines, restaurants, and private employers). The latter set of restrictions represent a nongovernmental solution to the externalities created by smokers. Can you think of other activities that generate negative externalities that are regulated in a similar manner?

4. Your decision about which college to attend is an example of a non-repeat, major purchase about which few individuals have full information. Do you feel like you made a good choice? Is there any way for you to know that you made the best choice? What sources did you use to obtain information about the various colleges and universities? How many of these sources were provided by the market? by the government? Does poor information pose a problem for the market for higher education?

5. In general, it has been argued that private sector markets will allocate too few resources to public goods like national defense. Do you think the public sector allocates too few, too many, or just the right amount of resources to such goods? What is your evidence? How should you go about determining the socially optimal amount of public goods to produce? Does government intervention necessarily imply that the good will be produced efficiently?

6. Consider each of the following quotes:

    "Following the example set by the ending of Prohibition, we should legalize marijuana, cocaine, and certain other drugs we have failed to control. Excise taxes and punishments could hold drug use to tolerable levels and discourage their use prior to engaging in activities that might harm others." (Gary Becker, economist)

    "Drug use is out of control in our society. Making it legal would only reinforce the erroneous perception that drugs such as marijuana and cocaine can be used without consequences." (Lee I. Dogoloff, Executive Director, American Council for Drug Education)

    Assume you are the vice president of the United States and have to cast a vote to break a tie in the Senate on the issue of legalization of marijuana and cocaine. In a single paragraph, state your decision, and carefully and clearly support your position. Be sure to address both points of view expressed above.

Harcourt Brace & Company

CHAPTER 6

The Economics of Collective Decision Making

TRUE OR FALSE

T F

☐ ☐ 1. Well-organized special interest groups may be able to use the political process for their own gain even though the action is inefficient and results in a net social loss.

☐ ☐ 2. The shortsightedness effect implies that a policy providing immediate, readily identified benefits at the expense of costs in the future that are difficult to identify tends to be very attractive to a legislator seeking reelection.

☐ ☐ 3. Logrolling and pork-barrel legislation are rules designed to prevent individual legislators from getting special interest policies for their districts passed.

☐ ☐ 4. Rent seeking is when an individual spends time and money in an effort to influence government policy in their favor.

☐ ☐ 5. When an individual votes, they will attempt to gain all available information about the candidate and the issues involved.

☐ ☐ 6. The efficiency of the political process would be enhanced if the costs of government action (taxes) were more closely linked to the benefits people receive from government action.

☐ ☐ 7. Government failure strengthens the case for use of the market system.

☐ ☐ 8. An individual voter has a strong economic incentive to fight special interest legislation with his or her own time and money because such legislation is costly to all members of society.

☐ ☐ 9. The majority of government income transfer programs are directed toward the poor.

☐ ☐ 10. The assumption that politicians behave in a self-interested fashion is premised largely on the fact that politicians who fail to do so will often also fail to be reelected.

☐ ☐ 11. A voter usually must choose among candidates whose positions represent complex bundles of goods, services, and costs to the voter.

☐ ☐ 12. When voters pay in proportion to benefits received, all voters gain from productive (i.e., efficient) government action.

T F

☐ ☐ 13. The exchange between politicians of political support for issues (vote trading) is called pork-barrel legislation.

☐ ☐ 14. Even if a policy is inefficient, government is likely to enact it if the benefits are concentrated in a small interest group and if the costs are widespread.

☐ ☐ 15. Even if a policy is efficient, government is *not* likely to enact it if the costs are concentrated in a small interest group and if the benefits are widespread.

PROBLEMS AND PROJECTS

1. Exhibit 1 presents data on the benefits received by three voters for two different proposals up for vote, A and B. Also shown in the table are two possible tax-sharing arrangements for each project. The equal tax is if they split the total cost of the project equally, while the benefit tax is the case where each person pays the same percent of the total tax bill as the percent of the benefits they receive from the project.
   a. Proposal A creates a total benefit of $200, and the total cost of the project (as shown by the total tax needed) is $150. Is project A efficient? Is project B efficient?
   b. Suppose only the equal tax plans are considered and majority rule is used to make the decisions. Would proposal A pass (win majority approval) under the equal tax-sharing arrangement? Would proposal B pass under the equal tax-sharing arrangement?
   c. Are the outcomes in part b consistent with the criterion of efficiency in part a?
   d. Under the benefit tax shown, each taxpayer is assessed the same proportion of the total tax as the proportion of the benefits they receive from the project. For example, Bob receives one-half the benefits from project B ($50 of $100), so is charged one-half the total tax ($60 of $120). Under the ben-

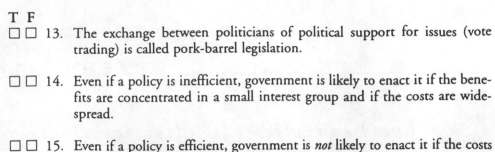

	EXHIBIT 1					
	PROPOSAL A			PROPOSAL B		
VOTER	BENEFIT	EQUAL TAX	BENEFIT TAX	BENEFIT	EQUAL TAX	BENEFIT TAX
Adam	$140	$50	$105	$5	$40	$6
Bob	40	50	30	50	40	60
Cathy	20	50	15	45	40	54
Totals	$200	$150	$150	$100	$120	$120

Harcourt Brace & Company

efits tax plan, would proposal A pass? Would proposal B pass under the benefits tax?
e. Are the outcomes in part d consistent with the criterion of efficiency in part a? If you want government to pass only efficient projects, would it be better to use equal taxes or taxes in proportion to benefits received?

2. Exhibit 2 shows the net benefits (benefits minus tax cost) from three different government projects for three districts.
a. By looking at the Totals row at the bottom of the table, which of these projects are efficient? Which are inefficient?

EXHIBIT 2

| REPRESENTATIVE OF DISTRICT | NET BENEFITS (+) OR COSTS (–) TO DISTRICT | | |
	NEW ROAD IN DISTRICT A	NEW PARK IN DISTRICT B	NEW DAM IN DISTRICT C
A	$+10	$–5	$–2
B	–6	+9	–2
C	–6	–5	+13
Totals	–2	–1	+9

b. If each project was put up for vote individually (by majority rule), which would pass? Which would fail?
c. Suppose you were the representative of district A and wanted to get your new road passed. You only need one more vote for a majority. Would both you and the representative of district B be willing to "trade" votes to get your projects passed? That is, would you be willing to vote for B's park if he voted for your road? Would he agree to the trade as well?
d. Now, consider a "pork-barrel" bill that contained all three projects. How would each representative vote on the total bill containing all three projects?

3. Consider the supply and demand for public sector action, and decide whether each of the following illustrates
(1) rent-seeking behavior by private parties,
(2) vote-seeking behavior by elected officials, or
(3) the rational ignorance effect.
____ a. Members of Congress rejected bills that would have restricted the lobbying activities of political action coalitions (PACs).
____ b. Election results are often distorted by poorly informed voters and low voter turnouts.
____ c. Liquor wholesalers in most states have lobbied for state laws that compel retailers to buy their liquor supplies only from the nearest available wholesaler, instead of shopping around.
____ d. Many voters support import tariffs and quotas on foreign goods even though such protectionism costs consumers over $80 billion in 1988.

Harcourt Brace & Company

___ e. A steel company sends a $50 million campaign contribution to a legislator in a year in which a bill is being debated that would affect the steel industry.

4. Exhibit 3 shows the classification of government actions into four types depending upon how concentrated or widespread the benefits and costs of the action are.
   a. For which types of action is government likely to work the best (that is most consistent) with economic efficiency?
   b. For which type of action is government likely to have a bias toward adopting the actions even if they are inefficient?
   c. For which type of action is government likely to have a bias against adopting the actions even if they are efficient?

EXHIBIT 3

	Distribution of Benefits	
	Widespread	Concentrated
Distribution of Costs Widespread	Type 1	Type 2
Concentrated	Type 4	Type 3

Classify each of the following as type 1, 2, 3, or 4 according to the above exhibit.
d. A $1 tax on every citizen to provide large subsidies to tobacco farmers
e. A 10 percent tax on the profits of major gasoline retailers (BP, Shell, Exxon, etc.) to finance government-funded research on solar energy
f. An increase in the income tax to finance an increase in national defense spending
g. A $5 increase in student tuition to finance increases in professor salaries
h. A law allowing consumers to buy prescription drugs on the advice of their pharmacist without a visit to a medical doctor (who are strongly represented by the American Medical Association)
i. A 1 percent increase in Social Security taxes on current workers to finance large benefit increases for those currently receiving Social Security payments
j. Reductions in subsidies to sugar farmers to finance the increases in Social Security benefits

Harcourt Brace & Company

MULTIPLE CHOICE

The following quotation relates to questions 1 and 2.

"The ideal policy, from the viewpoint of the state, is one with identifiable beneficiaries, each of whom is helped appreciably, at the cost of many unidentifiable persons, none of whom is hurt very much." (George Stigler, *A Dialogue on the Proper Economic Role of the State*)

1. This statement is probably
   a. incorrect because voters are well informed on a wide range of political issues.
   b. incorrect because the political process dilutes the influence of special interest groups, since like other citizens, their members have only one vote.
   c. correct because the well-informed voter will favor policies that cater to the views of small groups of people.
   d. correct because voters who have a strong personal interest in an issue will tend to support candidates who cater to their views, whereas most other voters ignore the issue.

2. Which of the following groups does the above quotation suggest would have the most influence on public sector action?
   a. taxpayers
   b. nonunion workers
   c. special interest groups
   d. consumers

3. Economists use the term *shortsightedness effect* to describe which one of the following phenomena?
   a. Politicians tend to support actions that have immediate and easily recognized current benefits.
   b. Individuals are apt to spend their income on goods that bring immediate personal benefits.
   c. Voters elect politicians on the basis of campaign promises, regardless of what they may do once they are in office.
   d. Politicians support the programs of special interest groups in order to get elected; however, special interest support may be detrimental later, costing politicians popularity after the programs are implemented.

4. Economic theory leads us to expect that the typical voter will be uninformed on many issues because
   a. most issues are so complex that voters will be unable to understand them.
   b. even though information is free, most voters do not care.
   c. information is costly, and the individual voter casting a well-informed vote can expect negligible personal benefit.
   d. citizen apathy about political matters is inevitable, except when decisions are made by referendum.

5. Public choice theory suggests that politicians will be most likely to favor redistribution of income from
   a. the rich to the poor.
   b. disorganized individuals to well-organized special interest groups.
   c. middle-income taxpayers to both rich and the poor.
   d. well-organized business and labor groups to consumers.

6. Giving local governments more power is less dangerous than giving the same power to the national government because
   a. local governments generally have more strict constitutional rules they must operate under.
   b. it is easier to vote in local elections than national elections.
   c. only national-level governments are allowed to use coercive force.
   d. higher exit options exist at the local level—it is easier for people to move away from a bad local government.

7. Assume that you are a member of the U.S. House of Representatives from your home state and district. Which of the following best explains why you have a strong incentive to get the federal government to finance pork-barrel projects in your district?
   a. Most of the benefits of pork-barrel projects within your district will accrue to your constituents, while most of the costs will be imposed on voters from other districts.
   b. Most of the costs of pork-barrel projects within your district will be imposed on your constituents, while most of the benefits will accrue to voters from other districts.
   c. Pork producers are a powerful political lobby that will influence the actions of legislators in all districts.
   d. This is a trick question; in a representative democracy, there is little incentive for legislators to support pork-barrel projects.

8. The theory of public choice
   a. analyzes the likelihood that various public sector alternatives will be instituted.
   b. assumes that economic incentives influence the choices of voters.
   c. applies the tools of economics to the collective decision-making process.
   d. all of the above

9. When analyzing public sector decision making, economic theory assumes that voters, politicians, and government officials will
   a. respond to changes in personal benefits and costs when making public sector choices.
   b. pursue the public interest even when it conflicts with their private interests.
   c. pursue primarily public interests since competition is less intense in the public sector.
   d. do none of the above.

10. Public choice theory indicates that competitive forces between candidates in elections provide a politician with a strong incentive to offer voters a bundle of political goods that she believes
    a. is best for the economic and political situations the country faces.
    b. will most likely clear the legislative process.
    c. will increase the welfare of society.
    d. will increase her chances of winning elections.

11. When voters pay in proportion to the benefits received from an economic action of the government, if the government activity is productive,
    a. all voters will gain.
    b. only a smaller proportion of voters will gain.
    c. less than a simple majority of voters will gain.
    d. approximately 50 percent of the voters will gain.

12. In which case is the political process most likely to result in the acceptance of productive programs and rejection of unproductive political activities?
    a. when the benefits are highly concentrated and costs widespread among voters
    b. when the costs are highly concentrated and the benefits widespread among voters
    c. when both the benefits and costs are widespread among voters
    d. when the benefits accrue primarily in the future, while the costs are more visible during the current period

13. When is representative democracy most likely to lead to the adoption of an inefficient government program?
    a. when the program provides substantial benefits to a small proportion of voters and the costs are widespread among voters
    b. when both the benefits and costs of the program are widespread among voters
    c. when the program is financed by a user charge
    d. when a close relationship exists between the personal benefits received from the program and the tax cost imposed on each voter

14. Legislators often gain by bundling a number of projects benefiting local districts at the expense of general taxpayers. Such legislation is called
    a. market failure legislation.
    b. the rational ignorance effect.
    c. public goods legislation.
    d. pork-barrel legislation.

15. Which of the following refers to when legislators trade votes on legislation?
    a. logrolling
    b. the special interest effect
    c. rational ignorance
    d. the shortsightedness effect

Harcourt Brace & Company

16. Which of the following is a predictable side effect of increased government activity (e.g., taxes and subsidies) designed to redistribute income among citizens?
    a. improvement in the operational efficiency of government agencies
    b. budget surpluses
    c. reduction in the poverty rate
    d. an increase in rent-seeking activity

17. Legislation that offers immediate and easily recognized benefits, at the expense of uncertain costs that are in the distant future (such as financing by government debt), is often enacted even when economic inefficiency results. This can be expected because of
    a. a lack of incentive for operational efficiency in the public sector.
    b. market failure.
    c. the special-interest effect.
    d. the shortsightedness effect.

18. Public choice analysis indicates that
    a. because government action provides public goods, it always increases the wealth of the citizenry.
    b. unconstrained democratic governments often enact special-interest programs that waste resources and impair the standard of living.
    c. constitutional rules limiting public-sector activity generally lower the economic efficiency of the overall economy.
    d. Politicians and voters are better able to judge the public interest than their own private interest.

DISCUSSION QUESTIONS

1. Do you find the public choice theory of political behavior convincing? What do you see as its strengths? its weaknesses? Do you think most politicians are motivated by personal self interest? Cite evidence in support of your answer.

2. Why are well-organized special interest groups likely to be politically powerful? Why will vote-seeking politicians have an incentive to cater to their views?

3. "Government bureaucrats are only as important as the size of their departments, so they will always spend their entire budget allocation to avoid having their budgets cut in the next year."
    a. Do you agree with this quote? Why or why not?
    b. If bureaucrats act this way, what are the implications for the efficiency of government-run bureaus? Will they minimize their costs?

4. What are the major factors that contribute to market failure? What are the major factors that contribute to government failure? Which type of failure do you think is more common? more costly?

Harcourt Brace & Company

5.   In recent years there has been a widespread discontent with the large size of income transfer programs in the United States. Welfare programs for the poor are subject to much heated criticism, whereas other transfer programs, like farm subsidies, are less often and less heatedly criticized. At the same time, large transfer programs like Social Security and Medicare are labeled as politically "untouchable." What explains why there is a greater clamor to cut welfare programs rather than farm subsidy programs? To what extent can public choice theory explain the difference? In an era when many are calling for substantial reductions in income transfer programs, why is it considered politically impossible to cut Social Security or Medicare?

Harcourt Brace & Company

CHAPTER 7

Demand and Consumer Choice

TRUE OR FALSE

T F

☐ ☐ 1. The price of diamonds exceeds that of water; therefore, consumers derive more total utility from diamonds than from water.

☐ ☐ 2. The price of diamonds exceeds that of water; therefore, consumers derive more marginal utility from one additional diamond than from one additional unit of water.

☐ ☐ 3. The law of diminishing marginal utility suggests that you would value the third milkshake on a given day less than the second.

☐ ☐ 4. The market demand curve is a horizontal summation of the demand curves of all individuals in the market.

☐ ☐ 5. Economic theory suggests that when deciding whether to buy a $25 shirt, you will consider the value you get from the shirt relative to the value of the other items that you could buy with the $25.

☐ ☐ 6. Consumer surplus is generally equal to the price paid for an item.

☐ ☐ 7. The income and substitution effects are the two effects leading consumers to change their consumption of a good when its price changes.

☐ ☐ 8. If a university faces an elastic demand for enrollment and lowers its tuition (price), the university's total tuition revenue will decrease.

☐ ☐ 9. Because income is limited due to scarcity, when a consumer uses some of their income to purchase a good, they give up the use of that income to purchase other goods.

☐ ☐ 10. Generally, the marginal benefit derived from a good increases with the rate of consumption.

☐ ☐ 11. A risk-averse person is less likely to purchase insurance than a risk-loving person.

☐ ☐ 12. The opportunity cost of time is an important factor in consumer decisions.

T F

☐ ☐ 13. When demand is inelastic, an increase in the price of a good causes total revenue (or total expenditure) to fall.

☐ ☐ 14. The demand for Ford automobiles is more elastic than the demand for automobiles in general.

☐ ☐ 15. The short-run demand for a good is generally more elastic than the long-run demand.

☐ ☐ 16. To maximize its revenue, a firm would set its price at the level where demand is unitary elastic (elasticity equals one).

PROBLEMS AND PROJECTS

1. The following questions relate to the price elasticity of demand.
   a. The most basic version of the price elasticity formula states that the price elasticity of demand is equal to the percentage change in quantity divided by the percentage change in price [$e = \%\Delta Q \div \%\Delta P$]. The law of demand states, however, that whenever price rises (+), quantity demanded falls (–); and whenever price falls (–), quantity demanded rises (+). What does this imply about the true sign of the price elasticity of demand? Is it always negative or positive? If your local clothing store had a 50-percent-off sale (that is, reduced its prices by 50 percent) and as a result it sold 25 percent more shirts, what is the price elasticity of demand?
   b. Economists generally ignore the sign of price elasticity (that is, we generally use the absolute value). The larger the computed elasticity number, the more elastic (or less inelastic) the demand for the product, while the smaller the number, the less elastic (or more inelastic) the demand for the product. In addition, we term elasticity as either elastic, inelastic, or unitary elastic depending upon whether the elasticity value is greater than, less than, or equal to one, respectively. If the demand for cigarettes has an elasticity of 0.6, while the demand for oranges has an elasticity of 2.3, how would you classify these demands? If the demand for apples had an elasticity of 2.1, would you say that the demand for apples is more or less elastic than the demand for oranges?
   c. Whenever you are given specific quantities and prices, you will have to find the percentage changes yourself to plug into the elasticity formula. Economists generally use a special "arc" formula for finding these percentage changes. For example, to find the percentage change in quantity, we would take the difference between the two quantities [$Q_2 - Q_1$] and divide it by the average of (or midpoint between) the two quantities [which can be found as $(Q_1 + Q_2) \div 2$]. The percentage change in price is found in a similar manner by taking the difference in the two prices divided by the average of the two prices. If price falls from $9 to $7, what is the percentage change

in price using this formula? If quantity rises from 30 to 50, what is the percentage change in quantity using this formula? Now use these percentage changes to find the elasticity of demand. Is demand elastic or inelastic?

2. The first two columns of Exhibit 1 indicate Keri's marginal benefit she derives from consuming additional pairs of jeans. Remember, marginal benefit is simply Keri's maximum amount that she would be willing to pay for that specific pair

EXHIBIT 1

(1) QUANTITY	(2) MARGINAL BENEFIT		(3) PRICE	(4) QUANTITY PURCHASED	(5) TOTAL EXPENDITURE	(6) PRICE ELASTICITY OF DEMAND
1	$40		$10	_____	_____	
2	30		20	_____	_____	
3	20		30	_____	_____	
4	10		40	_____	_____	

of jeans. Follow the questions below to fill in the missing information in the exhibit.

a. In the space provided, graph Keri's marginal benefit curve for jeans from the data given in columns (1) and (2). Do Keri's preferences reflect the law of diminishing marginal utility? How can you tell?

b. Economic theory states that a consumer will purchase all units of a product for which their maximum willingness to pay (that is, their marginal benefit) is greater than or equal to the price of the good. Using the marginal benefit curve you have graphed, fill in the quantity of jeans Keri will purchase in column (4) at the different prices given in column (3).

c. A demand curve simply shows how many units of a good a person will purchase at different prices. This is the data you now have in columns (3) and (4). If you were to graph Keri's demand curve for jeans, how would it compare to Keri's marginal benefit curve that you drew in part a?

d. Keri's total spending (total expenditures) on jeans is equal to the number of pairs of jeans she purchases times the price she pays for each pair. Columns (3) and (4) show how many pairs she will buy at different prices. Fill in Keri's total spending in column (5) for each different price and quantity combination along her demand curve.

e. When the price rises from $10 per pair of jeans to $20 per pair, what happens to Keri's total spending on jeans? For a price increase to cause this to happen to total expenditures, what must Keri's price elasticity of demand be, elastic, inelastic, or unitary elastic?

Harcourt Brace & Company

f. When the price rises from $20 per pair of jeans to $30 per pair, what happens to Keri's total spending on jeans? For this to happen, what must Keri's price elasticity of demand be, elastic, inelastic, or unitary elastic?

g. When the price rises from $30 per pair of jeans to $40 per pair, what happens to Keri's total spending on jeans? For this to happen, what must Keri's price elasticity of demand be, elastic, inelastic, or unitary elastic?

h. Double check your answers to parts e through g by using the price elasticity formula to calculate Keri's price elasticity of jeans for each price change. Place the results of your calculations in column (6). Do your values correspond to your answers above?

3. The table on the left side of Exhibit 2 shows the quantity of compact discs that both Ann and Bob will purchase at different prices. Follow the questions below to fill in the remaining information in the exhibit.

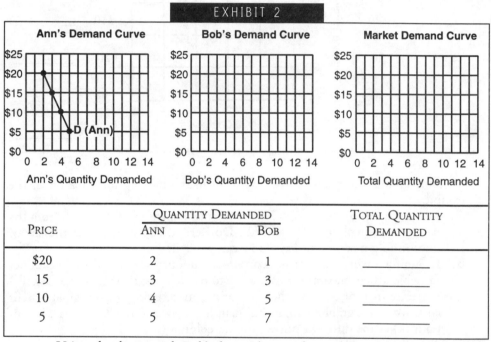

EXHIBIT 2

PRICE	QUANTITY DEMANDED		TOTAL QUANTITY DEMANDED
	ANN	BOB	
$20	2	1	_____
15	3	3	_____
10	4	5	_____
5	5	7	_____

a. Using the data, graph Bob's demand curve for compact discs (Ann's demand curve is already graphed as an example).

b. Assume that the entire market consisted of only Ann and Bob. The total market demand curve can be found by summing up the individual demands in the market. First, fill in the column for the total quantity demanded, then graph the market demand curve in the space provided.

c. At a price of $10 per compact disc, how many will Ann purchase? How many will Bob purchase? What is the total number of compact discs purchased by both Ann and Bob at a price of $10?

d. Suppose the price of compact discs rises from $10 to $15. How will Ann's purchases change? How will Bob's purchases change? How will the total purchases change? Whose purchases are more responsive to the price change,

Harcourt Brace & Company

Ann or Bob? Who would you say has the more elastic demand for compact discs?

4. Exhibit 3 shows the quantity of beer sold at Sammy's pub at different prices for beer. Use the data shown to answer the following questions.
   a. Fill in Sammy's total revenue for each price of beer shown.

	EXHIBIT 3		
PRICE	QUANTITY OF BEER SOLD	TOTAL REVENUE	ELASTICITY OF DEMAND
$1	600	_____	
2	400	_____	
3	200	_____	

   b. When Sammy raises his price from $1 to $2, what happens to his total revenue? For a price increase to cause this to happen to total revenue, what must be the elasticity of demand, elastic, inelastic, or unitary elastic? Use the formula to calculate the price elasticity of demand to confirm your answer.
   c. When Sammy raises his price from $2 to $3, what happens to his total revenue? For a price increase to cause this to happen to total revenue, what must be the elasticity of demand, elastic, inelastic, or unitary elastic? Use the formula to calculate the price elasticity of demand to confirm your answer.
   d. As a student in economics, Sammy asks you whether lowering the price of his beer is a good idea to generate more revenue. Is it? Does your answer depend on what price he is currently charging?
   e. Generally, customers leave tips for their waiter or waitress as a percent of their total purchase in dollars. If you were the waiter or waitress serving all of these beers, what price would you want Sammy to set in order for you to make the most money in tips? Explain your reasoning.
   f. As Sammy raised his price from $2 to $3, his revenue fell from $800 to $600. Suppose the demand for Sammy's beer had been less sensitive to price (that is, more inelastic), so that the price increase would have only caused his beer sales to fall to 300 at a price of $3 instead of 200. Would Sammy's revenue still have fallen when he raised price?
   g. If Sammy lowered his price from $2 to $1, his revenue would fall from $800 to $600. Suppose the demand for Sammy's beer had been more sensitive to price (that is, more elastic), so that the price reduction would have caused his beer sales to rise to 900 at a price of $1 instead of 600. Would Sammy's revenue still have fallen when he lowered price?

5. Exhibit 4 on page 74 shows the possible demand curves for a product, D_1 and D_2. Use the information in the exhibit to answer the following questions.

Harcourt Brace & Company

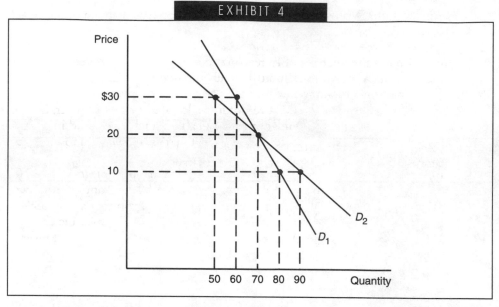

EXHIBIT 4

a. If the demand curve for this product was D_1, and price rose from $20 to $30, what would happen to the quantity purchased? If the demand curve for this product was instead D_2, and price rose from $20 to $30, what would happen to the quantity purchased? Given your answers, which demand curve would you consider more *elastic*? Which demand curve would you consider more *inelastic*?

b. If the demand curve for this product was D_1, and price fell from $20 to $10, what would happen to the quantity purchased? If the demand curve for this product was instead D_2, and price fell from $20 to $10, what would happen to the quantity purchased? Given your answers, which demand curve would you consider more *elastic*? Which demand curve would you consider more *inelastic*?

c. Does your conclusion about which demand curve is more elastic or inelastic depend upon which direction price changed? That is, are your answers to parts a and b the same?

6. John owns a restaurant that serves a lunch buffet. He currently charges $5 for the buffet and has 20 regular customers who come each day. His daily lunch revenue is $100 ($5 per person times 20 people). In an attempt to increase his revenue, he lowers the price to $4. John's regular customers are very happy about the price reduction, as it means they will each be paying less for their lunch each day.

a. How much revenue will John lose from his 20 regular customers as a result of reducing the price from $5 to $4, assuming they all continue to eat there each day?

b. If 3 new customers come each day now that the price is $4, will that be enough new customer revenue to make up for the lost revenue on John's regular customers? By how much will John's *total* daily lunch revenue change?

c. If, instead, 5 new customers come each day now that the price is $4, will that be enough new customer revenue to make up for the lost revenue on John's

Harcourt Brace & Company

regular customers? By how much will his *total* daily lunch revenue change in this case?

d. If, instead, 10 new customers come each day now that the price is $4, will that be enough new customer revenue to make up for the lost revenue on John's regular customers? By how much will his *total* daily lunch revenue change in this case?

e. In all three cases presented above, John has lowered price. However, in one case his daily revenue fell, in another it remained unchanged, and in another it increased. Can you relate your answers to parts b through d to the price elasticity of demand?

f. Instead of lowering his price, suppose John raises his price from $5 to $10. For a price increase, the change in his revenue can be decomposed into two parts: (1) the increased revenue on those customers who stay at the higher price and (2) the lost revenue from those customers who leave. Do this for the case where John loses 10 of his 20 regular customers as a result of raising price. Based upon your answer, what do you think would happen to his revenue if only 5 customers left? If 15 customers left? Can you relate these answers for a price increase to the price elasticity of demand?

7. Fill in the missing entries in Exhibit 5 based upon your knowledge about the relationship between demand elasticity, changes in price, and changes in total revenue (or total expenditure).

EXHIBIT 5

PRICE ELASTICITY	CHANGE IN PRICE	CHANGE IN TOTAL REVENUE
0.2	down	_____
3.5	_____	down
1.0	up	_____
0.9	_____	up
_____	down	no change
6.3	down	_____

MULTIPLE CHOICE

1. A 15 percent increase in the price of beef reduces the quantity of beef consumed by 30 percent. Thus, the demand for beef is _____ and total consumer expenditure (or total firm revenue) will _____ as a result of the price increase. (Fill in the blanks.)
   a. elastic; increase
   b. elastic; decrease
   c. inelastic; increase
   d. inelastic; decrease

2. Which of the following is true about marginal benefit?
   a. A consumer's marginal benefit is equal to the height of her demand curve.
   b. Consumers will continue to purchase up until the point where marginal benefit equals price.
   c. Marginal benefit declines as consumption increases because of the law of diminishing marginal utility.
   d. All of the above are true.

3. Jane received a 10 percent increase in her salary and purchased 20 percent more jewelry. For Jane, jewelry
   a. has an income elasticity of two.
   b. is a normal good.
   c. is a luxury good.
   d. is all of the above.

4. An inferior good is distinguished by
   a. a negative price elasticity of demand.
   b. a positive price elasticity of demand.
   c. a positive income elasticity of demand.
   d. a negative income elasticity of demand.

5. If Joe's income increased and as a result he purchased more wine and less fast food,
   a. wine is a normal good and fast food an inferior good for Joe.
   b. wine is an inferior good and fast food a normal good for Joe.
   c. both wine and fast food are inferior goods for Joe.
   d. both wine and fast food are normal goods for Joe.

6. "After eating nothing but fast-food hamburgers on spring break, I was anxious to return home and eat something different." This statement most clearly reflects the law of
   a. the budget constraint.
   b. consumer irrationality.
   c. greater demand elasticity with time.
   d. diminishing marginal utility.

7. If the price elasticity of demand for grapes was 2.5,
   a. the demand for grapes would be considered inelastic.
   b. an increase in the price of grapes would decrease total consumer spending on grapes.
   c. consumer purchases are less sensitive to a change in the price of grapes than to a change in the price of bananas, which have a price elasticity of 1.6.
   d. the income elasticity for grapes must also be 2.5.

8. If a 50 percent increase in the price of hula hoops led to a 10 percent reduction in the quantity of hula hoops purchased, the price elasticity of demand is
   a. 5 and the demand for hula hoops is elastic.
   b. 0.2 and the demand for hula hoops is elastic.
   c. 5 and the demand for hula hoops is inelastic.
   d. 0.2 and the demand for hula hoops is inelastic.

9. "Because of the unseasonably cold weather, Florida orange growers expect (1) fewer bushels of oranges to be harvested, (2) a higher market price for oranges, and (3) larger total revenues from this year's crop." This statement would most likely be correct if
   a. the demand for Florida oranges was elastic.
   b. the demand for Florida oranges was unitary elastic.
   c. the demand for Florida oranges was inelastic.
   d. the income elasticity of Florida oranges was negative.

10. If given a choice between receiving $100 in cash or playing a game in which a coin is flipped and receiving $200 if it is heads and nothing if it is tails,
    a. a risk-averse person would choose to play the coin-flip game.
    b. a risk-loving person would choose to receive the $100 in cash for certain.
    c. a risk-neutral person would be indifferent between the two alternatives.
    d. none of the above are true.

11. Use the diagram below to answer this question.

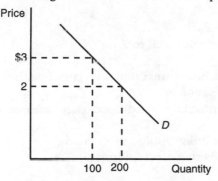

For this demand curve, the price elasticity of demand is
    a. more elastic at $3 than at $2.
    b. more elastic at $2 than at $3.
    c. identical at $2 to that at $3.
    d. equal to 1.0 over the range from $3 to $2.

12. A car wash currently sells 30 car washes a day at a price of $5. Total daily revenue is now $150. If they lower their price to $3,
    a. total revenue will fall if the number of washes sold only rises to 40.
    b. total revenue will remain unchanged if the number of washes sold rises to 50.
    c. total revenue will increase if the number of washes sold rises to 60.
    d. all of the above are true.

Harcourt Brace & Company

13. Coach Ballford: "To increase our revenue from football games, we need to lower ticket prices." University President Smith: "Coach, that would be counterproductive, a reduction in ticket prices would reduce our revenue, not increase it." Which of the following best explains this disagreement?
    a. The coach thinks that demand is elastic, while the university president thinks that demand is inelastic.
    b. The coach thinks that demand is inelastic, while the university president thinks that demand is elastic.
    c. The coach believes that lower ticket prices will increase attendance, but the university president must not believe attendance will increase when prices are lowered.
    d. While both the coach and the president believe demand is of unitary elasticity, they disagree about how much attendance will rise.

14. All else equal, if a firm raises its price by 20 percent and the firm's *total revenue* rises by 40 percent,
    a. demand must be elastic.
    b. demand must be inelastic.
    c. demand must be unit elastic.
    d. the price elasticity of demand must be equal to 2.

15. Which of the following is **not** a fundamental that underlies consumer behavior?
    a. Goods can be substituted for one another.
    b. Consumers make decisions purposefully based upon past experience and knowledge.
    c. The law of diminishing marginal utility applies to all goods.
    d. Consumers always make choices with perfect information.

16. Terri currently consumes 10 hamburgers and 2 shirts per month. At her current rates of consumption, her marginal utility of hamburgers is 10 and her marginal utility of shirts is 50. If the price of hamburgers is $2 each, while the price of a shirt is $25, Terri
    a. is maximizing her utility.
    b. could improve her total utility by buying fewer hamburgers and more shirts.
    c. could improve her total utility by buying fewer shirts and more hamburgers.
    d. could improve her total utility by spending less on both goods.

17. If taking an airplane from Pittsburgh to Miami cost $600 and takes 5 hours, while taking a bus would cost $150 and takes 50 hours, the minimum value of your time that would make it worthwhile to fly would be
    a. $1 per hour.
    b. $3 per hour.
    c. $10 per hour.
    d. $12 per hour.

Harcourt Brace & Company

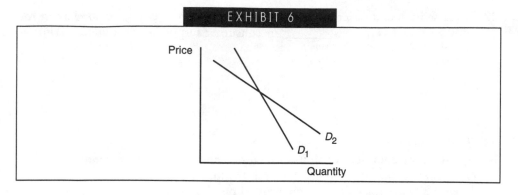

EXHIBIT 6

18. Exhibit 6 illustrates two possible demand curves for a product, D_1 and D_2. Which of the following is true regarding these demand curves?
   a. Demand curve D_1 represents a demand curve that is relatively more elastic than demand curve D_2.
   b. Demand curve D_1 represents a demand curve that is relatively more inelastic than demand curve D_2.
   c. Demand curve D_1 represents a demand curve that shows consumer purchases being more responsive to a change in the price of the good than demand curve D_2.
   d. Both are examples of unitary elastic demand curves.

19. Making drugs, such as cocaine, illegal results in a higher price than would be present if the drugs were legal. All else constant, the higher price results in drug users spending
   a. more on drugs if the demand for drugs is inelastic.
   b. more on drugs if the demand for drugs is elastic.
   c. less on drugs if the demand for drugs is inelastic.
   d. more on drugs if the demand for drugs is unitary elastic.

20. If the price of steak rises from $6 to $10 per pound, and the quantity purchased falls from 90 to 70 pounds, the price elasticity of demand (in absolute value) is
   a. 0.2.
   b. 0.5.
   c. 1.0.
   d. 2.0.

21. When the price elasticity of demand is greater than one, it means that demand is
   a. inelastic and the percent change in quantity is greater than the percent change in price.
   b. inelastic and the percent change in quantity is less than the percent change in price.
   c. elastic and the percent change in quantity is greater than the percent change in price.
   d. elastic and the percent change in quantity is less than the percent change in price.

Harcourt Brace & Company

22. If Russell values a ticket to a rock concert at $100 and is able to purchase it for only $40, he has received _____ in consumer surplus on his purchase. (Fill in the blank.)
    a. $40
    b. $60
    c. $100
    d. $140

23. The market demand for a good is
    a. the horizontal sum of all individual demand curves for the good.
    b. generally upward sloping, unlike individual demand curves.
    c. usually a vertical line at a quantity of one hundred.
    d. the average amount purchased by each individual in the market.

24. Bob goes out to dinner three times per week, usually either to the local steak house or a Chinese restaurant in town. If the steak house were to raise its prices, Bob would probably (1) be less inclined to eat at the steak house and more inclined to eat at the Chinese restaurant when he did go out and (2) eat out fewer times per week because at the higher prices he cannot afford to eat out as much.
    a. Part 1 is an example of the substitution effect, part 2 of the income effect.
    b. Part 1 is an example of the income effect, part 2 of the substitution effect.
    c. Part 1 is an example of the law of diminishing marginal utility, part 2 of the substitution effect.
    d. Part 1 is an example of the proportions hypothesis, part 2 of the income effect.

25. The price elasticity of demand for automobiles measures the responsiveness of
    a. consumer purchases to a change in the price of automobiles.
    b. consumer purchases to a change in the quality of automobiles.
    c. supplier production levels to a change in the price of automobiles.
    d. consumer purchases of automobiles to a change in their income.

26. Which of the following is true regarding the price elasticity of demand?
    a. Demand is generally more elastic in the long run than in the short run.
    b. Along a single demand curve, demand elasticity decreases as you move down the curve (to lower prices).
    c. A demand curve that is flatter (has a less steep slope) is relatively more elastic than a demand curve that has a steeper slope.
    d. All of the above are true.

DISCUSSION QUESTIONS

1. A recent newspaper reported that grocery stores are now selling floor space to firms for advertising. A sign on the floor of the supermarket with the brand name of the product increases sales of that product by 30 percent. The sign consists of nothing but the logo of the brand.

Harcourt Brace & Company

    a.   Why is such advertising effective?

    b.   How does a firm's large investment in establishing a brand name affect their incentive to keep product quality high?

    c.   More generally, what are the social costs of advertising? What are the social benefits?

2. For each of the following pairs of products, indicate which you think will have the lower price elasticity of demand. Explain your reasoning.

    a.   salt or tacos

    b.   Volkswagens or all automobiles

    c.   short-run electricity or long-run electricity

    d.   physician services or bus transportation

3. "Rich people spend much of their income on useless items. If consumers limited their purchases to those items they needed, we would have fewer economic problems."

    a.   What items do people spend their money on that are not necessary? Do you buy things you do not need? If so, why?

    b.   How can you determine if an item is useful or needed? Are demand and usefulness the same thing? How about a need and a want?

4. The following questions relate to the diamond/water paradox, which is a famous "puzzle" in economics.

    a.   Explain in your own words why diamonds are more expensive than water, despite the fact that water is essential for life, while diamonds are not. Which law of economics helps to explain why diamonds are more expensive than water?

    b.   What does a product's price measure, the total value created by the product or the value of an additional unit? Explain. What would measure total value?

    c.   If your professor gave you a gallon jug of water in class, would you bother carrying it home? How about a diamond? What is the least valuable thing you do with water each day?

5. Why is the price elasticity of demand always negative? Is the income elasticity of demand always negative too? Explain.

6. Goods are classified as having either elastic, inelastic, or unitary elastic demands based upon the value of the price elasticity coefficient. For each of these three cases, explain whether the percent change in quantity is greater than, less than, or equal to the percent change in price. How do these differences relate to the differing effect a price change can have on total revenue (or total expenditure), depending upon the value of price elasticity?

7. When is maximizing revenue the same as maximizing profit for a firm? Can you think of specific real-world situations where this condition is likely to be met? What price should a firm charge if it wishes to maximize revenue?

Harcourt Brace & Company

CHAPTER 8

Costs and the Supply of Goods

TRUE OR FALSE

T F

☐ ☐ 1. It is possible for a firm to be making an accounting profit but an economic loss.

☐ ☐ 2. Economic profit differs from accounting profit because it excludes opportunity costs (such as the opportunity cost of equity capital and forgone wages) from the calculation of profit.

☐ ☐ 3. The corporate form of business organization has two advantages: limited liability and the ease of ownership transfer.

☐ ☐ 4. The short run is a period of time so short that at least one factor of production is fixed.

☐ ☐ 5. A worker's marginal product is the change in total output that results from employing that worker.

☐ ☐ 6. The law of diminishing returns states that eventually each additional unit of a variable input employed with a fixed amount of other inputs will result in less additional output.

☐ ☐ 7. Average fixed costs (AFC) will always decline as output is expanded in the short run.

☐ ☐ 8. The change in total cost resulting from the production of one additional unit is called average variable cost.

☐ ☐ 9. Average total cost (ATC) will always increase when marginal cost (MC) is increasing.

☐ ☐ 10. As a firm expands output in the short run, total variable costs increase, but total fixed costs remain the same.

☐ ☐ 11. A firm is minimizing its per-unit costs of production if it operates where marginal cost (MC) equals average total cost (ATC).

☐ ☐ 12. A firm's total cost (TC) may be found by subtracting total variable cost (TVC) from total fixed cost (TFC).

☐ ☐ 13. The curve that shows how a firm's per-unit costs change over the long-run as plant size is expanded is the LRATC curve.

☐ ☐ 14. When a firm's per-unit costs fall as its plant size increases in the long run, it is said to be experiencing diseconomies of scale.

T F

☐ ☐ 15. A restaurant's average total cost (ATC) curve would shift upward if the price of food ingredients fell.

☐ ☐ 16. A good decision maker will always consider sunk costs in his decisions.

PROBLEMS AND PROJECTS

EXHIBIT 1

REVENUES		COSTS	
Sales	$57,000	Wholesale clothing	$30,000
		Equipment	2,000
		Labor	15,000
		Utilities and insurance	1,000
Total revenues	$57,000	Total costs	$48,000

1. Exhibit 1 represents the annual income statement of Joe's Clothing Store. Joe worked full time in the store and invested $30,000 of his own money to buy the store and stock it with merchandise. He recently turned down an offer of a salaried position paying $10,000 per year to manage another store. He did not pay himself a salary during the year. According to Exhibit 1,
   a. what were Joe's *accounting* profits?
   b. what major items did he exclude from his costs from an economic stand-point?
   c. if Joe could have earned 10 percent interest on his $30,000 by keeping it in the bank, how much interest is he losing per year by keeping the money invested in the store?
   d. recalculate Joe's total costs in light of your answers to b and c.
   e. what was the *economic* profit or loss of Joe's Clothing Store?

2. Exhibit 2 shows how a firm's total product, TP (which is the same as the firm's total output), changes as additional units of labor (L) are employed with a fixed amount of other resources in the short run.
   a. Fill in the missing data in the table for marginal product (MP) and average product (AP).
   b. Plot this firm's MP and AP curves in the space provided.
   c. At what level of labor usage does this firm begin to experience diminishing returns?

Harcourt Brace & Company

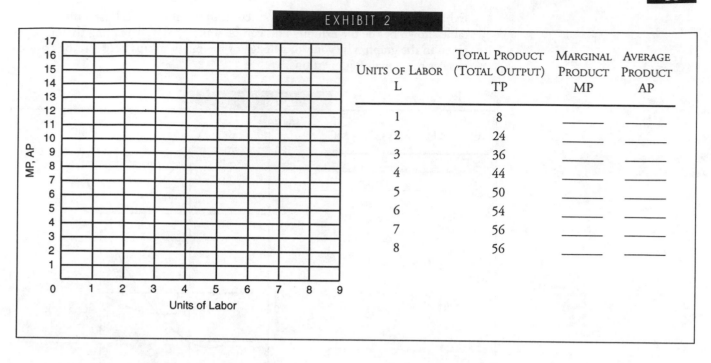

EXHIBIT 2

UNITS OF LABOR L	TOTAL PRODUCT (TOTAL OUTPUT) TP	MARGINAL PRODUCT MP	AVERAGE PRODUCT AP
1	8	_____	_____
2	24	_____	_____
3	36	_____	_____
4	44	_____	_____
5	50	_____	_____
6	54	_____	_____
7	56	_____	_____
8	56	_____	_____

3. Susan owns a small shop and produces dining room sets. Exhibit 3 presents data on her total costs at various output levels.
   a. Complete Exhibit 3 (you will need a calculator for this problem).
   b. At what output level is Susan's average total cost at a minimum?
   c. At what output level do diminishing returns begin for Susan?
   d. Using your own paper, graph Susan's average total cost, average variable cost, and marginal cost curves.

EXHIBIT 3

COSTS AND OUTPUT

OUTPUT (PER WEEK)	TOTAL COST	TOTAL FIXED COST	TOTAL VARIABLE COST	AVERAGE TOTAL COST	AVERAGE VARIABLE COST	MARGINAL COST
1	$100	$50	_____	_____	_____	_____
2	140	_____	_____	_____	_____	_____
3	177	_____	_____	_____	_____	_____
4	216	_____	_____	_____	_____	_____
5	265	_____	_____	_____	_____	_____
6	324	_____	_____	_____	_____	_____
7	399	_____	_____	_____	_____	_____
8	496	_____	_____	_____	_____	_____

Harcourt Brace & Company

4. Exhibit 4 shows a firm's costs of production in the short run. First, complete the table shown beside the exhibit. This can be done by simply reading the numbers given in the graph. Use your knowledge of the relationships between the costs to answer the remaining questions.

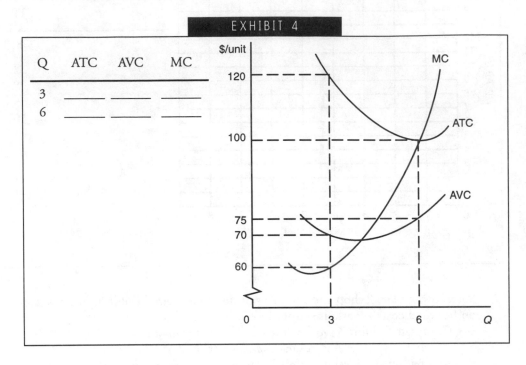

EXHIBIT 4

Q	ATC	AVC	MC
3	___	___	___
6	___	___	___

a. For an output level of 3 units, what is the total cost of production? What are the total variable costs and total fixed costs when the firm produces 3 units?
b. For an output level of 6 units, what is the total cost of production? What are the total variable costs and total fixed costs when the firm produces 6 units?
c. You know the total cost of producing 6 units and also the marginal cost of producing the sixth unit. Can you find the total cost of producing 5 units? [Hint: Remember the definition of marginal cost.]
d. What would this firm's total fixed costs be at an output level of 10 units? 15 units?
e. Find the average fixed cost (AFC) for output levels of 3 and 6 units. Are there two ways you can get these numbers? Do they produce identical results?
f. In the exhibit, shade in the rectangular area that represents the total cost of producing 3 units. Which part of this area represents total variable costs? Which part represents total fixed costs?

5. Below is a list of problems to help you learn the relationship between the costs and productivity measures in this chapter. Each problem is independent. That is, answer each question separately because it does not depend on the other answers.
a. If a restaurant can serve 30 tables with 3 waiters and 35 tables with 4 waiters, the marginal product of the fourth waiter is _____.

Harcourt Brace & Company

b. If a garbage collection company employs 2 workers on a garbage truck and they pick up 300 cans of trash, the average product of labor is _____.

c. If a firm's total fixed cost (TFC) is $100 and its total variable cost (TVC) is $200 when it produces 30 units, its *average total cost* (ATC) is _____.

d. If ATC is $5 and AVC is $2, then AFC is _____.

e. If average variable cost (AVC) is $5 when a firm produces 20 units, its total variable cost is _____.

f. If the total cost (TC) of producing 10 units is $40 and the total cost of producing 11 units is $45, the marginal cost (MC) of producing the eleventh unit is _____.

g. If a firm's total fixed cost (TFC) is $350 when it produces 4 units, its total fixed cost when it produces 5 units is _____.

h. If a firm's total fixed cost (TFC) is $200 when it produces 50 units, its average fixed cost (AFC) is _____.

i. If a firm's average variable cost (AVC) is $100 when it produces 5 units and its total fixed cost (TFC) is $200, the firm's total cost (TC) is _____.

j. If a local fast-food restaurant sells 25 hamburgers and its total costs are $50, its per-hamburger cost is _____.

k. If a university's total variable cost (TVC), such as professors' salaries and chalk, is $5,000,000 when it has 1,000 students and the total fixed costs (TFC), such as buildings, is $1,000,000, the per-student total cost is _____.

MULTIPLE CHOICE

1. The law of diminishing returns indicates why
    a. beyond some point, the extra utility derived from additional units of a product will yield the consumer smaller and smaller amounts of additional satisfaction.
    b. the firm's total fixed costs do not change with output in the short run.
    c. a firm's long-run average total cost curve is U-shaped.
    d. a firm's marginal costs will eventually increase as the firm expands output in the short run.

2. The short run is a time period of insufficient length for the firm to change its
    a. output.
    b. amount of labor employed.
    c. plant size and heavy equipment.
    d. price.

3. Sunk or "historical" costs are
    a. costs associated with current operational decisions.
    b. costs that have already been incurred as the result of past decisions.
    c. costs that add to the firm's marginal costs.
    d. costs that form the major component of the firm's variable costs.

Harcourt Brace & Company

4. Advantages of the corporate form of business organization include
    a. the ease of transferring ownership in a corporation.
    b. the limited liability concept that protects the stockholder from potential debts incurred by the corporation.
    c. the lack of employee shirking that occurs in corporations.
    d. both a and b.

5. The average variable cost curve and average total cost curve become closer together as output increases because
    a. the marginal cost curve intersects the average total cost curve at its minimum.
    b. average fixed cost remains constant as output rises.
    c. average fixed cost, which is the difference between them, declines with output.
    d. output is rising more rapidly than inputs are being increased.

6. Which of the following factors would **not** shift the cost curves of an automobile company upward?
    a. a regulation requiring all automobiles be equipped with improved safety equipment
    b. an increase in the price of steel used to make automobiles
    c. an increase in the property tax on buildings and equipment used by the automobile company
    d. An employee develops an new method of installing doors on the cars that requires half as many workers as before.

7. The firm's average total costs will be a minimum at the output level where
    a. the firm just begins to confront diminishing returns to the variable factors.
    b. the marginal costs are a minimum.
    c. the firm's average fixed costs are at their minimum.
    d. the marginal cost curve crosses the firm's average total cost curve.

8. The law of diminishing returns states that
    a. as we continually add variable factors to a fixed amount of other resources, output eventually increases at a decreasing rate.
    b. as we increase plant size, costs must diminish.
    c. the additional output generated by the employment of additional units of a variable input eventually decline.
    d. both a and c are correct.

Questions 9 through 15 refer to the following cost curves for one very small firm in a large market.

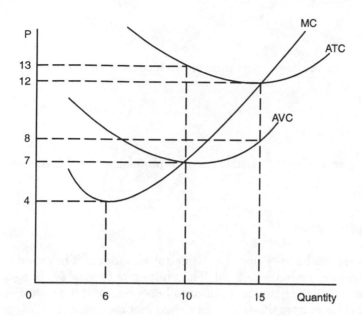

9. If the firm produces 10 units of output, its average total cost is
    a. 6.
    b. 7.
    c. 12.
    d. 13.

10. If the firm produces 15 units of output, its average fixed cost is
    a. 4.
    b. 5.
    c. 6.
    d. 60.

11. If the firm produces 10 units of output, its total cost is
    a. 7.
    b. 13.
    c. 70.
    d. 130.

12. If the firm produces 10 units of output, its total fixed cost is
    a. 6.
    b. 60.
    c. 70.
    d. 130.

13. The marginal cost of producing the tenth unit is
    a. 7.
    b. 13.
    c. 70.
    d. 130.

14. This firm minimizes its per-unit costs of production at an output level of
    a. Q = 6.
    b. Q = 10.
    c. Q = 15.
    d. none of the above.

15. Diminishing returns to the variable factor of production for this firm set in at
    a. Q = 6.
    b. Q = 10.
    c. Q = 15.
    d. none of the above.

16. A homeowner will be away from her house for six months. The monthly mort-gage payment on the house is $300. The utilities, *to be paid by the owner,* cost $100 per month if the house is occupied; otherwise zero. If the owner wishes to minimize her losses from the house, she should rent the house for as much as the market will bear, as long as monthly rent is greater than which of the following? (Assume wear and tear to be zero regardless of whether the house is occupied.) [Hint: Remember the concept of sunk cost.]
    a. $0
    b. $100
    c. $200
    d. $400

17. Suppose you value watching a movie at $5. You rent it from your local movie rental store for $3.50 for one night. You do not get a chance to watch it, so you decide to keep it an extra day and pay a late fee of $2. Your decision is
    a. incorrect; you paid $5.50 to watch a movie you valued at only $5. You should have taken the movie back.
    b. incorrect; you should have returned the movie and rented it later.
    c. correct; the $3.50 paid for the first night is a sunk cost and is not relevant in your decision to keep it an additional night.
    d. correct; you value watching the movie at $5 per night, so keeping it an extra day increases your value of the movie to $10.

18. Which of the following factors is most likely to shift the cost curves of an Iowa corn farmer downward?
    a. an increase in the price of fertilizer
    b. an increase in the tax on diesel fuel, which is used by the farmer
    c. the development of a new, more efficient corn harvester
    d. the adoption of a regulation requiring farmers to treat their crops with three new pesticides.

Harcourt Brace & Company

19. Which of the following is true?
    a. Economic profits are generally lower than accounting profits.
    b. Economic profits are generally greater than accounting profits.
    c. Economic profits are generally equal to accounting profits.
    d. Economic profits plus accounting profits must equal zero.

20. When a firm increases its plant size in the long run and its per-unit costs fall, this is called
    a. diminishing returns and is shown by the downward sloping portion of the MP curve (or the upward sloping portion of the MC curve).
    b. constant returns to scale and is shown by the flat portion of the LRATC curve.
    c. diseconomies of scale and is shown by the upward sloping portion of the LRATC curve.
    d. economies of scale and is shown by the downward sloping portion of the LRATC curve.

21. When the owner of a business invests his or her own money in the business, they give up the interest this money could be earning in the bank. This forgone interest is called
    a. the marginal cost of diminishing financial services.
    b. the opportunity cost of equity capital.
    c. the opportunity cost of labor services.
    d. interest expense and is included as a cost in the accounting statements of the business.

22. Ron works for Betty at Betty's Pizza Palace, Betty has many work rules, and Ron believes if there were fewer rules and more flexibility, he could do a better job. Betty probably has the rules because
    a. Ron, like her other employees, is a residual claimant.
    b. due to the principal-agent problem, some employees are likely to shirk when the owner is absent.
    c. she is maximizing sales rather than profits.
    d. with regard to their jobs, employees seldom know what is best.

23. Which of the following is true?
    a. Under the partnership form of business organization, the owners are not personally liable for the debts of the business.
    b. When employees also own a business, their incentive to shirk is removed.
    c. The limited liability of stockholders under the corporate business structure makes it easier to raise equity capital.
    d. Under the corporate form of business organization, the owners of the firm are personally liable for its debts.

24. Mary owns her own business and works full time in the store without paying herself a salary. She has $20,000 of her own money invested in the store that she withdrew from her savings account, which earned 10 percent interest. She was offered a job last year making $28,000 per year but turned it down. If Mary's accounting statements show revenues of $100,000 and accounting costs of $60,000, then Mary's
    a. accounting profit is $20,000 and her economic profit is zero.
    b. accounting profit is $40,000 and she is making an economic loss of $8,000.
    c. accounting profit is $40,000 and her economic profit is $10,000.
    d. accounting and economic profit is $40,000.

25. When an economist says a firm is earning zero economic profit, this implies that the firm
    a. will be forced out of business in the near future unless market conditions change.
    b. is earning a zero rate of return on its assets.
    c. is earning as high a rate of return now as could be earned in other industries.
    d. has an accounting profit of zero.

26. The long run is a period of
    a. at least one year.
    b. sufficient length to allow a firm to expand output by hiring additional workers.
    c. sufficient length to allow a firm to alter its plant size and capacity and all other factors of production.
    d. sufficient length to allow a firm to transform economic losses into economic profits.

27. As output is expanded, if MC is more than ATC,
    a. ATC must be at its minimum.
    b. ATC must be at its maximum.
    c. ATC must be increasing.
    d. ATC must be constant.

28. Mr. Hudson notes that if he produces 10 pairs of shoes per day, his average fixed cost (AFC) is $14 and his marginal cost $8; if he produces 20 pairs of shoes per day, his MC is $15. What is his AFC when output is 20 pairs of shoes per day?
    a. $5
    b. $7
    c. $8
    d. $15

29. Bill lives in Montana and likes to grow zucchini. He applies fertilizer to his crop twice during the growing season and notices that the second layer of fertilizer increases his crop but not as much as the first layer. What economic concept best explains this observation?
    a. the law of diminishing marginal utility
    b. the law of diminishing returns

Harcourt Brace & Company

   c. return equalization principle

   d. the principal-agent problem

30. Larger firms will often have lower minimum per-unit costs than smaller firms because

   a. employee shirking is less of a problem.

   b. large-scale output allows greater specialization for both labor and machines in the production process.

   c. mass production techniques, with high setup and development costs, are appropriate only when a small output is planned.

   d. all of the above are correct.

DISCUSSION QUESTIONS

1. a. What are the reasons that economic profit differs from accounting profit?

   b. In the real world, which reason do you think is the most significant?

   c. Could it make economic sense for a firm to leave an industry when the firm's accounting profits are positive? when its economic profits are positive? Explain both answers.

2. a. Suppose you compute the average weight of the students present at the start of class. Then a student weighing 175 pounds shows up late, and your computed average rises. If another student weighing only 145 pounds shows up, could your computed average rise again, even though the second late student weighs less than the first?

   b. Suppose you are part way through a course, and then your course grade falls because you do poorly on an assignment. Will your course grade necessarily rise back up again if you do better on the next assignment than you did on the last one?

   c. Decide whether the following is true or false and explain: If average cost is falling (rising), then we can conclude that marginal cost is also falling (rising).

3. What are the main reasons that per-unit production costs are often lower for larger firms than for small firms in the same industry? Why don't the small firms go bankrupt because of their higher production costs?

4. How would each of the following influence the cost of producing new housing?

   a. an increase in the price of lumber

   b. the development of a new lighter brick that reduced labor requirements without increasing the costs of material

   c. a reduction in the price of cement

   d. a new "occupational safety" regulation that required all construction workers to wear safety glasses, aluminum hats, and steel-toed shoes.

   e. passage of state legislation requiring all contractors to pay a $10,000 licensing fee.

Harcourt Brace & Company

5. a. Suppose some friends of yours buy a trailer. After some time, you ask them if they are glad they bought the trailer and they respond, "No, we wouldn't buy one again, but we spent so much on it that we do travel more now." Does their reasoning make sense? If so, why? If not, why not, and why do you think they do travel more now?

    b. Decide whether you agree or disagree with the following and explain: "In deciding whether to produce more of an item, a firm should consider total cost in the long run, but only variable cost in the short run."

6. What are the advantages of corporations compared to proprietorships? the disadvantages?

7. Consider the following three statements:
    (1) "I have to keep driving my old car in order to make up for the loss that I took when the transmission went out." [Hint: Remember the relevance of sunk costs.]
    (2) "It does not make sense to keep operating an old machine when new machines can produce more efficiently."
    (3) "Accounting costs yield valuable information, but they are not the relevant cost consideration when making business decisions."

    a. How would an economist assess the above statements? What economic principles would be used to assess them?

    b. Do you agree or disagree with the economist's assessment? Does the economic way of thinking overlook important real-world considerations?

    c. When economists discuss rational decision-making principles, like setting marginal benefit equal to marginal cost, are they describing human behavior? or are they proscribing it? Is there a normative content to economist's discussion of rational decision making?

8. In 1911, Thomas Edison wrote in *The Wall Street Journal:*

    > Thirty years ago my balance sheet showed me that I was not making much money. My manufacturing plant was not running to its full capacity. I couldn't find a market for my products. Then I suggested that we undertake to run our plant on full capacity and sell the surplus products in foreign markets at less than the cost of production. Every one of my associates opposed me. I had my experts figure out how much it would add to the cost of operating the plant if we increased this production 25 percent. The figures showed that we could increase the production 25 percent at an increased cost of only about 2 percent. On this basis I sent a man to Europe who sold lamps there at a price less than the cost of production in Europe.

    a. When Edison suggested that he would sell in foreign markets "at less than the cost of production," of what cost was he speaking?

    b. What was happening to Edison's marginal cost as he expanded output by 25 percent?

    c. Edison's pricing idea was opposed by his associates. Assuming that he was motivated by profit, who was right—Edison or his associates? Explain.

    Harcourt Brace & Company

9. a. What is the nature of the principle agent problem? How does the principle agent problem affect the cost efficiency of large corporations in the market sector? Can you think of factors that limit the ability of corporate managers to follow policies that are inconsistent with economic efficiency (cost effectiveness)?

    b. Use your answers to part a to discuss the phenomenon of extremely high salaries for corporate managers, who often have "golden parachute" clauses in their contracts that guarantee them large payments if they are forced to leave the corporation.

Harcourt Brace & Company

PERSPECTIVES IN ECONOMICS

MARGINAL-COST POLICY MAKING AND THE GUY NEXT DOOR

by Thomas L. Wyrick

[From *The Wall Street Journal*, April 12, 1984, abridged. Reprinted with permission of Thomas L. Wyrick, Southwest Missouri State University.]

Imagine yourself in a supermarket when the manager announces that for the next five minutes bottles of your favorite soft drinks will be sold two for $1 rather than the regular price of $1 each. "Buy one, get one free."

Back at home, a half-hour later, a neighbor with unexpected company calls to ask if you would sell him a bottle of the same soda. You agree, but before he gets there you must decide how much to charge him. Three possibilities come to mind—$1, 50 cents, or nothing—but there doesn't seem to be any way of knowing which is appropriate.

It doesn't take long to narrow your choices to two. Only the most altruistic would figure that the neighbor was getting the free bottle anyway, and shouldn't have to pay for it.

If you concentrate on the average price per bottle, then 50 cents will seem correct. After all, it is impossible to say which bottle was purchased and which one was "free," so it may appear reasonable to split the difference and charge your neighbor 50 cents.

But before the neighbor arrives, you have two bottles of soda. Once he leaves you will have one bottle and 50 cents, if you charge according to average cost. Since the two-for-one sale was only a one-time thing, it will be necessary to spend an additional 50 cents of your own money to replace the bottle once it is gone.

So averaging costs to set a price reduces your wealth by the difference between replacement cost for soda and its average cost to you.

Now, you may charge the neighbor 50 cents just to prevent hard feelings in case he later learns about the two-for-one special. But that is the consequence of placing friendship above economic considerations. If the deal is purely an economic one, then it is proper to charge the neighbor $1. This represents the soda's replacement cost, or the marginal cost incurred by you when selling the soda.

Sound simple? That's because it is. Unfortunately, however, government officials often have difficulty translating such ideas into policy.

Our nation's energy policies have usually been based on the naive view that firms set prices according to their average costs of doing business. Instead, profit-seeking firms use marginal-cost pricing. Thus policies can (and often do) have consequences opposite to those intended.

Recall the experience with oil price controls in the 1970s. The price of domestic crude oil was held down to artificially low levels to try to lower the costs of producing gasoline. As everyone knows, though, gasoline prices have declined (rather than increased) since President Reagan abolished controls in early 1981. This is contrary to what price controllers had expected, so they generally explain the (three-year) decline as temporary.

But a different explanation emerges from the marginal-cost pricing perspective. Oil refiners produce gasoline (and other products) from crude oil purchased from both domestic and foreign sources. Controls held the price of U.S. oil to $2 or $3 a barrel while foreign suppliers charged $36 or more in 1979. Refiners rationally bought all of the U.S. crude available, and turned to OPEC members only as a last resort.

Like a person selling soda to his neighbor, however, refiners charge customers a price based on their marginal costs of selling oil. That is, because Exxon or Texaco had only a limited amount of $2 oil available, a sale of that oil meant they had to rely on OPEC sources to replenish their inventories. Since that meant an additional (marginal) outlay of $36 a barrel, then the price of gasoline had to be high enough to reflect this cost rather than the lower controlled price.

So price controls on oil allowed refiners to pay less than a market price on some of their inputs, while they charged a market price on all of their output. Thanks to Congress, refiners' profits were at an all-time high during the price-control years. Of course, U.S. landowners and others who sold crude to refiners were harmed in proportion to the latter's gain.

The 1981 removal of price controls gave domestic owners of oil reserves more incentive to find and sell crude, and they responded in kind. As new domestic supplies came into competition with foreign oil, OPEC and others were forced to lower their prices to the current range of $28 to $29. This lowered refiners' marginal costs of doing business, and allowed them to lower the price of gasoline.

Meanwhile, because of the average cost-marginal cost confusion, Congress remains unwilling to remove price controls from certain categories of natural gas. Doing so, it is thought, would result in price increases for consumers perhaps by 50 percent or more within a few months.

In reality, however, controls cause owners of artificially low-priced gas to hold down production, so pipeline companies must turn to more expensive (uncontrolled) sources to satisfy customer demands. That drives up the latter's utility companies, and pushes up prices to consumers.

Decontrol would allow all natural gas to sell for the same price. The owners of decontrolled gas would increase production to profit from higher prices, and the now familiar dynamic would be seen again. Lessened demand for higher-priced gas on the margin would bring down the market price of gas. And lower marginal costs for pipelines would ultimately help reduce the heating bills of consumers.

The lesson to be learned is that market participants respond to marginal costs, not average costs. If a firm's costs rise by X dollars when it produces and sells one more unit of output, then price will tend toward X dollars regardless of the firm's costs averaged over all units of output.

Policy makers intent on helping consumers, borrowers and others would do well to stop trying to control the various components of production costs. Such efforts usually end up reducing the total supply of the good or service in question, and customers pay higher retail prices as a result. Public officials should spend more effort understanding how the private economy works; then they wouldn't waste so much energy trying to fix it.

Harcourt Brace & Company

DISCUSSION

1. How much would *you* have charged your neighbor for the bottle of soda? Why?

2. Wyrick seems to be arguing that getting rid of price controls on crude oil actually helped *reduce* the retail price of gasoline. How is this possible? Why is the role of marginal cost crucial in all of this?

3. Do you agree with Wyrick's predication that removing price controls from natural gas would decrease natural gas prices rather than increase them (even though an increase is what most people seem to expect)? Why or why not?

Harcourt Brace & Company

CHAPTER 9

Price Takers and the Competitive Process

TRUE OR FALSE

T F

☐ ☐ 1. In a price-taker market, all firms produce an identical product and each firm comprises only a very small portion of the total market.

☐ ☐ 2. If a price-taker firm wants to sell its output, it must accept the market price, but it can sell as much output as it wishes at that market price.

☐ ☐ 3. For a price-taker firm, its marginal revenue from the sale of an additional unit is generally less than the market price.

☐ ☐ 4. A profit-maximizing, price-taking firm will expand output to the point where marginal cost equals the market price.

☐ ☐ 5. In a price-taker market, each individual firm confronts a perfectly elastic demand curve that is a horizontal line at the market price.

☐ ☐ 6. A price-taker firm's short-run supply curve is equal to the firm's average total cost curve.

☐ ☐ 7. The short-run market supply curve for a price-taker market is equal to the horizontal summation of the marginal cost curves (above AVC) for all firms in the industry.

☐ ☐ 8. In the short run, price-taker firms will expand their output and earn higher profits, when the market price increases.

☐ ☐ 9. Whenever short-run economic profits are present in a price-taker market, new firms will enter and the market price will fall until all firms earn only zero economic profit in the long run.

☐ ☐ 10. Price takers always produce at the level of output at which average total costs are a minimum in both the short and long run.

☐ ☐ 11. Economic losses cause firms to exit from an industry in the long run, and the market supply declines until zero economic profits are restored.

☐ ☐ 12. A price-taking firm earning zero economic profit will generally go out of business unless it expects to earn positive economic profits in the long run.

☐ ☐ 13. In a constant cost industry, an increase in demand will cause price to rise in the long run because the long-run market supply curve is upward sloping.

☐ ☐ 14. When a firm shuts down in the short run, its total cost will fall to zero.

☐ ☐ 15. If price currently is less than ATC but above AVC, the firm should remain open in the short run but shut down in the long run.

PROBLEMS AND PROJECTS

1. Exhibit 1 shows the total cost schedule for a firm in a price-taker market.
   a. If the market price is $25, the firm's total revenue is the number of units sold times the market price. Fill in the missing values for the firm's total revenue.
   b. Marginal revenue is the *change* in total revenue that results from producing and selling one additional unit. Fill in the missing values for the firm's marginal revenue. Because this is a price-taker firm, what is marginal revenue equal to?
   c. Marginal cost is the *change* in total cost that results from producing and selling one additional unit. Fill in the missing values for the firm's marginal cost.
   d. The firm's profit is equal to total revenue minus total cost. Fill in the missing values for the firm's profit.
   e. The profit maximization rule is that a firm should produce and sell all units up until the point where marginal cost equals marginal revenue (MC = MR).

EXHIBIT 1

Output	Total Revenue	Marginal Revenue	Total Cost	Marginal Cost	Profit
0	$ 0	x	$20	x	−$20
1	25	$25	30	$10	− 5
2	50	25	35	5	+ 15
3	_____	_____	45	_____	_____
4	_____	_____	65	_____	_____
5	_____	_____	95	_____	_____
6	_____	_____	135	_____	_____

   Given your answer to part b above, how can this rule be restated for a price-taker firm?
   f. It will not be true in every case that there will be a specific unit for which MC exactly equals MR. Thus, the profit maximization rule more appropriately stated is that a firm should produce all units for which marginal revenue (or price, for a price-taker firm) exceeds marginal cost. The logic of this rule is that when a unit is produced that adds more to revenue than it adds to cost, the result will be an increase in profit. Looking at the table, is it true that when a unit's marginal revenue exceeds marginal cost, producing and selling the unit results in higher total profit? What happens when units are produced for which marginal revenue is less than marginal cost?

Harcourt Brace & Company

g. Looking at the total profit column, what level of output maximizes this firm's profit? Using the marginal-cost/marginal-revenue rule, what level of output maximizes this firms profit? Do they yield the same answer?

h. Suppose the market price rose to $40. What new level of output would maximize this firm's profit? [Hint: You can either recalculate the total revenue and total profit columns to find this answer or (easier) use the marginal-cost/marginal-revenue rule.]

i. When there is a specific unit for which MC = MR, how does producing this last unit change the firm's profit? Check your answer by computing the total profit at a price of $40 for output levels of 5 and 6 units.

2. Exhibit 2 depicts a ziwi fruit farm that has a river running along the west side of the property boundary. Because ziwi fruit grows better near water, each row planted further away from the river costs more to grow because of the additional fertilizer and watering needed. Shown in the exhibit are the costs for each row. The first row of fruit planted next to the river costs $10, the second row out costs

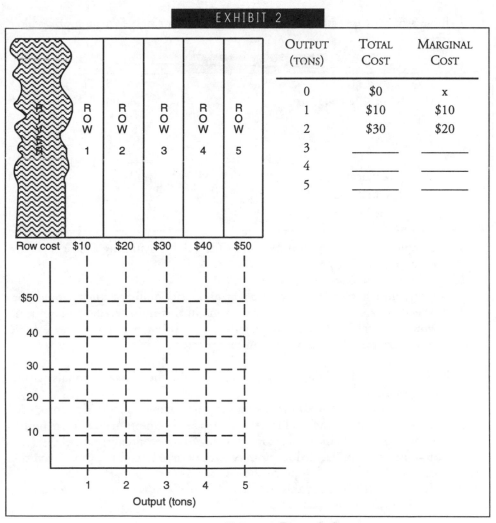

OUTPUT (TONS)	TOTAL COST	MARGINAL COST
0	$0	x
1	$10	$10
2	$30	$20
3	_____	_____
4	_____	_____
5	_____	_____

EXHIBIT 2

Row cost $10 $20 $30 $40 $50

Harcourt Brace & Company

$20, the third row costs $30, and so forth. Further assume that each row plant-ed results in one ton of ziwi fruit.

a. If the farmer wishes to produce one ton of output, he will plant only row one. His total cost will be $10. If the farmer wishes to produce two tons of output, he will plant both rows one and two, for a total cost of $30 ($10 + $20). Fill in the remaining spaces in the table for total cost.

b. Fill in the remaining spaces in the table for marginal cost. Now in the space pro-vided, graph the ziwi fruit farm's marginal cost curve with the data in the table.

c. If the market price of ziwi this year is $30, draw in the figure the demand curve facing this ziwi fruit farm. What level of output should be produced to maximize profits?

d. At the profit-maximizing level of output, what is the firm's total cost? What is the firm's *average total cost* per ton? Given that they are receiving a price of $30 per ton, how much profit are they earning *per ton*?

e. Multiply the per ton profit by the number of units sold to calculate the firm's total profit. Now, calculate the firm's total revenue and compare it to their total cost to find total profit. Are your answers the same?

3. Exhibit 3 presents selected information relating to a single firm in a price-taker market.

EXHIBIT 3	
Price	$8
Total Revenue	8,000
Output	_____
Average Total Cost	8
Total Cost	_____
Marginal Revenue	_____
Marginal Cost	_____
Total Profit	_____

a. Complete the missing information in the exhibit assuming the firm is cur-rently maximizing profits.

b. Is this firm in *long-run* equilibrium?

c. If this firm is representative of all firms in the industry, what would you expect to happen to the number of firms in this industry in the long run? Would it increase, decrease, or stay the same? [Hint: Remember the exhibit shows economic profit, not accounting profit.]

4. Exhibit 4 shows a firm in a price-taker market. Use the diagrams to answer the following questions

a. If this firm wants to maximize its profits, how many units should it produce?

b. What will be the firm's total revenue at this level of output? total cost? profit?

c. Shade in the area in the exhibit corresponding to the economic profit of this firm.

d. Suppose the firm decided to produce fifty units. How much profit would it earn? Is this more or less profit than in part b?

e. How many firms are in this industry? [Hint: Compare total market output to this firm's output and remember all firms are identical.]

Harcourt Brace & Company

EXHIBIT 4

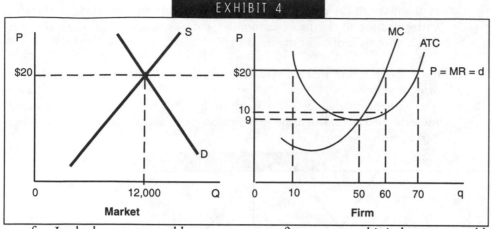

f.   In the long run, would you expect more firms to enter this industry or would you expect some firms to leave? What price would you expect to be present in this market in the long run? (You may assume it is a constant cost industry.)

5.   Exhibit 5 depicts the market conditions experienced by representative firms in three different price-taker markets. Use the diagrams to answer the following questions.

EXHIBIT 5

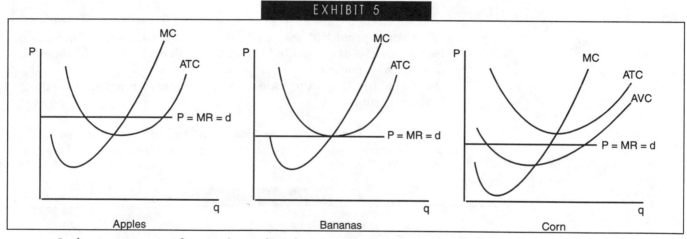

a.   Is the representative firm in the apple industry earning an economic profit, an economic loss, or earning zero economic profit? What would you expect to happen to the number of firms in this industry in the long run? Indicate in the diagram the profit-maximizing level of output and shade in the area corresponding to the firm's economic profit or loss.

b.   Is the representative firm in the banana industry earning an economic profit, an economic loss, or earning zero economic profit? What would you expect to happen to the number of firms in this industry in the long run? Indicate in the diagram the profit-maximizing level of output.

c.   Is the representative firm in the corn industry earning an economic profit, an economic loss, or earning zero economic profit? What would you expect to happen to the number of firms in this industry in the long run? Indicate

Harcourt Brace & Company

in the diagram the profit-maximizing level of output and shade in the area corresponding to the firm's economic profit or loss. Should the firm shut down or remain open in the short run?

6. Exhibit 6 shows a firm in a price-taker market. Use the diagrams to answer the following questions.
   a. The current market demand is given by D_1. Suppose market demand increases to D_2. Indicate the new market price and draw the new demand curve for this firm.

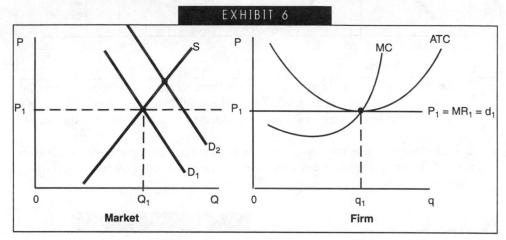

EXHIBIT 6

   b. What has happened to the profitability of this firm? Will it increase or decrease its level of output? Indicate in the graph the new level of output the firm should produce to maximize profit.
   c. What would you expect to happen to the number of firms in this industry in the long run?

7. Suppose you own a small hotel near a ski resort. The left-hand panel of Exhibit 7 depicts the market supply of rooms and the demand for rooms in the winter,

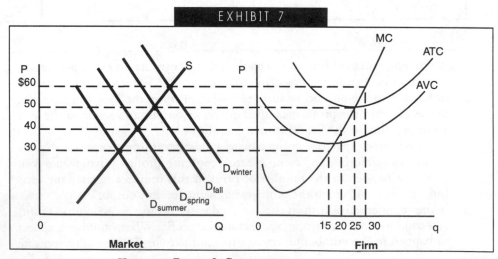

EXHIBIT 7

Harcourt Brace & Company

spring, summer, and fall. The right-hand panel depicts your unit costs per room rented; these costs are the same for each season.

a. Use the diagrams in Exhibit 7 to help you complete the following table. For the profit column, simply indicate whether your profits for the season are positive (+), negative (−), or zero (0).

SEASON	PRICE	NUMBER OF ROOMS RENTED	PROFITS
Winter	_____	_____	_____
Spring	_____	_____	_____
Summer	_____	_____	_____
Fall	_____	_____	_____

b. Should you keep your hotel open all year? During which seasons should you shut down? How many rooms will you rent during the summer? Explain your reasoning.

c. Given that you earn negative profits in some seasons and positive profits in other seasons, how would you decide whether or not to remain in this industry in the long run?

MULTIPLE CHOICE

1. In a price-taker market,
    a. all firms in the market charge different prices depending upon their respective costs of production.
    b. there are generally a small number of very large firms.
    c. the firms all produce identical products
    d. firms will usually make economic losses in the long run.

2. A firm that must sell its output at a market-determined price is called a
    a. price-taker firm.
    b. price-searcher firm.
    c. price-setter firm.
    d. price-maker firm.

3. For a firm in a price-taker market, the firm's demand curve is
    a. a horizontal line at the market price that is equal to the firm's marginal revenue curve.
    b. an upward-sloping line that is equal to the firm's marginal cost above AVC.
    c. a downward-sloping line that lies below the firm's marginal revenue curve.
    d. undefined because it cannot determine the price it charges for its output.

4. To maximize profits, a firm should always produce the level of output where
    a. marginal cost equals average total cost.
    b. average total cost equals price.
    c. marginal cost equals marginal revenue.
    d. marginal revenue equals price.

5. If you were the owner of a price-taker firm operating at an output level where the marginal cost of producing another unit was $5, and the market price was $7, then
    a. you could increase your profit by expanding output.
    b. you could increase your profit by decreasing output.
    c. you are maximizing your profit at your current output level.
    d. you will be able to earn positive economic profits in the long run.

6. A price-taker firm is currently producing 50 units of output at an average total cost of $3 per unit. If the market price is $7, then the firm's total economic profit is
    a. $4.
    b. $150.
    c. $200.
    d. $350.

7. For a price-taker firm, marginal revenue is
    a. equal to price.
    b. equal to zero when the market is in long-run equilibrium.
    c. equal to the change in total revenue divided by the change in output.
    d. both *a* and *c*.

8. If a firm in a price-taker market is earning zero economic profit, it
    a. will shut down in the long run but not the short run.
    b. will also be earning zero accounting profit.
    c. is doing as well as typical firms in other markets.
    d. will shut down in the short run.

9. If marginal revenue exceeds marginal cost at the current level of output, profit will increase when output is expanded because
    a. other firms in the industry will shut down as the firm expands output.
    b. the market price will rise as the firm expands output.
    c. producing and selling an additional unit will add more to total revenue than it adds to total cost.
    d. marginal cost will decline as output is expanded.

10. Historically, most economists have referred to markets where firms are price takers as
    a. purely competitive markets.
    b. monopoly markets.
    c. open-door markets.
    d. price-searcher markets.

Harcourt Brace & Company

11. Which of the following is true?
    a. When firms in a price-taker market are earning zero economic profit, they will shut down.
    b. When firms in a price-taker market are earning positive economic profits, new firms will enter the industry causing the market price to fall until the firms in the industry are earning only zero economic profit.
    c. When firms in a price-taker market are earning economic losses, some firms will exit the industry causing the market price to rise until the remaining firms are earning zero economic profit.
    d. Both b and c are true.

12. Beginning from a point of long-run equilibrium, an increase in the market demand for wheat would result in
    a. an increase in the market price of wheat.
    b. existing wheat producers increasing output in the short run and earning positive economic profits.
    c. new firms entering the wheat industry in the long run.
    d. all of the above.

13. If the market price in a price-taking industry was currently above the average total cost of production for firms in the industry,
    a. firms in the industry would earn short-run economic profits that would be offset by long-run economic losses.
    b. new firms would enter the industry, which would drive price down to the average total cost of production in the long run.
    c. firms in the industry would earn positive economic profits in the long run.
    d. most firms in the industry would shut down in the long run.

14. Which of the following statements is correct?
    a. In order to maximize profits in the short run, a price taker should always produce at the output level where marginal cost is equal to price.
    b. In long-run equilibrium, a price taker will produce at an output level where average total cost is at its minimum.
    c. A price taker will remain open in the short run, even if it is earning an economic loss, so long as price is sufficient to cover average variable cost.
    d. All of the above.

15. When consumer demand for a good produced in a price-taker market decreases,
    a. firms in the industry will continue to produce at the same output levels as before.
    b. total market output will generally rise, but each individual firm will reduce its output.
    c. the market price of the good will rise, causing additional resources to flow into the industry in the long run.
    d. some firms will shut down in the long run, making their resources available for the production of other goods.

Harcourt Brace & Company

16. (I) A firm's short-run supply curve is equal to its average variable cost curve above marginal revenue. (II) The short-run supply curve for a price-taker market is the horizontal sum of the supply curves of all firms in the industry.
    a. I is true; II is false.
    b. I is false; II is true.
    c. Both I and II are true.
    d. Both I and II are false.

17. The long-run supply curve is
    a. a horizontal line for a constant-cost industry.
    b. upward sloping for a decreasing-cost industry.
    c. downward sloping for an increasing-cost industry.
    d. all of the above.

18. If the demand for a product increases in an increasing cost industry, as the market adjusts in the long run, production costs for all firms will
    a. rise as new firms enter the industry.
    b. fall as new firms enter the industry.
    c. remain unchanged.
    d. fall as firms exit the industry.

19. If firms in a price-taker industry were forced to install antipollution devices that increased their production costs, we should expect
    a. the cost curves for the firms in this industry to shift downward.
    b. the market price of the product to decrease.
    c. that the firms in the industry would suffer long-run economic losses.
    d. that the firms in the industry would earn normal economic profits in the long run, as the higher production costs were passed along to consumers in the form of higher prices.

20. A price-taker market tends toward a state of long-run equilibrium in which firms earn only a normal rate of return (zero economic profits) because
    a. firms will keep their prices low under fear of government regulation.
    b. with firms able to enter and leave the industry freely, competition will drive prices down to the level of production costs.
    c. by definition, production costs always rise to equal the market price.
    d. mismanagement on the part of owners generally results in the firms not equating marginal revenue and marginal cost.

21. Which portion of the marginal cost curve is used to create a firm's short-run supply curve?
    a. the entire marginal cost curve
    b. the marginal cost curve above its intersection with the average variable cost curve because below this price, firms will shut down in the short run
    c. the marginal cost curve above its intersection with the marginal revenue (demand) curve
    d. the marginal cost curve above its intersection with the average total cost curve because below this price, firms will shut down in the short run

22. You are the owner of an ice cream shop that earns profit most of the year except during the cold winter months. During the month of December, your rent and other fixed costs amount to a total of $200. If you remain open, your total variable costs (workers, ice cream cones, etc.) will amount to $300. If you would be able to sell 100 ice cream cones at $4 each during December, then
    a. to maximize profits, you should remain open in December.
    b. to maximize profits, you should shut down in December.
    c. you will be able to avoid making a loss by shutting down in December.
    d. you should go out of business in the long run if there is any single month in which you do not earn a profit.

23. FYI Sanitation is currently eight months into a year-long lease contract on a garbage truck at a cost that averages $500 per month. Other variable costs (fuel, workers, etc.) for operating the truck amount to $300 per month. If the monthly revenue from operating the truck is $400, and these conditions are expected to continue into the future, to maximize its profit, FYI Sanitation should
    a. stop operating the truck immediately and not renew the lease for next year.
    b. continue operating the truck indefinitely.
    c. continue operating the truck until the lease expires, then not renew the lease for next year.
    d. stop operating the truck now but renew the lease and begin operating the truck again next year.

24. "I have been making furniture for twenty-seven years. I have never heard of either marginal cost or marginal revenue. Fancy economic theories mean nothing to me. I just know how to do well in business. Whenever I can sell something for more than it cost me to produce it, I make it, and whenever I can't sell it for enough to cover my cost, I don't. That's how I stay in business and earn income for my family. Common sense and watching the market are good enough for me." For producers like this, economic models
    a. accurately describe their behavior and allow predictions to be made as to how they will respond to changes in market conditions.
    b. indicate nothing about the behavior of such producers.
    c. will generally only apply if the person has a college education.
    d. do not apply because the producers do not understand the terminology.

25. If consumers suddenly began desiring more apples and fewer oranges,
    a. the market price of apples would rise, creating short-run economic profits in the apple industry. Current firms will expand output and new firms will enter the industry.
    b. the market price of oranges would fall, creating short-run economic losses in the orange industry. Current firms will reduce output and some will go out of business in the long run.
    c. neither *a* nor *b* are correct.
    d. both *a* and *b* are correct.

Harcourt Brace & Company

26. The schedule of total cost for a firm in a price-taker market is given in Exhibit 8. If the market price for this product is $50, which of the following output levels should this firm produce if it wants to maximize its profit?
   a. 1
   b. 2
   c. 3
   d. 4

EXHIBIT 8	
OUTPUT	TOTAL COST
0	$ 25
1	65
2	95
3	140
4	195
5	255

Exhibit 9 depicts a firm in a price-taker market. Use this exhibit to answer questions 27 through 29.

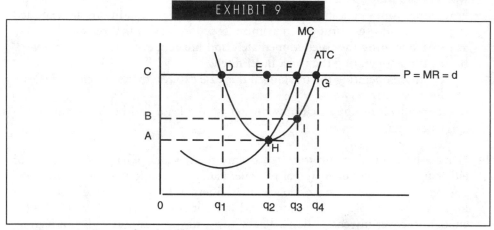

EXHIBIT 9

27. To maximize profit, the firm should produce an output level of
   a. q_1.
   b. q_2.
   c. q_3.
   d. q_4.

28. At the profit-maximizing level of output, the firm will earn [Hint: Areas in the exhibit are referenced by the four letters on the corners of the respective area.]
   a. an economic profit of AHEC.
   b. an economic profit of BIFC.
   c. an economic loss of AHEC.
   d. an economic loss of BIFC.

29. Given the current market conditions, in the long run,
   a. new firms will enter the industry and market price will fall.
   b. firms will exit the industry and market price will rise.
   c. firms will neither enter or exit because the market is in long-run equilibrium.
   d. firms will maintain their current level of economic profit.

30. Exhibit 10 shows a representative firm in a price-taker market. Which of the following is true regarding the situation depicted in the exhibit?

Harcourt Brace & Company

a. This firm shown is earning zero economic profit.
b. The industry is in long-run equilibrium.
c. Firms will neither enter nor exit the market.
d. All of the above.

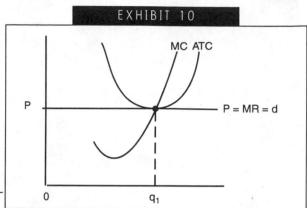

EXHIBIT 10

Exhibit 11 depicts a firm in a price-taker market. Use this exhibit to answer questions 31 through 33.

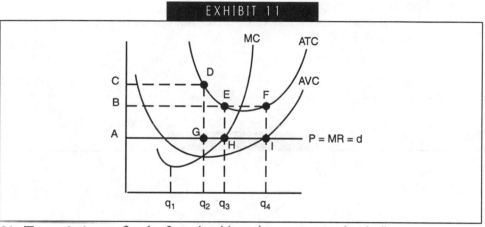

EXHIBIT 11

31. To maximize profit, the firm should produce an output level of
    a. zero; the firm should shut down immediately.
    b. q_2.
    c. q_3.
    d. q_4.

32. At the profit-maximizing level of output, the firm will earn
    a. an economic profit of AHEB.
    b. an economic loss of AGDC.
    c. an economic loss of AHEB.
    d. an economic loss of AIFB.

33. Given the current market conditions, in the long run,
    a. new firms will enter the industry and market price will fall.
    b. firms will exit the industry and market price will rise.
    c. firms will neither enter nor exit because the market is in long-run equilibrium.
    d. firms will continue to suffer economic losses.

34. Exhibit 12 shows a representative firm in a price-taker market. Which of the following is true regarding the situation depicted in the exhibit?
    a. This firm should shut down immediately.

EXHIBIT 12

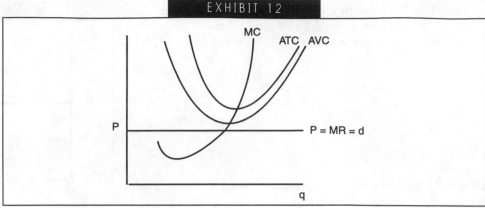

    b.   This firm is earning positive economic profit.
    c.   This firm is able to cover its variable cost but not its total cost.
    d.   All of the above.

EXHIBIT 13

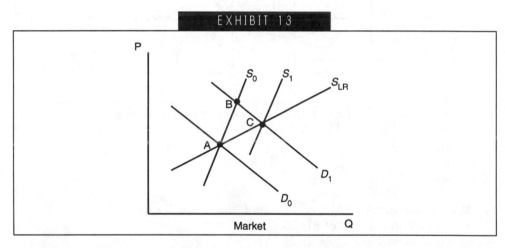

35. Which of the following best describes the series of events shown in Exhibit 13? The original conditions prior to the change are shown by D_0 and S_0 (point A) and S_{LR} is the market long-run supply curve.
    a.   an increase in demand and an expansion in the number of firms in an increasing cost industry
    b.   an increase in demand and an expansion in the number of firms in a decreasing cost industry
    c.   an increase in demand and an expansion in the number of firms in a constant cost industry
    d.   none of the above

DISCUSSION QUESTIONS

1. Why don't price-taker firms have more control over the price they charge for their output? Can you think of several real-world industries that are price-taker markets?

2. Do you think most real-world firms attempt to maximize their profit? How do you think a nonprofit firm (and industry) would respond to changes in the price of the product produced? Would the response be any different? How can you reconcile the fact that most business people probably do not know these economic models, but yet the models are very accurate predictors of their behavior?

3. How does the dynamic process of competition increase prosperity? What important variables are omitted from the simple economic model of a price-taker market?

4. Use the price-taker model to explain fully how a reduction in demand for shrimp would affect (a) the economic profit or loss of shrimp producers and (b) the market price and output in both the short and long run. Use diagrams relating the adjustments of the producers (firms) to the market in explaining your answer.

5. Use the price-taker model to explain fully how an increase in demand for eggs would affect (a) the economic profit or loss of egg producers and (b) the market price and output in both the short and long run. Use diagrams relating the adjustments of the producers (firms) to the market in explaining your answer.

6. Our economy is in a continuous process of change: New firms start up and many existing firms go out of business.
   a. When a firm goes out of business, does it increase or decrease efficiency?
   b. Who loses when a firm goes out of business? Who gains?
   c. If a firm is producing a good or service at a loss, how is it affecting national wealth? Explain.
   d. The government occasionally rescues bankrupt firms, such as Chrysler and many savings and loan associations. Do you approve of these bailouts? Why or why not?

CHAPTER *10*

Price-Searcher Markets with Low Entry Barriers

TRUE OR FALSE

T   F

☐ ☐ 1. Unlike price takers, price searchers do not maximize profits by producing at the point where marginal revenue is equal to marginal cost.

☐ ☐ 2. Entry and exit of firms drive economic profits to zero in the long run in competitive price-searcher markets.

☐ ☐ 3. Price discrimination is the term used to describe a situation where a firm is charging the same price to all of its customers.

☐ ☐ 4. The marginal revenue curve for a price searcher is equal to the firm's downward-sloping demand curve.

☐ ☐ 5. Economic models of profit maximization do not fully capture the role played by entrepreneurs.

☐ ☐ 6. Monopolistic competition is a term that has historically been used when referring to competitive price-searcher markets.

☐ ☐ 7. Competition provides firms with a strong incentive to develop improved products and discover lower-cost methods of production.

☐ ☐ 8. The entry of firms into a competitive price-searcher market generally does not affect the demand curve for firms already operating in that market.

☐ ☐ 9. In the long run, a firm in a competitive price-searcher market produces at the point where price is equal to average total cost.

☐ ☐ 10. Competitive price searchers often emphasize quality, location, and advertising as competitive weapons (in addition to price competition).

☐ ☐ 11. A market is said to be contestable when barriers to entry and exit are high.

☐ ☐ 12. To effectively price discriminate, a firm must be able to prevent resale among its customers.

Harcourt Brace & Company

115

T   F

☐ ☐ 13. A competitive price searcher will charge a price equal to marginal cost.

☐ ☐ 14. For a firm with a downward-sloping demand curve, marginal revenue is less than price because to sell additional units, price must be reduced on other units that could have been sold at a higher price.

☐ ☐ 15. A firm currently sells three units at a price of $5. If the firm must lower its price to $4 to sell four units, the marginal revenue derived from producing and selling the fourth unit is $4.

PROBLEMS AND PROJECTS

EXHIBIT 1

Price	Quantity Demanded	Total Revenue	Marginal Revenue	Total Cost	Marginal Cost	Profit
$65	0	_____	xxx	$ 40	xxx	_____
60	1	_____	_____	90	_____	_____
55	2	_____	_____	110	_____	_____
50	3	_____	_____	135	_____	_____
45	4	_____	_____	164	_____	_____
40	5	_____	_____	204	_____	_____
35	6	_____	_____	254	_____	_____

1. Suppose that you produce and sell tables in a localized market. Past experience permits you to estimate your demand and marginal cost schedules. This information is presented in Exhibit 1.
   a. Fill in the missing values for revenue, cost, and profit.
   b. If you wanted to maximize your profit, what price should you charge? How many tables would you sell at that price?
   c. At the profit-maximizing level of output, what is the relationship between the price you are charging and the marginal cost of producing the last table?
   d. If all the firms in the market for tables face similar costs, what would you expect to happen to your demand in the long run?

2. Exhibit 2 indicates the demand and cost conditions facing a firm.
   a. Is this firm a price taker or a price searcher? Explain how you can tell the difference.
   b. Illustrate the firm's profit-maximizing price and output on the diagram.

Harcourt Brace & Company

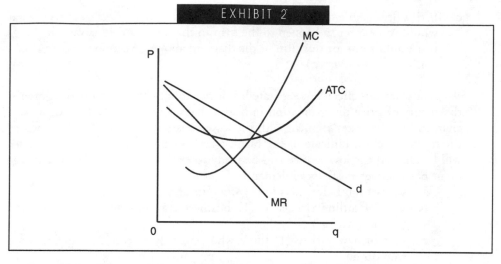

EXHIBIT 2

c. If the firm produces at the output you indicated in part b, will the firm be making a profit or a loss? Show the area that represents this profit or loss in the diagram.

d. If this firm is in a contestable market (one with low barriers to entry), what would you expect to happen to the firm in the long run? Illustrate the long-run equilibrium for this firm in the diagram above. (Assume the firm is in a constant cost industry.)

3. Exhibit 3 indicates the demand and cost conditions facing a firm in a competitive price-searcher market.

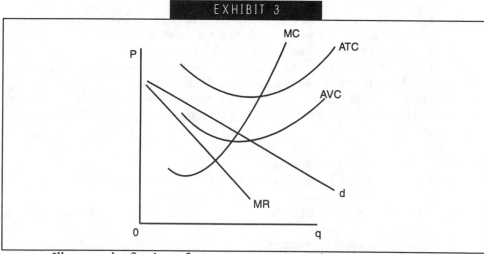

EXHIBIT 3

a. Illustrate the firm's profit-maximizing price and output on the diagram.

b. If the firm produces at the output you indicated in part a, will the firm be making a profit or a loss? Show the area that represents this profit or loss in the diagram.

Harcourt Brace & Company

c. If this firm is in a contestable market (one with low barriers to entry), what would you expect to happen to the firm in the long run? Illustrate the long-run equilibrium for this firm in the diagram above. (Assume the firm is in a constant cost industry.)

4. When a seller can effectively separate his or her total market into two segments, the theory of price discrimination indicates that a higher product price will be charged in the market segment with the lower elasticity of demand. For each of the markets below, indicate in the blank which segment, (1) or (2), you think will be charged the lower price and be ready to explain why you think that segment has a higher elasticity of demand.

_____ a. sales of football tickets to (1) students and (2) alumni

_____ b. sales of airline tickets to (1) business travelers and (2) vacationers (leisure travelers)

_____ c. sales of new cars to (1) those who presently own a car and (2) those who do not

_____ d. sales of cosmetic surgery to (1) the poor and (2) the rich

MULTIPLE CHOICE

1. Which of the following is a major difference between a competitive price searcher and a price taker?
   a. Price takers need to compete through advertising since they cannot choose their own price, whereas competitive price searchers compete primarily through their pricing policies.
   b. Price takers are exposed to competition because of low barriers to entry, whereas competitive price searchers are somewhat immune from competition due to relatively high barriers to entry.
   c. Price takers can never earn economic profits, whereas competitive price searchers can earn economic profits in the short run.
   d. Price takers produce identical goods, whereas competitive price searchers produce goods that are differentiated from the goods produced by their competitors.

2. For the competitive price searcher,
   a. price will exceed marginal cost at the profit-maximizing level of output.
   b. price will equal average total cost in the long run.
   c. economic profit will be driven to zero in the long run by the entry and exit of firms.
   d. all of the above are correct.

Harcourt Brace & Company

3. Only undertaking an activity when it adds more to revenue than to cost is the decision rule a profit-maximizing firm will use when deciding upon
    a. the level of output to produce.
    b. the amount of advertising to undertake.
    c. the level of product quality (for example, how many years it is designed to last).
    d. all of the above.

4. The marginal revenue curve lies below the demand curve for a competitive price searcher because
    a. in order for a competitive price searcher to sell an extra unit, it must cut the price on all units. The lowered price offsets the additional revenue from the extra unit sold, so the marginal revenue is lower than the price.
    b. in order for a competitive price searcher to sell an extra unit, it must increase its advertising. The cost of advertising offsets the extra revenue generated by the extra sales, so the marginal revenue is lower than the price.
    c. whenever a competitive price searcher discovers a profit-maximizing pricing policy, the economic profit it generates attracts new competitors into the industry, driving marginal revenue below the price.
    d. none of the above. The marginal revenue curve *is* the demand curve for a competitive price searcher.

5. Suppose you were asked to determine whether a firm was a price taker or a competitive price searcher by looking at a graph of the firm's cost and revenue curves. The key is that for the competitive price searcher,
    a. the firm's marginal revenue curve lies above and to the right of the demand curve, not below and to the left.
    b. there are only total costs, not variable costs, on the graph.
    c. the firm's demand curve is downward sloping, not a horizontal line.
    d. all of the above.

6. A competitive price-searcher market is characterized by
    a. firms being able to choose their price and no barriers preventing firms from entering or leaving the market.
    b. firms being able to choose their price and high barriers preventing firms from entering or leaving the market.
    c. firms having to accept the market price for their product and high barriers preventing firms from entering or leaving the market.
    d. firms having to accept the market price for their product and no barriers preventing firms from entering or leaving the market.

7. If a price-searcher firm can sell 4 units at a price of $6 or it can sell 5 units at a price of $5, the marginal revenue from the fifth unit is
    a. $1.
    b. $5.
    c. $6.
    d. $25.

Harcourt Brace & Company

8. The fact that barriers to entry are low in competitive price-searcher markets means that if current firms are making economic losses,
   a. these losses will remain in the long run because firms will not exit the market.
   b. some current firms will exit the market, causing the demand curves that face the remaining firms to increase.
   c. new firms will enter the market, causing the demand curves that face the existing firms to decrease.
   d. new firms will enter the market, causing no change in the demand curves that face the existing firms in the market.

9. Which of the following is true when *long-run* equilibrium conditions are present in price-taker and competitive price-searcher markets?
   a. MR = MC in both price-taker and competitive price-searcher markets.
   b. P = ATC in both price-taker and competitive price-searcher markets.
   c. P = MC in both price-taker and competitive price-searcher markets.
   d. Both *a* and *b*, but not *c*.

10. A market in which the costs of entry and exit are low is called a
    a. regulated market.
    b. monopoly market.
    c. market with high barriers to entry.
    d. contestable market.

11. In **both** price-taker and competitive price-searcher markets, short-run economic profits will lead to
    a. firms being able to sustain those economic profits into the long run.
    b. the exit of firms from the market and the eventual restoration of zero long-run economic profits.
    c. the entry of additional firms into the market and the eventual restoration of zero long-run economic profits.
    d. none of the above.

12. In order for a firm to be able to engage in price discrimination, it must be able to
    a. identify and separate groups with different price elasticities of demand.
    b. prevent resale of the product between customer groups.
    c. maximize profits at the point where average total cost is minimized.
    d. do both *a* and *b*, but not *c*.

Harcourt Brace & Company

13. Some economists have argued that competitive price-searcher industries are allocatively inefficient relative to price-taker industries because
    a. unlike price takers, price searchers fail to produce at the point where marginal revenue is equal to marginal cost.
    b. competition forces price takers to find the most efficient method of production, while product differentiation allows competitive price searchers to stay in business even when their methods of production are inefficient.
    c. unlike price takers, price searchers do not produce at the minimum of their average total cost curves.
    d. price searchers need to pay higher salaries to their managers because of the greater amount of entrepreneurship required in price-searcher industries.

14. Other economists have argued that the allocative inefficiency of competitive price searchers apparent in mechanical models is misleading. They argue that such mechanical models fail to account for
    a. the entry and exit of firms in the long run, which drives economic profits to zero, thereby eliminating any short-run, allocative inefficiencies in competitive price-searcher industries.
    b. the possibility that the higher prices paid by consumers in competitive price-searcher industries are compensated by greater choice of goods or locations than would be present in an allocatively "efficient" industry.
    c. the spillover effects on the advertising industry, which would shrink substantially if competitive price searchers did not need to advertise so much.
    d. the fact that most competitive price-searcher industries are contestable markets, so competitive price searchers react to competitive pressures whether or not numerous competitors actually operate in the market.

15. If economic profits were present in a competitive price-searcher industry,
    a. production inefficiency would develop, causing costs to increase until the profits had been eliminated.
    b. firms would operate in the short run, but they would be forced out of business in the long run as competition eliminated the economic profit.
    c. competition from new entrants would occur until the economic profits had been eliminated.
    d. the firms would eventually find these profits offset by long-run economic losses.

16. The practice of price discrimination has which of the following effects?
    a. Groups with the higher elasticity of demand will pay higher prices.
    b. Groups with the lower elasticity of demand will pay higher prices.
    c. With price discrimination, total output and allocative efficiency will fall.
    d. Groups will pay identical prices that are exactly equal to the firm's marginal cost.

Harcourt Brace & Company

17. Neither price takers nor competitive price searchers will be able to earn long-run economic profit because
    a. with low entry barriers, the entry and exit of firms result in prices that are equal to per-unit costs in the long run.
    b. competition from new firms will result in higher prices in the market, which offset any economic losses they earn.
    c. in both markets, firms charge a price equal to marginal cost.
    d. in both markets, firms produce products that are identical to the products produced by their competitors.

Questions 18 through 20 refer to Exhibit 4, which depicts the demand, marginal revenue, and cost curves facing a firm in a competitive price-searcher industry.

EXHIBIT 4

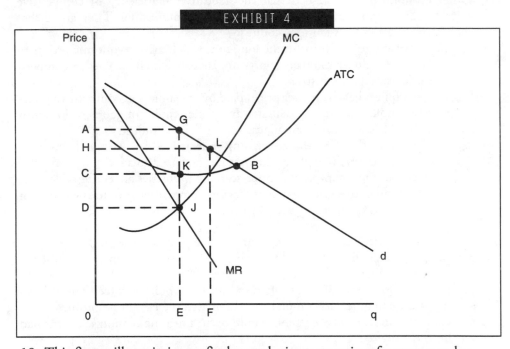

18. This firm will maximize profits by producing a quantity of output equal to
    a. E and charging a price equal to A.
    b. E and charging a price equal to D.
    c. F and charging a price equal to H.
    d. F and charging a price equal to C.

19. The firm is currently earning an
    a. economic profit equal to the area CKGA.
    b. economic profit equal to the area DJGA.
    c. economic loss equal to the area CKGA.
    d. economic loss equal to the area DJGA.

Harcourt Brace & Company

20. In the long run, we would expect
   a. the firm's ATC curve to fall as firms enter the industry, forcing the firm to increase its efficiency.
   b. the firm's demand curve to decrease as firms enter the industry due to the presence of positive economic profits.
   c. the firm's demand curve to increase as firms exit the industry due to the presence of economic losses.
   d. the firm's demand curve to shift such that marginal revenue and marginal cost intersect at quantity F—the point where average total cost is at a minimum.

Questions 21 through 23 refer to Exhibit 5, which depicts the demand, marginal revenue, and cost curves facing a firm in a competitive price-searcher industry.

EXHIBIT 5

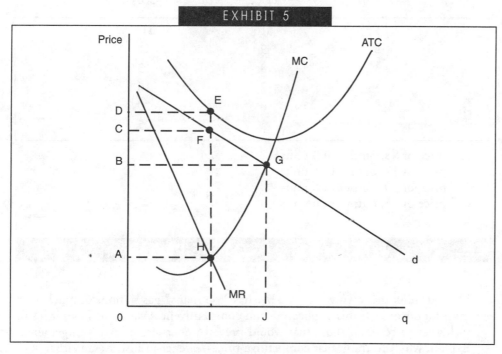

21. This firm will maximize profits by producing a quantity of output equal to
   a. I and charging a price equal to A.
   b. I and charging a price equal to C.
   c. I and charging a price equal to D.
   d. J and charging a price equal to B.

22. The firm is currently earning an
   a. economic profit equal to the area AHFC.
   b. economic profit equal to the area CFED.
   c. economic loss equal to the area AHED.
   d. economic loss equal to the area CFED.

Harcourt Brace & Company

23. In the long run, we would expect
    a. more firms to enter this industry until zero economic profits are restored.
    b. firms to exit this industry until zero economic profits are restored.
    c. the number of firms to remain constant and existing firms will continue to suffer economic losses in the long run.
    d. the number of firms to remain constant and existing firms will continue to earn economic profits in the long run.

24. Given the data shown in Exhibit 6, what price and output level would a profit-maximizing price searcher choose?

	EXHIBIT 6	
OUTPUT	PRICE	TOTAL COST
1	$10	$10
2	9	11
3	8	13
4	7	16
5	6	20
6	5	25

    a. price of $8, output of 3 units
    b. price of $7, output of 4 units
    c. price of $6, output of 5 units
    d. price of $5, output of 6 units

DISCUSSION QUESTIONS

1. Do you think the town where you live has "too many" gas stations or quick-stop mini food stores? Is this duplication and competitiveness wasteful? Does it result in higher prices than those that would prevail under alternative arrangements? Explain why you think that competitive price-searcher industries are either
    a. wasteful and inefficient, or
    b. consistent with efficiency and a consumer-directed economy.

2. a. List some real-world examples of price discrimination.
    b. Do you think price discrimination is more or less common in the sale of services than in the sale of physical goods? Why might this be the case?
    c. Phone prices are generally lower on weekends than on weekdays. Do you think this is price discrimination? Explain.

3. What is meant by competition? How does competition in price-taker industries differ from the competition that occurs in competitive price-searcher industries?

Why is competition important if markets are to work efficiently? Can competition protect the consumer from sellers who sell differentiated products?

4. List five industries or markets that you feel are characterized by competitive price searching. Pick two of them and describe the form of competition in those industries. Do these firms compete through price-cutting, advertising, location, or quality differences? Do you feel that competition in these industries delivers good-quality products for good prices? Why or why not?

5. Is advertising wasteful or productive? To what extent do commercials like those produced for the soft drink industry provide information to the customer? Why is such advertising effective? Make a list of advertising campaigns that you regard as useful because of the information they provide. Make a list of advertising campaigns that you regard as socially wasteful.

6. What is a contestable market? If there was only one firm presently in an industry, but there was no barriers preventing other firms from entering, would you expect this firm to price its products *as if* it were in competition with other firms? Explain your reasoning.

Harcourt Brace & Company

CHAPTER 11

Price-Searcher Markets with High Entry Barriers

TRUE OR FALSE

T   F

☐ ☐ 1. Government licensing, patent laws, economies of scale, and control over an essential resource are four potential sources of high entry barriers in a market.

☐ ☐ 2. In the long run, the profits of a monopolist will be eliminated by the entry of new competitors.

☐ ☐ 3. Unlike other firms, a profit-maximizing monopolist will not produce the level of output where MC = MR.

☐ ☐ 4. Since an unregulated monopolist is assured of economic profit, there is little incentive for such a firm to produce efficiently.

☐ ☐ 5. Patent laws result in higher prices to consumers, but they also encourage more investment in research and development.

☐ ☐ 6. The level of output produced by a monopolist will exceed the level of output produced if the industry was instead comprised of many competitive firms.

☐ ☐ 7. An oligopoly is an industry dominated by a small number of rival sellers.

☐ ☐ 8. Collusion is likely to be more successful if barriers to entry are high and the number of producers in the industry is small.

☐ ☐ 9. A cartel is an organization of sellers attempting to act as a single monopolist.

☐ ☐ 10. A competitive firm has more market power than a monopolist because it competes with a larger number of rival sellers.

☐ ☐ 11. Theoretically, price regulation could improve efficiency and resource allocation by forcing a monopolist to charge a price equal to her average (or marginal) cost of production.

☐ ☐ 12. Practically speaking, the advantages of government regulation are greatly limited because of imperfect information about cost and demand conditions.

☐ ☐ 13. Historically, regulatory agencies have sometimes been used as vehicles to maintain high prices and limit competition.

☐ ☐ 14. Reducing artificial barriers to entry (eliminating licensing requirements, for example) would reduce some of the inefficiencies associated with monopolies and oligopolies in industries currently protected by such barriers.

PROBLEMS AND PROJECTS

1. Exhibit 1 indicates the demand and long-run cost conditions in an industry.

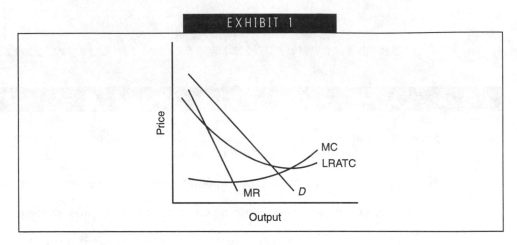

EXHIBIT 1

a. Explain why the industry is likely to be monopolized. [Hint: Look at the shape of the LRATC curve.]
b. Indicate the monopolist's profit-maximizing output level and label it Q.
c. Indicate the price that a profit-maximizing monopolist would charge and label it P.
d. Indicate the area representing the profits of the monopolist

2. The food service at many university campuses is operated by a single firm. Suppose that Exhibit 2 indicates the monthly demand for meals and total operating costs for the food service firm on your campus.
a. Fill in the firm's TR, MR, and MC schedules.
b. What price (of those shown) would a profit-maximizing monopolist choose?
c. Is the monopolist making economic profits? If so, how large per month?

EXHIBIT 2

SALES (IN 1,000s)	PRICE (PER MEAL)	TR	MR (PER 1,000)	TOTAL COST	MC (PER 1,000)
4	$1.60	_____	xx	$6,000	xx
5	1.40	_____	_____	6,400	_____
6	1.30	_____	_____	6,800	_____
7	1.20	_____	_____	7,300	_____
8	1.10	_____	_____	8,000	_____
9	1.00	_____	_____	9,000	_____
10	0.90	_____	_____	10,200	_____

Harcourt Brace & Company

d. Suppose that the university competitively auctioned the food service rights to the highest bidder. What is the *maximum* amount this firm would be willing to pay for this license for one year? Who would reap the monopoly profits under this arrangement?

3. Exhibit 3 indicates the demand, marginal revenue, marginal cost, and average cost curves for a monopolist.
    a. To maximize profits, what price would the monopolist set? What is the profit-maximizing level of output? Shade in the area that represents the monopolist's profit or loss.
    b. What are the socially ideal levels of price and output in this market (as might be obtained if the market were a competitive price-taker market)?

EXHIBIT 3

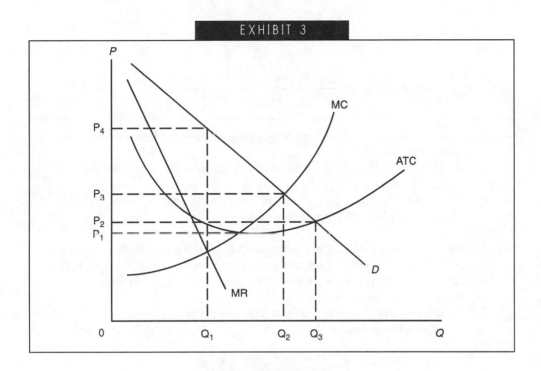

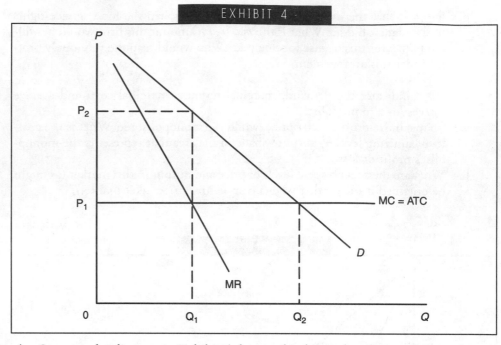

EXHIBIT 4

4. Suppose the diagram in Exhibit 4 depicts the demand and cost conditions in an oligopoly market.
   a. If the firms in this industry were to compete, what would be the resulting market price and quantity?
   b. If the firms in this industry were to successfully collude, what would be the resulting market price and quantity?

5. Exhibit 5 shows the long-run, per-unit costs (LRATC) for producing newspapers for a *single* firm. Use the information in the exhibit to answer the following questions.
   a. Using the LRATC curve, at what level of output does a newspaper minimize its per-newspaper cost?
   b. Demand curve A shows the total demand for newspapers in city A, which has a small population. If this is the only newspaper in the city, and it pro-

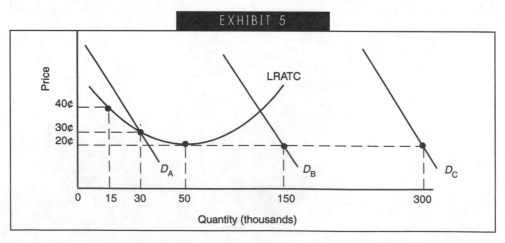

EXHIBIT 5

Harcourt Brace & Company

duces 30,000 newspapers to satisfy the entire city's demand, what will be the newspaper's per-unit cost?

c. Suppose the city council was worried about having a monopoly provider of newspapers and decided to break this firm up into two smaller newspapers, each producing 15,000 units. How will the per-newspaper costs for each of these two smaller firms compare to the per-newspaper cost for the one large firm?

d. In larger cities, there generally tends to be more than one newspaper in the city. Consider cities B and C, whose demands are also shown in the exhibit. In city B, could one newspaper produce the entire market output at a lower cost than several smaller firms? How many different newspaper firms might we expect to be present in city B? city C?

6. Consider a university town in which two stores sell textbooks, Tom's Texts and Bob's Books. Both stores purchase textbooks from distributors at a cost of $20 per textbook and are considering whether to set their price at either $30 or $40. Because the quantity sold at each store will depend upon not only the price they set but also on the price set by the rival firm, Exhibit 6 shows the quantity of textbooks (Q) sold by each store for all four possible combinations of prices. Use the information in the exhibit to answer the following questions.

a. The case where Tom's Texts sets its price at $30, while Bob's Books sets its price at $40 is given in the lower left. In this case, Tom's Texts will sell 900 books and Bob's Books will sell 100 books. Profits for each firm will be equal to the number of units sold times the profit earned on each book. Tom's Texts earns $10 profit on each book ($30 price minus cost per book of $20) and sells 900 books, for a total profit of $9,000. Bob's Books earns $20 profit on each book ($40 price minus cost per book of $20) and sells 100 books, for a total profit of $2,000. These values for profit are indicated in the table. For each of the other cases, find profit for both stores and put your answers in the spaces provided in the table.

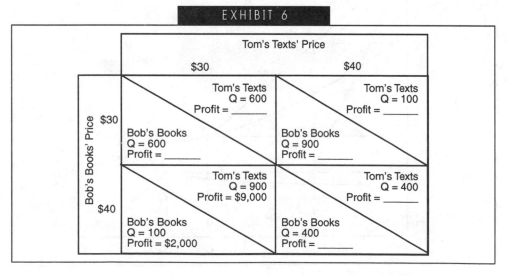

EXHIBIT 6

Harcourt Brace & Company

b. Suppose that Tom's Texts was almost certain that Bob's Books was going to set their price at $30. Given a $30 price at Bob's Books, what price should Tom's Texts set to maximize their profits?

c. Instead, suppose that Tom's Texts was almost certain that Bob's Books was going to set their price at $40. Given a $40 price at Bob's Books, what price should Tom's Texts set to maximize their profits?

d. Given your answers to parts b and c, does the profit-maximizing price for Tom's Texts depend upon the price set by Bob's Books?

e. Now, view this problem from the standpoint of Bob's Books. What is the price Bob's Books should charge to maximize their profit? Does it depend upon what price they expect Tom's Texts to set?

f. As the previous questions have uncovered, both stores will choose to set their textbook price at $30 regardless of what the other firm does. How much profit does each firm make in this case? Suppose that the owners of both stores secretly met and agreed to collude, both raising price to $40. Would both stores earn more profit if they collude?

g. Do you think this collusive agreement would be stable? Does Tom's Texts have an incentive to cheat on the agreement and lower price? Bob's Books?

7. Exhibit 7 indicates the demand, marginal revenue, marginal cost, and average cost curves for a monopolist. Use the exhibit to answer the following questions regarding government price regulation of a monopolist.

a. In the absence of regulation, what price would the monopolist set to maximize profits? What is the profit-maximizing level of output? Is the monopolist making an economic profit?

b. If a regulatory agency wanted to use average cost pricing to regulate the monopolist, what price would it set? What level of output would the

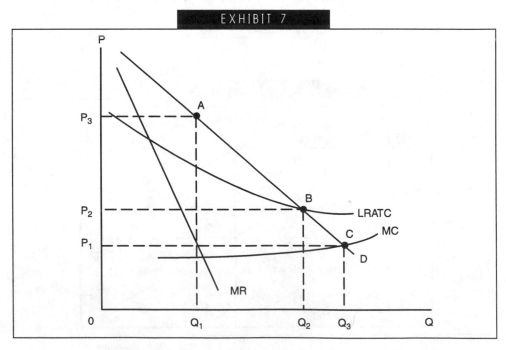

EXHIBIT 7

Harcourt Brace & Company

monopolist produce at that price? What level of economic profit would the monopolist earn at this regulated outcome?

c. If a regulatory agency wanted to use marginal cost pricing to regulate the monopolist, what price would it set? What level of economic profit would the monopolist earn at this regulated outcome? What level of output would the monopolist produce at that price?

MULTIPLE CHOICE

1. A monopoly is best defined as
   a. a single seller of a product that has characteristics very similar to the products produced in other industries.
   b. a single seller of a well-defined product for which there are no good substitutes operating in a market with high barriers to entry.
   c. a market in which a small number of rival sellers produce the entire market output.
   d. any firm operating in a contestable market.

2. Which of the following firms best fits the definition of a monopoly?
   a. McDonald's, because it is the only firm who produces the Big Mac
   b. a local cable company who has been granted the only license to sell cable in a city by the town council
   c. Ford Motor Company, because there are significant economies of scale in the production of automobiles
   d. Harvard University, because it has a reputation as being one of the top universities in the country

3. Which of the following is **not** a barrier that limits the entry of potential competitors into a market?
   a. government licensing
   b. control over an essential resource
   c. an elastic demand for a product
   d. patent rights

4. When significant economies of scale are present in the production process, an industry will tend naturally toward monopoly because
   a. one firm will be able to produce the entire market output at a lower cost than several smaller firms.
   b. marginal revenue will be less than market price, giving firms the incentive to equate marginal cost with price instead of equating marginal cost and marginal revenue.
   c. economies of scale can only be present when firms produce identical products and there is no reason to have more than one firm producing the same exact product.
   d. consumers will be unwilling to compare the prices charged by several different firms.

5. How will the price and output of an unregulated monopolist compare with the ideal levels that might be reached if the market was competitive?
   a. The output of the monopolist will be larger and the price lower.
   b. The output of the monopolist will be larger and the price higher.
   c. The output of the monopolist will be smaller and the price lower.
   d. The output of the monopolist will be smaller and the price higher.

6. Allowing firms to receive patents on new inventions
   a. increases the price consumers pay for patented products.
   b. gives firms a greater incentive to conduct research and development to invent new products.
   c. results in much lower prices than would be present if other firms were allowed to compete.
   d. does both *a* and *b*, but not *c*.

7. Which of the following is true?
   a. A monopolist is always guaranteed to earn positive economic profits regardless of their cost of production or the price they charge.
   b. A monopolist will charge the highest price possible for their product because no matter what price they charge, people will still have to buy it.
   c. A monopolist has no incentive to find more cost-efficient methods of production because they are protected from competition from other sellers.
   d. None of the above are correct.

8. Which of the following statements accurately describes a difference between a firm that is a monopolist and one that is in a competitive, open price-taker market?
   a. Marginal revenue and price are equal for a price taker, but not a monopolist.
   b. Monopolists can earn economic profits in the long-run, price takers cannot.
   c. A price takers sells its output at a price equal to marginal cost, while a monopolist sells its output at a price higher than marginal cost.
   d. All of the above.

9. To maximize profit, the monopolist whose cost and demand conditions shown in Exhibit 8 should charge a price of
   a. $4.
   b. $5.
   c. $6.
   d. $7.

EXHIBIT 8		
PRICE	OUTPUT	TOTAL COST
$7	1	$7
6	2	8
5	3	10
4	4	13
3	5	17

Harcourt Brace & Company

10. Which of the following statements accurately describes a difference between a firm that is a monopolist and one that is in a competitive price-searcher market?
    a. A competitive price searcher produces at the output level where marginal cost equals marginal revenue, a monopolist does not.
    b. A monopolist faces a downward-sloping demand curve, a competitive price searcher does not.
    c. A monopolist charges a price higher than marginal cost, a competitive price searcher does not.
    d. In the long run, a competitive price searcher will earn zero economic profit because of low entry barriers, while a monopolist may earn positive economic profits in the long run.

EXHIBIT 9

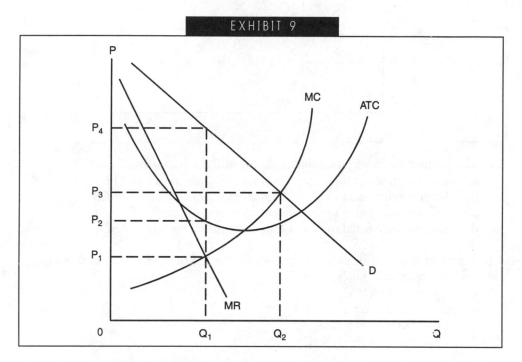

11. To maximize profits, the monopolist shown in Exhibit 9 would
    a. produce output of Q_1 and charge a price of P_1.
    b. produce output of Q_1 and charge a price of P_2.
    c. produce output of Q_2 and charge a price of P_3.
    d. produce output of Q_1 and charge a price of P_4.

Harcourt Brace & Company

EXHIBIT 10

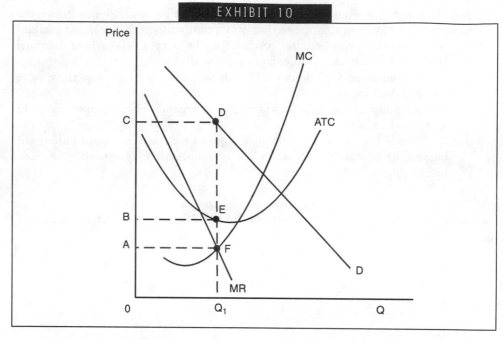

12. The profit-maximizing monopolist shown in Exhibit 10 would
    a. charge a price equal to C and earn an economic profit of AFDC.
    b. charge a price equal to C and earn an economic profit of AFEB.
    c. charge a price equal to C and earn an economic profit of BEDC.
    d. charge a price equal to A and earn an economic profit of AFDC.

13. A market situation in which only a small number of mutually interdependent, rival sellers exists is known as a(n)
    a. oligopoly market.
    b. monopoly market.
    c. open price-taker market.
    d. competitive price-searcher market.

14. In general, an organization of sellers designed to coordinate supply decisions so that the joint profits of the members is maximized is called a(n) _____. If they are successful, the total market output and price will most closely approximate the output and price in a(n) _____ market. (Fill in the blanks.)
    a. cooperative; open price-taker
    b. cartel; monopoly
    c. cartel; open price-taker
    d. OPEC; competitive price-searcher

15. To increase joint profits, a cartel will attempt to
    a. restrict output in order to increase the market price of the good produced.
    b. restrict output in order to decrease the market price of the good produced.
    c. expand output in order to increase the market price of the good produced.
    d. expand output in order to decrease the market price of the good produced.

Harcourt Brace & Company

16. The oil industry is dominated by a cartel known as OPEC, and the cocaine industry is dominated by the Columbian cocaine cartel. If these cartels are being successful,
    a. the price of oil is higher than if the cartel did not exist, but the price of cocaine is lower.
    b. the price of cocaine is higher than if the cartel did not exist, but the price of oil is lower.
    c. both goods have higher prices than if the cartels did not exist, and both have lower levels of total output.
    d. both goods have higher prices than if the cartels did not exist, and both also have higher levels of total output.

17. Laws designed to prevent monopoly and promote competition are known as
    a. antitrust laws.
    b. statutory amendments.
    c. fair-pricing legislation.
    d. breakup bills.

18. Which of the following would increase the likelihood that firms in an industry could successfully collude?
    a. a large number of firms in the industry
    b. unstable demand conditions in the industry
    c. high barriers to entry in the industry
    d. product characteristics that make it difficult for firms to detect other firms who cheat on the agreement

19. (I) Oligopolistic firms have an incentive to collude to increase profits. (II) Oligopolistic firms have an incentive to cheat on collusive agreements to increase profits.
    a. I is true; II is false.
    b. I is false; II is true.
    c. Both I and II are false.
    d. Both I and II are true.

20. If a local government began licensing funeral homes in the area, effectively making them into a cartel, we would expect
    a. the price of funeral services to rise, and the number of funerals performed in the area to fall.
    b. the price of funeral services to rise, and the number of funerals performed in the area to increase as well.
    c. the price of funeral services to fall, and the number of funerals performed in the area to increase.
    d. the price of funeral services to fall, and the number of funerals performed in the area to fall as well.

21. A major problem with regulatory agencies is that they
    a. have no real legal power over the industries they are supposed to regulate.
    b. tend to be too tough on the firms they are regulating, forcing them into a loss position.
    c. often underestimate the firm's cost of production and consequently force regulated firms into a loss position.
    d. often come to represent the interests of established firms in the industry and use their power to limit competition.

22. An expansion in the number of plumbers in a local area has resulted in lower profits. The local plumbing contractors have called a meeting to discuss ways to improve their long-run profitability. Of the four plans being discussed seriously, which would most likely increase their long-run profits?
    a. passage of legislation requiring *new* contractors to be licensed, which would require passing a stiff licensing exam and paying a $5,000 fee
    b. an "off-the-record" agreement that each plumbing contractor would increase his or her prices by an average of 7 percent
    c. passage of legislation requiring the local government to share the cost of installing all private sewage systems
    d. repeal of the current tax on installations of plumbing units

23. For which of the following reasons do regulatory agencies sometimes fail to bring the price and output of a natural monopoly to the ideal level?
    a. The regulatory agency does not have all the information concerning a firm's true costs.
    b. Monopolists may conceal profits by inflating the costs of production by spending money to achieve personal objectives (a very nice office building, for example).
    c. Regulatory agencies often come to reflect the views of the industries they are supposed to regulate.
    d. All of the above.

24. Economic theory suggests that government-operated monopolies will
    a. be highly efficient and follow policies that are in the consumers' interest.
    b. be dominated by persons who, while seeking to serve the public interest, are not hard nosed enough to run a business efficiently.
    c. be inefficient because of poor incentives for operational efficiency.
    d. favor the consumer at the expense of special interest groups in and out of government.

DISCUSSION QUESTIONS

1. In a famous antitrust case, the government charged the DuPont Company with attempting to monopolize the cellophane industry. The company argued that, while it was the major producer of cellophane, it was competing in the broader market of "flexible packaging," a very competitive industry. Waxed paper, glass-

ine, and aluminum foil all had sizable shares of the flexible packaging market. Would you consider DuPont a monopolist? How might you go about determining whether, in fact, DuPont was competing in the flexible wrap industry?

2. What are the advantages of regulating the activities of a monopolist? The major problems? Why does regulation, over time, tend to become a source of economic inefficiency?

3. What are the major sources of monopoly? Can a monopolized industry sometimes be transformed into a competitive industry? Why may it sometimes be costly to break up a monopoly into several smaller independent firms? Explain.

4. Use economic analysis to evaluate the government-operated firm as an alternative to monopoly. What factors will influence the price, output, and operational efficiency of the public sector firm? Explain.

5. Explain why firms in an oligopolistic industry have an incentive to collude but yet also have an incentive to cheat on collusive agreements.

6. What are the main similarities and differences in the economic outcomes between the major market structures we have covered (open price-taker markets, competitive price-searcher markets, oligopoly, and monopoly)? Address in your answer
    a. the price a firm will charge,
    b. the level of output produced,
    c. the role of profits and losses in both the short and long run,
    d. the types of products and different types of competition among firms, and
    e. the number of firms in each market.

PERSPECTIVES IN ECONOMICS

THE PARABLE OF THE PARKING LOTS

by Henry G. Manne

[From *Public Interest*, No. 23 (Spring 1971), pp. 10–15, Copyright © by National Affairs Inc., 1971. Reprinted by permission.]

In a city not far away there was a large football stadium. It was used from time to time for various events, but the principal use was for football games played Saturday afternoons by the local college team. The games were tremendously popular and people drove hundreds of miles to watch them. Parking was done in the usual way. People who arrived early were able to park free on the streets, and late comers had to pay to park in regular improvised lots.

There were, at distances ranging from 5 to 12 blocks from the stadium, approximately 25 commercial parking lots all of which received some business from Saturday afternoon football games. The lots closer to the stadium naturally received more football business than those fur-

ther away, and some of the very close lots actually raised their price on Saturday afternoons. But they did not raise the price much, and most did not change prices at all. The reason was not hard to find.

For something else happened on football afternoons. A lot of people who during the week were students, lawyers, school teachers, plumbers, factory workers, and even stock brokers went into the parking lot business. It was not a difficult thing to do. Typically a young boy would put up a crude, homemade sign saying "Parking $3." He would direct a couple of cars into his parent's driveway, tell the driver to take the key, and collect the three dollars. If the driveway was larger or there was yard space to park in, an older brother, an uncle, or the head of the household would direct the operation, sometimes asking drivers to leave their keys so that shifts could be made if necessary.

Some part-time parking lot operators who lived very close to the stadium charged as much as $5.00 to park in their driveways. But as the residences-turned-parking-lots were located further from the stadium (and incidentally closer to the commercial parking lots), the price charged at game time declined. In fact houses at some distance from the stadium charged less than the adjacent commercial lots. The whole system seemed to work fairly smoothly, and though traffic just after a

Harcourt Brace & Company

big game was terrible, there were no significant delays parking cars or retrieving parked cars.

But one day the owner of a chain of parking lots called a meeting of all the commercial parking lot owners in the general vicinity of the stadium. They formed an organization known as Association of Professional Parking Lot Employers, or APPLE. And they were very concerned about the Saturday parking business. One man who owned four parking lots pointed out that honest parking lot owners had heavy capital investments in their businesses, that they paid taxes, and that they employed individuals who supported families. There was no reason, he alleged, why these lots should not handle all the cars coming into the area for special events like football games. "It is unethical," he said, "to engage in cutthroat competition with irresponsible fender benders. After all, parking cars is a profession, not a business." The last remark drew loud applause.

Thus emboldened he continued, stating that commercial parking lot owners recognize their responsibility to serve the public's needs. Ethical car parkers, he said, understand their obligations not to dent fenders, to employ only trustworthy car parkers, to pay decent wages, and generally to care for the customers' automobiles as they would the corpus of a trust. His statement was hailed by others attending the meeting as being very statesmanlike.

Others at the meeting related various tales of horror about non-professional car parkers. One homeowner, it was said, actually allowed his fifteen-year-old son to move other peoples' cars around. Another said that he had seen an $8,000 Cadillac parked on a dirt lawn where it would have become mired in mud had it rained that day. Still another pointed out that a great deal of the problem came on the side of the stadium with the lower-priced houses, where there were more driveways per block than on the wealthier side of the stadium. He pointed out that these poor people would rarely be able to afford to pay for damage to other peoples' automobiles or to pay insurance premiums to cover such losses. He felt that a professional group such as APPLE had a duty to protect the public from their folly in using those parking spaces.

Finally another speaker reminded the audience that these "marginal, fly-by-night" parking lot operators generally parked a string of cars in the driveways so that a driver had to wait until all cars behind his had been removed before he could get out. This, he pointed out, was quite unlike the situation in commercial lots where, during a normal business day, people had to be assured of ready access to their automobiles at any time. The commercial parking lots either had to hire more attendants to shift cars around, or they had to park them so that any car was always accessible, even though this meant that fewer cars could park than the total space would actually hold. "Clearly," he said, "driveway parking constitutes unfair competition."

Emotions ran high at this meeting, and every member of APPLE pledged $1 per parking space for something mysteriously called a "slush fund." It was never made clear exactly whose slush would be bought with these funds, but several months later a resolution was adopted by the city council requiring licensing for anyone in the parking lot business.

The preamble to the new ordinance read like the speeches at the earlier meeting. It said that this measure was designed to protect the public against unscrupulous, unprofessional and undercapitalized parking lot operators. It required, *inter alia*, that anyone parking cars for a fee must have a minimum capital devoted to the parking lot business of $25,000, liability insurance in an amount not less than $500,000, bonding for each car parker, and a special driving test for these parkers (which incidentally would be designed and administered by APPLE). The ordinance also required, again in the public's interest, that every

lot charge a single posted price for parking and that any change in the posted price be approved in advance by the city council. Incidentally, most members were able to raise their fees about 20 percent before the first posting.

Then a funny thing happened to drivers on their way to the stadium for the next big game. They discovered city police in unusually large numbers informing them that it was illegal to pay a non-licensed parking lot operator for the right to park a car. These policemen also reminded parents that if their children were found in violation of this ordinance it could result in a misdemeanor charge being brought against the parents and possible juvenile court proceedings for the children. There were no driveway parking lots that day.

Back at the commercial parking lots, another funny thing occurred. Proceeding from the entrance of each of these parking lots within twelve blocks of the stadium were long lines of cars waiting to park. The line got larger as the lot was closer to the stadium. Many drivers had to wait so long or walk so far that they missed the entire first quarter of the big game.

At the end of the game it was even worse. The confusion was massive. The lot attendants could not cope with the jam up, and some cars were actually not retrieved until the next day. It was even rumored about town that some automobiles had been lost forever and that considerable liabilities might result for some operators. Industry spokesmen denied this, however.

Naturally there was a lot of grumbling, but there was no argument on what had caused the difficulty. At first everyone said there were merely some "bugs" in the new system that would have to be ironed out. But the only "bug" ironed out was a Volkswagen that was flattened by a careless lot attendant in a Cadillac Eldorado.

The situation did not improve at subsequent games. The members of APPLE did not hire additional employees to park cars, and operators near the stadium were not careful to follow their previous practice of parking cars in such a way as to have them immediately accessible. Employees seemed to become more surly, and a number of dented-fender claims mounted rapidly.

Little by little, too, cars began appearing in residential driveways again. For instance, one enterprising youth regularly went into the car wash business on football afternoons, promising that his wash job would take at least two hours. He charged five dollars, and got it—even on rainy days—in fact, especially on rainy days. Another homeowner offered to take cars on consignment for three hours to sell them at prices fixed by the owner. He charged $4.00 for this "service," but his subterfuge was quickly squelched by the authorities. The parking situation remained "critical."

Political pressures on the city council began to mount to "do something" about the inordinate delays in parking and retrieving cars on football afternoons. The city council sent out a stern note of warning to APPLE, and the local university's computer science department to look into the matter. This group reported that the managerial and administrative machinery in the parking lot business was archaic. What was needed, the study group said, was less goose quills and stand-up desks and more computers and conveyor belts. It was also suggested that all members of APPLE be hooked into one computer so that cars could be readily shifted to the most accessible spaces.

Spokesmen for the industry took up the cry of administrative modernization. Subtle warnings appeared in the local papers suggesting that if the industry did not get its own house in order, heavy-handed regulation could be anticipated. The city council asked for reports on failures to deliver cars and decreed that this would include any failure to put a driver in his car within five minutes of demand without a new dent.

Some of the professional operators actually installed computer equipment to handle their ticketing and parking logistics problems. And some added second stories to their parking lots. Others bought up additional space, thereby raising the value of vacant lots in the area, but many simply added a few additional car parkers and hoped that the problem would go away without a substantial investment of capital.

The commercial operators also began arguing that they needed higher parking fees because of their higher operating costs. Everyone agreed that costs for operating a parking lot were certainly higher than before the licensing ordinance. So the city council granted a request for an across-the-board ten percent hike in fees. The local newspaper editorially hoped that this would ease the problem without still higher fees being necessary. In a way, it did. A lot of people stopped driving. They began using city buses, or they chartered private buses for the game. Some stayed home and watched the game on TV. A new study group on fees was appointed.

Just about then, several other blows fell on the parking lot business. But transportation to the area near the stadium was improved with a federal subsidy to the municipal bus company. And several new suburban shopping centers caused a loss of automobile traffic in the older area of town. But most dramatic of all, the local university, under severe pressure from its students and faculty, dropped intercollegiate football altogether and converted the stadium into a park for underprivileged children.

The impact of these events on the commercial parking lots was swift. Income declined drastically. The companies that had borrowed money to finance the expansion everyone wanted earlier were hardest hit. Two declared bankruptcy, and many had to be absorbed by financially stronger companies. Layoffs among car parkers were enormous, and APPLE actually petitioned the city council to guarantee the premiums on their liability insurance policies so that people would not be afraid to park commercially. This idea was suggested to APPLE by recent congressional legislation creating an insurance program for stock brokers.

A spokesman for APPLE made the following public statement: "New organizations or arrangements may be necessary to straighten out this problem. There has been a failure in both the structure of the industry and the regulatory scheme. New and better regulation is clearly demanded. A sound parking lot business is necessary for a healthy urban economy." The statement was hailed by the industry as being very statesmanlike, though everyone speculated about what he really meant.

Others in the industry demanded that the city bus service be curtailed during the emergency. The city council granted every rate increase the lots requested. There were no requests for rate decreases, but the weaker lots began offering prizes and other subtle or covert rebates to private bus companies who would park with them. In fact, this problem became so serious and uncontrollable that one owner of a large chain proclaimed that old-fashioned price competition for this business would be desirable. This again was hailed as statesmanlike, but everyone assumed that he really meant something else. No one proposed repeal of the licensing ordinance.

One other thing happened. Under pressure from APPLE, the city council decreed that henceforth no parking would be allowed on any streets in the downtown area of town. The local merchants were extremely unhappy about this, however, and the council rescinded the ordinance at the next meeting, citing a computer error as the basis for the earlier restriction.

The ultimate resolution of the "new" parking problem is not in sight. The parking lot industry in this town not very far from here is now said to be a depressed business, even a sick one. Everyone looks to the city council for a solution, but things will probably limp along as they are for quite a while, picking up with an occasional professional football game and dropping low with bad weather.

MORAL. If you risk your lot under an apple tree, you may get hit in the head.

DISCUSSION

1. In this fable, who was protected by the regulations? From what? At what cost?

2. Do you see similar situations in regulated businesses in your own area? in state or federally regulated industries? How are they similar? How do they differ? Who gains, and at what cost?

3. In this article, businesses that lobbied to protect themselves from competition ended up hurting themselves in the long run. Do you think that this is a typical result? Explain your answer.

Harcourt Brace & Company

CHAPTER 12

The Supply of and Demand for Productive Resources

TRUE OR FALSE

T F

☐ ☐ 1. Physical capital and human capital cannot be substituted for each other.

☐ ☐ 2. Attending college is an example of an investment in human capital.

☐ ☐ 3. The demand for a resource will be negatively related to its price partly because producers will substitute other factors of production for the resource as it increases in price.

☐ ☐ 4. If consumer demand for automobiles increases, the demand for resources used to produce automobiles will fall to offset the increase.

☐ ☐ 5. Marginal revenue product (MRP) is the change in the total revenue of a firm that results from the employment of one additional unit of a resource. It is equal to the marginal product (MP) of the resource multiplied by the firm's marginal revenue (MR).

☐ ☐ 6. The value of marginal product (VMP) is equal to marginal revenue product (MRP) for a price-searcher firm because for these firms, price (P) equals marginal revenue (MR).

☐ ☐ 7. The demand curve for a resource is equal to the MRP curve for the resource.

☐ ☐ 8. An employer will hire workers as long as their marginal revenue product is positive.

☐ ☐ 9. When multiple resources are employed, a firm will minimize its costs by equating marginal revenue product divided by the price for each resource (in other words, $MRP_A \div P_A = MRP_B \div P_B$).

☐ ☐ 10. The supply of a resource in the long run will generally be more inelastic than its supply in the short run.

☐ ☐ 11. The marginal products—and therefore wage rates—of employees will be positively influenced by the amount of physical capital per worker in a firm.

☐ ☐ 12. In a market economy, resource prices help to allocate a country's resources among the alternative industries in which they could be employed.

T F

☐ ☐ 13. Because of the law of diminishing marginal returns, a worker's marginal revenue product eventually declines as more workers are hired in a given plant.

☐ ☐ 14. The demand for a resource strongly depends upon the demand for the final good that the resource helps to produce. This is why the demand for a resource is called a derived demand.

PROBLEMS AND PROJECTS

1. Nicole sells building materials in a price-taker industry. Her firm receives $100 for each unit of material sold. Exhibit ! shows how Nicole's total output changes as additional units of labor are hired.

EXHIBIT 1

UNITS OF LABOR	TOTAL OUTPUT (PER WEEK)	MARGINAL PRODUCT (PER WEEK)	PRODUCT PRICE	TOTAL REVENUE	MARGINAL REVENUE PRODUCT (PER WEEK)
1	5	5	$100	$500	$500
2	9	_____	100	_____	_____
3	12	_____	100	_____	_____
4	14	_____	100	_____	_____
5	15	_____	100	_____	_____

a. Fill in the marginal product, total revenue, and marginal revenue product columns.

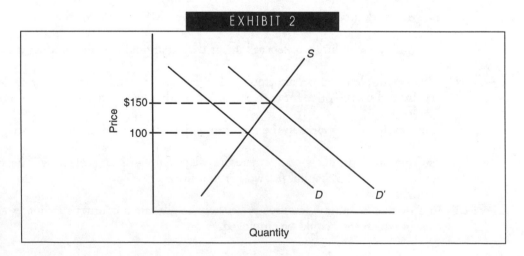

EXHIBIT 2

Harcourt Brace & Company

b. If she wants to maximize her profits, how many employees should Nicole hire if the market wage rate is $250 per week?

c. How many employees should Nicole hire if the wage rate goes up to $350 per week?

d. The supply-and-demand conditions in the building materials market are represented in Exhibit 2. Suppose that the demand for building materials increases as indicated by *D'* and Nicole can now sell her output for $150. Using the original wage rate of $250 per week from part b, what will happen to the number of employees Nicole hires?

2. Magic Carpet, Inc., produces and sells handmade oriental rugs in a price-taker industry. The firm receives $100 per square meter for each rug produced. Exhibit 3 shows how total output (in square meters) changes as additional units of skilled labor are hired.

EXHIBIT 3

UNITS OF SKILLED LABOR	TOTAL OUTPUT (SQUARE METERS PER WEEK)	MP	PRICE PER SQUARE METER	TR	MRP
1	5	5	$100	$500	$500
2	12	_____	100	_____	_____
3	18	_____	100	_____	_____
4	21.5	_____	100	_____	_____
5	24	_____	100	_____	_____
6	25	_____	100	_____	_____

a. Complete the table.

b. Given the equilibrium wage rate as $200 per week, indicate how many workers the firm would hire if it wanted to maximize profits.

c. How many workers would Magic Carpet hire if the market wage increased to $300 per week?

3. Use the diagrams on page 146 to indicate the changes in demand (D), supply (S), equilibrium price (P), and equilibrium quantity (Q) in response to the events in the resource markets. First, show in the diagrams how the described event or events affect demand and/or supply of the resource, and then fill in the table to the right of the diagrams using + to indicate an increase, − to indicate a decrease, and 0 to indicate no effect. [Hint: The diagrams are of the resource markets themselves; for example, the diagram in part a is of the market for high school math teachers.]

Harcourt Brace & Company

RESOURCE MARKET	EVENTS	DIAGRAMS	D	S	P	Q
a. High school math teachers	Wages for mathematicians employed in private industry rise.		___	___	___	___
b. Computers	Technological change raises the speed of computer calculations.		___	___	___	___
c. Computer technicians	The cost of obtaining computer training falls		___	___	___	___
d. Welders	Technological change lowers the cost of robots used to weld auto parts on auto assembly lines.		___	___	___	___
e. Agricultural land in Southern California	A vitamin C fad raises the price of oranges.		___	___	___	___

4. In the growing of corn, a farmer uses two fertilizers: Vitacorn and Cornpower. The farmer has estimated that at the current rate of usage of the two fertilizers, the marginal (physical) product of one ton of Vitacorn is 200 bushels per acre and the marginal product of one ton of Cornpower is 400 bushels per acre. The

Harcourt Brace & Company

best price quotations the farmer has been able to get are $800/ton for Vitacorn and $1,200/ton for Cornpower.

   a. From the above information, does the farmer's current usage of the two fertilizers meet the "condition for cost minimization when multiple resources are employed"?

   b. Suppose the farmer used one more ton of Cornpower and two fewer tons of Vitacorn. How would total output change? How would total cost change? Would this substitution be consistent with the goal of profit maximization?

   c. If the farmer continued to substitute Cornpower for Vitacorn, assume that the marginal product of Cornpower would fall. Would these changes lead toward fulfillment of the condition for cost minimization you discussed in part a? How?

5. XYZ Corporation is considering moving its plant from the United States to Mexico to cut its labor costs. Wage rates for labor are $10 per hour in the U.S. and $6 per hour in Mexico. Suppose the firm's current U.S. workers have a marginal product of 60, while Mexican workers would have a marginal product of 30.

   a. Find the ratio of marginal product to price (MP/P) for both U.S. and Mexican labor.

   b. For a given level of output, would the firm's costs be lower or higher if it were to produce in Mexico?

   c. How low would the wage rate have to be in Mexico to make the move profitable for the company?

MULTIPLE CHOICE

1. The short-run *supply* of a human resource will be more elastic the
   a. more elastic the demand for the product to be produced.
   b. more inelastic the demand for the product to be produced.
   c. lower the skill level necessary to perform the job.
   d. harder it is to acquire the skill and knowledge necessary to provide the resource.

2. A decrease in the demand for a final product will cause
   a. a decrease in demand for the resources used to produce the good.
   b. an increase in demand for the resources used to produce the good.
   c. firms to expand production of the good.
   d. an increase in the supply of resources used to produce the good.

3. The more elastic the demand for a final product,
   a. the more elastic will be the demand for the productive resources used.
   b. the less elastic the supply of resources used in producing the product.
   c. the less firms will reduce their usage of resources when the price of the resources increases.
   d. the higher the MRP of the resources used to produce the product.

Harcourt Brace & Company

4. Which of the following expresses the correct decision-making rule for a profit-maximizing firm hiring units of labor?
   a. If the MRP was rising, less labor would be employed as time passed.
   b. The firm should continue to hire workers as long as their MRP is greater than the wage rate.
   c. The firm should continue to hire workers until the total costs of all workers equals the total revenue from the output of the workers.
   d. The firm should continue to hire workers until the wage rate equals the price of the product.

5. Because the demand for a resource is highly dependent upon the demand for the final goods that the resource helps produce, the demand for a resource is called a(n)
   a. derived demand.
   b. independent demand.
   c. declining proportions demand.
   d. elastic demand.

6. Compared to the short-run demand, the long-run demand for a resource is
   a. less elastic.
   b. more elastic.
   c. equally elastic.
   d. either more or less elastic; we cannot predict which.

7. In a price-taker industry, the marginal revenue derived from the sale of an additional unit of the product is equal to the market price of the product. In these circumstances,
   a. value of marginal product is less than marginal revenue product.
   b. value of marginal product is greater than marginal revenue product.
   c. value of marginal product equals marginal revenue product.
   d. marginal product equals marginal cost.

8. If the cost of using skilled labor was twice the cost of using unskilled labor, and both were used by a profit-maximizing firm, the firm would adjust the quantity of each type of labor until
   a. the marginal product of each was the same.
   b. twice as much unskilled labor was used.
   c. half as much unskilled labor was used.
   d. the marginal product of skilled labor was twice that of unskilled labor.

9. If a firm used only two factors of production, labor (L) and capital (K), which of the following conditions would be present if the firm was minimizing its cost of production?
   a. $MP_L \div P_L = MP_K \div P_K$
   b. $MP_L \times P_L = MP_K \times P_K$
   c. $MRP_L = MRP_K$
   d. $MP_L = MP_K$

Harcourt Brace & Company

10. A change in the demand for a resource can be caused by which of the following?
    a. a change in the demand for the final product that uses the resource as a factor of production
    b. a change in the productivity of the resource
    c. a change in the price of *other* resources that could be used as substitutes for the resource in question
    d. all of the above

11. A firm currently employs 80 units of labor and 50 units of capital equipment to produce 3000 hamster cages. Given the current input levels utilized, the marginal product of labor is 40 and the marginal product of capital is 10. If we assume that labor costs $20 per unit and capital costs $10 per unit,
    a. the firm is using the appropriate mix of labor and capital to minimize its costs.
    b. the firm could lower its costs for the same level of output by using more labor and less capital.
    c. the firm could lower its costs for the same level of output by using more capital and less labor.
    d. the current MRP of capital exceeds the current MRP of labor.

12. During his administration, President Carter advocated a $1.46 billion aid program for college students from low- and middle-income families. The program was designed to halt the decline in college enrollments. If the program had been implemented, which of the following would have been the most likely outcome?
    a. Starting salaries for new college graduates would have risen because of an increase in the number of high-quality graduates.
    b. Starting salaries for college graduates would have been unaffected.
    c. The productivity of the labor force would fall as more young people chose to be students instead of workers.
    d. Starting salaries of new college graduates would have fallen as the supply of graduates increased.

13. If a college education did not increase worker productivity,
    a. no one would go to college.
    b. wages would tend to be the same for workers with and without a college education.
    c. wages would still be higher for workers with college degrees because of the cost of going to college.
    d. the total lifetime earnings of workers who go to college and those who do not would tend to be the same.

14. Economists refer to expenditures on training, education, and skill development designed to increase the productivity of an individual as
    a. overhead expenditures.
    b. investments in human capital.
    c. sunk expenditures.
    d. social capital.

Harcourt Brace & Company

15. If steel workers obtain a substantial wage increase, employment in the steel industry will be likely to fall the most if
   a. the demand curve for steel is highly inelastic.
   b. the demand curve for steel is highly elastic.
   c. the demand curve for steel workers is highly inelastic.
   d. there are no good substitutes for steel.

Use the information given in Exhibit 4 to answer questions 16 through 18. Assume the firm hires labor competitively and sells its product in a competitive price-taker market at a price of $2 per unit.

EXHIBIT 4

Units of Labor	Total Output
1	6
2	11
3	15
4	18
5	20
6	21

16. What is the marginal revenue product of the fifth unit of labor?
   a. $2
   b. $4
   c. $20
   d. $100

17. If the market wage rate is $5 per day, how many workers should the firm employ if it wants to maximize profits?
   a. three
   b. four
   c. five
   d. six

18. If the market wage rate rose to $7 per day, how many workers should the firm employ if it wants to maximize profits?
   a. three
   b. four
   c. five
   d. six

Harcourt Brace & Company

19. Jim Smith runs a company that sells encyclopedia sets for $200 each. When he employs 5 workers, they can sell 20 sets per week, while only 17 sets are sold when 4 workers are employed. What is the weekly marginal revenue product of the fifth worker?
    a. $3
    b. $200
    c. $600
    d. $4,000

20. Firms should hire additional units of a resource as long as the
    a. marginal product of the resource exceeds the price of the resource multiplied by the quantity of output produced.
    b. marginal product of the resource is less than the price of the resource.
    c. price of the output produced is positive.
    d. marginal revenue product of the resource exceeds the cost of employing an additional unit of the resource.

21. The marginal revenue product of a resource is best described as the
    a. selling price of the last unit of output produced.
    b. increment of total cost resulting from the use of an additional unit of the resource.
    c. marginal product of the resource divided by the unit price of the good produced.
    d. change in total revenue resulting from employing an additional unit of the resource.

22. Marginal revenue product (MRP) differs from the value of marginal product (VMP) because
    a. MRP equals MP times product price (P), while VMP equals MP times marginal revenue (MR).
    b. VMP equals MP times product price (P), while MRP equals MP times marginal revenue (MR).
    c. VMP equals MP times marginal cost (MC), while MRP equals MP times marginal revenue (MR).
    d. They do not differ; they are the same for every firm.

23. An increase in the demand for a resource
    a. will cause the price of that resource to fall.
    b. may be the result of a decrease in the demand for products utilizing this resource.
    c. will cause the price of the resource to fall by a smaller amount in the short run than in the long run.
    d. will increase the price of the resource and thereby increase the incentive of potential suppliers to provide the resource in the future.

Harcourt Brace & Company

24. Generally, the supply of a resource in the short run will be
    a. more elastic than in the long run.
    b. less elastic than in the long run.
    c. equally elastic as the supply of the resource in the long run.
    d. directly related to the elasticity of demand for the product that the resource helps produce.

25. A convenience store is considering renting a surveillance camera from a security company that would prevent $100 in shoplifting per year. The yearly rental rate for the camera is $150. To maximize profits, the firm should
    a. rent the camera because the firm wants to completely eliminate shoplifting.
    b. not rent the camera because the rental rate exceeds the value of shoplifting prevented.
    c. rent the camera if VMP exceeds MRP, but not rent the camera if VMP is less than MRP.
    d. Without knowing the rate of diminishing marginal returns, there is not enough information to answer the question.

DISCUSSION QUESTIONS

1. In recent years, the computer industry has grown quite rapidly as a result of technological advances. Suppose that the application of computers in the workplace continues at an accelerated rate.
   a. What would happen to the supply of computer technicians in the short run? in the long run?
   b. What would happen to the earnings of computer technicians in the short run? in the long run?
   c. What would happen in the long run to the supply and earnings of workers in industries that compete for the type of workers who become computer technicians?
   d. What would happen to the demand for inputs (for example, bookkeepers and clerks) for which computers are substitutes?

2. Is human labor really a "thing" that can be bought and sold like any other productive resource? What about the feelings of the human beings involved? While we can buy a person's time, we cannot buy his or her enthusiasm or loyalty so easily. What sort of advantages and disadvantages does the "human element" in purchasing labor inputs have?

3. a. Why is the amount demanded of a productive resource negatively related to the price of the resource? Why is the demand likely to be more elastic when buyers have more time to respond?
   b. If the price of unskilled labor rises, what will tend to happen to the demand for substitute resources? for complementary resources?

Harcourt Brace & Company

c.   Will the demand for unskilled labor be more or less elastic as a result of the demand change described in part b for substitute resources? for complementary resources?

4.   Some have argued that if wages really equal the marginal revenue product of the worker, the wage is "fair." Define marginal revenue product in your own words. Does the marginal revenue product of a worker reflect her or his contribution to output? What are the factors that raise marginal revenue products? Is it fair that those with the highest marginal revenue products also receive the highest wages? Why or why not?

Harcourt Brace & Company

CHAPTER *13*

Earnings, Productivity, and the Job Market

TRUE OR FALSE

T F

☐ ☐ 1. If all workers had identical levels of education, all workers would have equal earnings.

☐ ☐ 2. Immobility of labor can be a source of wage differentials.

☐ ☐ 3. Higher productivity generally leads to higher wages.

☐ ☐ 4. There is a strong negative relationship between earnings and education level.

☐ ☐ 5. Under a tournament pay system, the top performer receives a wage less than his or her marginal revenue product.

☐ ☐ 6. Employment discrimination can also be caused by discriminatory preferences on the part of a firm's customers or its employees.

☐ ☐ 7. Working conditions and other nonwage job characteristics are called nonpecuniary job characteristics.

☐ ☐ 8. Other things constant, the more dangerous a job, the lower the wage rate it will have. This is known as a compensating wage differential.

☐ ☐ 9. The average wage rate in the United States is high in comparison with that of other countries largely because of the large amount of physical and human capital with which the average American works.

☐ ☐ 10. If employers can hire equally productive minority employees at a lower wage than other workers (because other firms are discriminating against them), the profit motive gives them a strong incentive to do so.

☐ ☐ 11. When comparing wage differences across gender and racial groups, it is important to adjust for differences between the groups in education, experience, and other productivity-related factors.

☐ ☐ 12. When deciding whether to employ a worker, the employer will consider the total cost of the compensation (money wages plus fringe benefits) relative to the worker's marginal revenue product.

☐ ☐ 13. If a new government law mandated that employers provide free child care for their employees, we would expect workers to end up paying for this in the form of lower money wages from employers.

Harcourt Brace & Company

T   F

☐ ☐ 14. Automation is a major source of unemployment.

☐ ☐ 15. The rate of labor productivity growth in the United States is at its highest point in recent history due to the introduction of the computer.

PROBLEMS AND PROJECTS

1. For each of the following, decide whether the factor is likely to increase (+) or decrease (−) the *money* wages paid for the job relative to an identical job without that factor.

   _____ a. A job offers a very generous health-care plan that includes dental coverage.

   _____ b. A job requires the operation of very dangerous equipment.

   _____ c. A job is located in a very undesirable place to live.

   _____ d. A job comes with a company car for the employee to use.

   _____ e. A job is very insecure and is subject to frequent layoffs.

   _____ f. The employer matches all employee contributions to retirement funds for its workers.

2. Jane currently works for a company that pays her compensation all in the form of money wages (in other words, no fringe benefits). Bob works for another company in an identical job that also has fringe benefits like a health-care plan and free child care during working hours, but the job pays $5,000 less per year in money wages.

   a. Who earns the highest *money wages* per year?

   b. Who has the highest *total compensation* per year?

   c. If Bob had children and Jane did not, would this explain why Jane has chosen one job while Bob has chosen the other?

   d. If Jane were offered a job at Bob's company, would she take it? What would she need to consider?

3. Exhibit 1 is a hypothetical, demand-and-supply schedule for sophisticated pocket calculators in a price-taker industry.

   a. What will be the equilibrium quantity and price in this market? [Hint: You may use the graph lined area to plot the demand and supply to figure this out, or you can simply figure it by looking at the numbers.]

   b. Suppose that a new labor-saving technology is developed, resulting in an increase of 2,000 in quantity supplied at every price. What will happen to the equilibrium quantity and price?

   c. If the new technology reduces the quantity of labor used from 50 workers per thousand calculators produced to 40 workers per thousand calculators produced, what will happen to total employment in the industry?

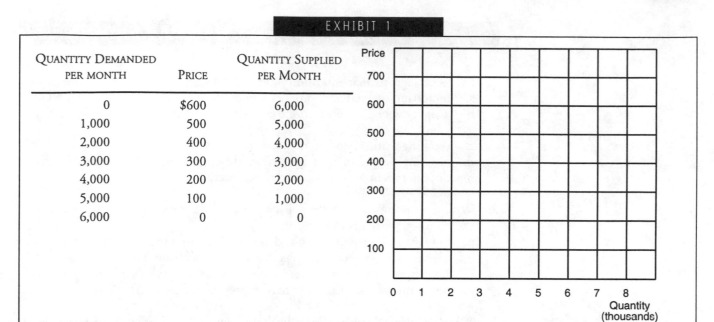

EXHIBIT 1

QUANTITY DEMANDED PER MONTH	PRICE	QUANTITY SUPPLIED PER MONTH
0	$600	6,000
1,000	500	5,000
2,000	400	4,000
3,000	300	3,000
4,000	200	2,000
5,000	100	1,000
6,000	0	0

d. Owing to the new technology, the computer industry substituted more machines for labor. Using your understanding of the answer to part c, refute or support the following statement: "If we continue to allow machines to replace workers, we will run out of jobs. Automation is a major cause of unemployment."

4. The text describes the following determinants of earnings differentials:
   a. differences in workers
      A1: worker productivity and specialized skills
      A2: worker preferences
      A3: race and gender discrimination
   b. differences in jobs
      B1: location of jobs
      B2: working conditions
      B3: opportunities for training and experience
   c. immobility of labor
      C1: temporary disequilibrium
      C2: institutional restrictions, such as licensing and unions

Indicate the main reason from the list above for each of the following wage differentials:
   ____ a. College graduates earn more than high school graduates.
   ____ b. Wages in Alaska are higher than in Florida in identical jobs.
   ____ c. Police officers in metropolitan areas with high violent crime rates earn higher wages than police officers elsewhere.
   ____ d. Graduate students teach classes at universities for much less money than they could earn at a regular job.

Harcourt Brace & Company

MULTIPLE CHOICE

1. Evidence suggests that education raises the earnings of the workforce mainly by
   a. increasing the marginal productivity of labor.
   b. keeping young people out of the labor force, thereby reducing the supply of labor.
   c. teaching workers how to demand more pay.
   d. teaching people to read and write, although education beyond this point does not seem to increase worker productivity.

2. Within an occupation, when a given job provides steadier work (fewer layoffs), the hourly wage tends to be
   a. lower than wage rates in jobs that are otherwise similar.
   b. higher than wage rates in jobs that are otherwise similar.
   c. no different from wage rates in jobs that are otherwise similar.
   d. determined by factors other than supply and demand.

3. Which of the following is most likely to decrease the market wage rate in a job category?
   a. The employer provides a generous pension plan.
   b. The work is widely viewed as safe and not stressful.
   c. The job is widely viewed as interesting and prestigious.
   d. All of the above.

4. The fact that some people will work hard to earn a lot of money while others will be content with much less income indicates that
   a. worker preferences are an important source of earning differentials.
   b. economics ranks one set of worker preferences as more desirable than another.
   c. some people can be paid less for doing hard work while others have to be paid a premium for doing a similar task.
   d. skill levels of laborers are a minor consideration in wage rate determination.

5. A compensation structure that generates much higher pay rates for the top performers, while those whose productivity is only a little lower receive substantial less compensation is called
   a. tournament pay.
   b. competing differentials.
   c. dueling executives.
   d. winner take all.

6. Assume that empirical evidence shows a difference in mean earnings between two groups, say, majority and minority workers. What conclusion may be drawn?
   a. The group with the lower earnings is being discriminated against.
   b. The group with the lower earnings is less productive.
   c. The group with the higher earnings has a larger quantity of human capital.
   d. Any of the above statements could, either partially or entirely, explain the difference in the mean earnings.

7. If a firm refuses to hire any minorities due to a personal prejudice, its profits
   a. will increase markedly.
   b. will decrease.
   c. will not be affected.
   d. will increase slightly.

8. Which of the following factors will probably lead to a decrease in the gap between male and female earnings in the future?
   a. As the labor force participation of women increases, their years of work experience will become more similar to men.
   b. In recent years, a higher proportion of women have been preparing for careers in higher paying professions.
   c. As women plan for more lengthy workforce participation, they will be more likely to invest in human capital and take other steps that will improve their chances for earnings advancements.
   d. All of the above.

9. From an employee's viewpoint, an increase in fringe benefits provided by the employer
   a. is never as valuable as a wage increase, costing the employer the same number of dollars.
   b. is always more valuable than a wage increase, costing the employer the same number of dollars.
   c. is also paid by the employer; therefore, it is always a good thing.
   d. involves a tradeoff with money wages since more of one can usually be gained by workers willing to accept less of the other.

10. Benefits mandated by the government are most likely paid for by
    a. the government through direct subsidies.
    b. the employer in the form of lower profits.
    c. the worker through reductions in other components of the wage package.
    d. material suppliers in the form of lower resource prices.

11. Economic theory suggests that the standard of living of American workers would rise if
    a. the minimum wage were doubled.
    b. automation was outlawed.
    c. the amount of physical capital increased.
    d. technological setbacks lowered output per worker hour.

Harcourt Brace & Company

12. Use statements I and II to answer this question. (I) Differences in worker productivity are one major reason why individual earnings differ. (II) Even if all workers were identical, differences in the desirability of jobs would still cause earnings differentials.
    a. Both I and II are true.
    b. I is true; II is false.
    c. I is false; II is true.
    d. Both I and II are false.

13. After correcting for differences in age, education, marital status, language, and regional characteristics, the earnings of women are not as great as those of men. This differential is due in part to
    a. discrimination against women in employment.
    b. work specialization within the family following traditional male-female patterns.
    c. both *a* and *b*.
    d. neither *a* nor *b*.

14. Which of the following *best* states the relationship between machinery and the earnings of labor?
    a. Machines tend to reduce the demand for labor, thereby reducing the earnings rate of labor.
    b. Production of machinery creates jobs, thereby increasing the demand for (and wages of) labor.
    c. High productivity per worker hour is a necessary ingredient for the attainment of high real earnings, and adoption of labor-saving machinery enhances the ability of labor to attain such high productivity.
    d. Output and real earnings can always be increased whenever a machine can be substituted for a function previously performed by labor.

15. If large numbers of young Americans thought the life of a cowhand was great (despite the hardships), we would expect
    a. an increase in the wages of cowhands.
    b. a decrease in the wages of cowhands since supply would be enlarged.
    c. no impact on wages, which are determined by supply and demand, not preferences.
    d. a decrease in the wages of cowhands since demand would be reduced.

16. If customers are racist but employers are not, then employment discrimination will be
    a. less profitable than nondiscrimination.
    b. more profitable than nondiscrimination.
    c. equally profitable as nondiscrimination.
    d. easier to eliminate than if employers were racist but customers were not.

Harcourt Brace & Company

17. Under a tournament pay scheme, the pay gap between a few "winners" (those who receive big promotions) and other employees exceeds the productivity differences between these two groups. The reason firms might use such a scheme is that they
    a. overestimate the productivity of those who receive big promotions and inadvertently pay them "too much."
    b. gain tax advantages by paying a few workers large salaries and using fringe benefits to compensate the rest of the employees.
    c. hope to raise the productivity of those who receive big promotions since marginal productivity adjusts to equal wages.
    d. hope to raise the productivity of all other workers, who will work harder trying to gain a big promotion.

18. Sue: "I much prefer eating at the El Grande Mexican restaurant to the others in town because all of their employees are Mexican and speak Spanish. It gives the place a real 'authentic' feel." Which of the following is true about the above statement?
    a. This is an example of customer-based discrimination for one group of employees over another.
    b. Despite customer preferences, we would expect the restaurants in town to hire equally from all racial and ethnic groups.
    c. If many customers felt the same way Sue does, there would be pressure for firms to satisfy this consumer preference in their hiring.
    d. Both *a* and *c* are correct.

DISCUSSION QUESTIONS

1. Suppose that a new invention halves the cost of making automobiles.
   a. What will happen to output in the auto industry?
   b. What will happen to auto-industry employment if demand for automobiles is elastic? inelastic?
   c. What will happen to output and employment elsewhere in the economy if the auto demand is elastic? inelastic?
   d. Is it more likely for the new invention to make auto-industry employment rise in the short run and fall in the long run or fall in the short run and rise in the long run? Explain.

2. Substantial differences, sometimes up to 150 percent, in wage rates for essentially the same kind of labor (for example, semiskilled labor) prevail between different industries even in the same locality.
   a. What are some of the causes of interindustry wage differentials? List an industry that illustrates each cause.
   b. Which kinds of industries are likely to be at the top of the wage scale? at the bottom?

Harcourt Brace & Company

3. If you owned a firm, how would you expect the wages and racial composition of your employees to compare with your competitors' employees if
   a. firms in general practice employment discrimination, but you do not.
   b. firms in general do not practice employment discrimination, but you do.
   c. Explain both answers.

4. A recent issue of importance has been that of illegal immigration from one country to another. Analyze the impact of such illegal immigration on (1) the immigrants, (2) the new employers of the immigrants, (3) workers who remained in the home country of the immigrants, and (4) workers in the country to which the immigrants came. Given this analysis, attempt to develop a solution for the issue of illegal immigration.

5. Sewer workers face extremely unpleasant working conditions. They work in sewage; have daily encounters with millions of cockroaches, thousands of rats, and other unpleasant vermin; and are forced to take very long hot showers at the end of every working day. In addition, the occupation is extremely hazardous. Sewer workers are not infrequently asphyxiated by toxic gases. (We will leave it to your imagination to determine the nature of those toxic gases.) In Los Angeles, the median salary (not the starting salary) for sewer workers is $25,000. The city of Los Angeles has no difficulty filling vacant sewer worker positions. How much would someone have to pay you to compensate you for the disamenities of being a sewer worker? By that estimate, how much would low-skilled workers in reasonably pleasant jobs earn? How much do you (reasonably) hope to earn after graduating from college? What is the wage differential between what you hope to earn and what low-skilled workers appear to be able to earn? Why do you suppose more low-skilled workers do not gain the skills necessary to improve their earnings potential?

6. According to the textbook, married women choose occupations that more easily accommodate their responsibilities at the home but that also pay relatively little. What are the characteristics of these occupations? Be specific. Can you think of any occupations dominated by men that also have these characteristics? Do you think the "greater flexibility" argument is the main determinant of which occupations are dominated by women? Why or why not?

Harcourt Brace & Company

THE SHRINKING PAY GAP

by June Ellenoff O'Neill

[From *The Wall Street Journal*, October 7, 1994, p. A12. Reprinted with permission from *The Wall Street Journal*. Copyright © Dow Jones & Co., Inc., 1994. All rights reserved.]

"Fifty-nine cents," the popular button said, a symbol of the stubborn fact that throughout the post-World War II period, women's wages hovered at around 60% of men's, despite an increasing proportion of women working outside the home. This gender gap did not decline through the 1960s and the 1970s despite the rise of the feminist movement, equal pay and employment legislation, and affirmative action.

But starting in the Reagan years, the gender gap in wages began to decline dramatically. By some measures the ratio of women's earnings to men's rose to nearly 80%; and even this number, I believe, overstates the gender gap between men and women with similar skills and training. Why did this dramatic narrowing in relative wages happen?

The answer has less to do with politics or protests than with the realities of the labor market. Although basic skills are acquired in school, it is in the labor market where specialized skills are developed that bring higher wages. During the three decades following World War II women entered the labor market in record numbers. But many of the new entrants had been out of the labor force for considerable periods of time, raising their children. These women diluted the skill level of the rapidly expanding group of employed women. This was the main reason why the gender gap in pay did not narrow during the postwar years.

More Nearly Equal. Today's working women, particularly those younger than 40, are much more nearly equal to men in work experience than were their mothers. Through delayed marriage, low fertility, and an increasing tendency for mothers of young children to work, women have acquired many more years of continuous work experience than was true in the past. (Close to 60% of married women with children under age six are now in the labor force; in 1960, the proportion was only 19%.)

And the work experience gained by these younger women is likely to have an even greater impact on their future earnings because their work experience has been more correctly anticipated. Many investment choices affecting careers are made at younger ages: years of schooling, subjects in school, other professional training. In the past, women were much less likely than men to invest in lengthy training because they assumed they would not be working enough years to justify it.

In fact, the National Longitudinal Surveys found that even in the late 1960s less than 30% of young women anticipated that they would be working at age 35, yet when this group actuary reached 35, more than 70% of them were in the labor force. Their underestimation of future work activity surely influenced their early career preparations (or lack thereof). More recent survey data show a dramatic change in expectations. The vast majority of young women now report an intention to work at age 35.

Those changing work expectations are reflected in rising female enrollments in higher education. In 1960, women received 35% of all bachelor's degrees in the U.S.; by the 1980s, they received somewhat

more than half of them. In 1968, women received 8% of the medical degrees, 3% of the MBAs and 4% of the law degrees granted that year. In 1986, they received 31% of the medical degrees and MBAs and 39% of the law degrees. This recent trend in schooling is likely to reinforce the rise in work experience and contribute to continuing increases in the relative earnings of women workers.

By 1980 the stage was set for the gender pay gap to narrow. It had already begun to narrow among younger women and men in the 1970s, and as the baby boomers became the dominant age group their experience and earnings began to influence the overall earnings statistics.

In a systematic analysis of the factors accounting for the narrowing of the gender gap, Solomon Polachek (professor of economics at SUNY Binghamton) and I found that the increase in women's years of work experience relative to men's could account for about 25% to 30% of the approximate 1% per year narrowing of the wage gap since the late 1970s. In addition, on-the-job training appears to have increased more for women than for men, so that women's earnings now rose more rapidly with experience than was once the case; this accounts for an added 35% to 40% of the convergence. That women's college and graduate attainment increased faster than men's also contributed significantly to the shrinking of the gap.

The gains women have made since 1980 are particularly striking considering that the past 10 to 15 years have been years of little growth in the overall wage level and a widening pay difference between skilled and unskilled workers. Low-skill male occupations, which are largely blue-collar, have experienced significant wage declines. Since relatively few women have entered these occupations, they avoided this particular downward drag on wages. The much greater concentration of men in blue-collar occupations accounted for about 20% of the overall wage convergence.

Despite the advances of the past decade, women still earn less than men. The hourly earnings of women were 74% of the earnings of men in 1992 when ages 25 to 64 are considered, up from 62% in 1979. At ages 25 to 34, where women's skills have increased the most, the ratio is 87%.

Economist Barbara Bergmann and others attribute the pay gap to "widespread, severe, ongoing discrimination by employers and fellow workers." But discrimination cannot be directly measured. Instead, researchers estimate the extent to which differences in productivity appear to explain the gap and then attribute the rest to discrimination. Such a conclusion is premature, however, when productivity differences are not accurately measured, which is usually the case.

For example, data are seldom available on lifetime patterns of work experience, and even less material is available on factors bearing on work expectations and the intensity and nature of work investments. As these are still the key sources of skill differences between men and women, there is considerable room for interpretation and disagreement.

When earnings comparisons are restricted to men and women more similar in their experience and life situations, the measured earnings differentials are typically quite small. For example, among people 27 to 33 who have never had a child, the earnings of women in the National Longitudinal Survey of Youth are close to 98% of men's. Among college graduates in the same survey, a differential of 11% narrowed to 6% after adjusting for gender differences in work experience, field of study and math test scores. In special Census surveys of people with science or engineering backgrounds, women's earnings are much closer to men's than in the general population.

In the past, women who chose careers were likely to find their paths filled with obstacles erected to preserve women's role in the home. But even then, these discriminatory barriers were probably not the major cause of pay differences between men and women. Rather, women's decisions about work were rooted in real economic forces affecting the family, particularly gender differences in the priority placed on market work vs. child care responsibilities.

The care of children is the household activity for which market alternatives may be least easily substituted, although increasingly child care has been shifted to the market through earlier school starting ages and greater use of group day-care arrangements. The time demands have been reduced, too, through declining fertility. The decline in fer-

tility is likely to have been in part a response to rising wage rates and the rising labor force participation of women. But modern contraceptives also played a role.

Comparative Advantage. What is more, over the years women's comparative advantage in the labor market has increased as the service sector has expanded, providing jobs that required mental acuity and social skills rather than physical strength. As the costs of denying employment to women have mounted, prejudices have diminished.

It is true that women and men still do not have the same earnings. But I believe that the differential is largely due to continuing gender differences in the priority placed on market work vs. family responsibilities. Until family roles are more equal, women are not likely to have the same pattern of market work and earnings as men. Technology has reduced the burden of housework, but child care remains a responsibility that is harder to shift to the market.

DISCUSSION

1. Which number is more relevant, the ratio of women's earnings to men's earnings for all workers or the ratio of women's earnings to men's earnings for individuals of similar backgrounds and jobs? Explain your answer. (Be careful, this question may be harder than you think it is.)

2. O'Neill attributes the decrease in the pay gap to increases in the work experience of women and other market factors. Do you agree? Do protests and demands for fair treatment have no impact on discrimination? Explain.

3. What is your own personal experience? Have you observed that women get paid less than men for similar work or that women are forced into lower-paying jobs by societal pressures or expectations? Do you agree with O'Neill that any such differences are decreasing? Why or why not?

Harcourt Brace & Company

CHAPTER 14

Investment, the Capital Market, and the Wealth of Nations

TRUE OR FALSE

T F

☐ ☐ 1. If an economy is to achieve a higher level of investment, an increase in personal saving will be required.

☐ ☐ 2. To expand the availability of capital requires reducing current consumption.

☐ ☐ 3. People generally have a positive rate of time preference—they value goods obtained sooner more highly than goods obtained later.

☐ ☐ 4. To a lender, the interest rate is the reward earned from delaying consumption, while to a borrower, it is the price paid for earlier availability.

☐ ☐ 5. The net present value of a payment to be received one year from now will fall if the interest rate falls.

☐ ☐ 6. An increase in the positive rate of time preference would raise the real interest rate in the economy.

☐ ☐ 7. If there were an increase in the demand for loans, the interest rate would increase, encouraging people to expand their savings so as to make more money available for loans.

☐ ☐ 8. The inflation premium represents the true real cost of borrowing money.

☐ ☐ 9. Higher risk usually lowers the interest rate agreed to by business decision makers.

☐ ☐ 10. The interest rate charged by a lender has three components: the inflationary premium, the risk premium, and the pure money interest rate component.

☐ ☐ 11. Changes in a corporation's stock price happen too slowly to give corporate officers much feedback on how market investors evaluate their investment decisions.

☐ ☐ 12. The value of an asset is equal to the present value of the expected net revenue that can be earned by the asset.

PROBLEMS AND PROJECTS

1. For each of the following pairs of countries, decide which would tend to have the higher rate of interest, assuming all else is equal except for the factor listed in the problem.

    ___ a. Country A has a higher rate of inflation than Country B.

    ___ b. Citizens in Country C have a higher positive rate of time preference than in Country D.

    ___ c. Citizens in Country E tend to save a higher proportion of their income than citizens in Country F.

    ___ d. In Country G, a much higher proportion of borrowers default on their loans than in Country H.

2. The owner of a small forest in Florida is raising trees as a cash crop. A forester friend mentions that a certain treatment applied to the trees, costing $500 now, will yield an extra 10,000 board feet of timber when the forest is harvested in 30 years. Harvesting and other costs will not change significantly.

    a. In the first case, assume that the owner expects the price per board foot to be $2 when the crop is harvested. Is this a worthwhile investment for the grower if the interest rate is 5 percent? 10 percent? 15 percent?

    b. Now, assume the interest rate is 15 percent, but the uncertainty is over the future price of the timber. At a 15 percent interest rate, is this a worthwhile investment for the grower if the expected price is $1 per board foot? $2 per board foot? $4 per board foot?

3. It was noted in the text that the price of an asset that earns a given payment each year forever is

    Asset price = annual earnings ÷ interest rate.

    The following formula can also be used to assess the present value of any fixed payments that will be earned each year forever.

    Present value = fixed annual payment ÷ interest rate

    Even when the payments do not last forever, this formula can be used to *approximate* present value whenever the payments last for a "fairly long" period of time. Try the following examples to see how well this simple formula works as an approximation.

    a. Recently, Life Cereal held a "Life Cereal Lifetime Allowance Sweepstakes." Each grand-prize winner was promised $2,000 per year for life. With a combined state and federal income tax rate of 50 percent, and an interest rate of 8 percent, what would be the approximate present value of the grand prize after taxes?

    b. A few years ago, households across the country received a letter from Ed McMahon (formerly of *The Tonight Show*) urging them to enter the American

Harcourt Brace & Company

Family Publishers sweepstakes, which offered America's "first TEN MILLION DOLLAR prize!" The winner of the prize was promised $333,333 per year for thirty years. At 7 percent interest, what is the approximate present value of this stream of receipts (you may ignore taxes in this problem)?

c. Suppose you or your parents borrow $150,000 to buy a new home. If the interest rate is 10 percent, what is the approximate size of the mortgage payments each year? (Hint: It will be necessary to rearrange the terms in the formula to find this answer.)

4. Use the appropriate discounting method to find the present value of each of the following cases. For all, assume an interest rate of 10 percent. (Hint: Use the formula for an asset price given above to approximate the cases when the payments last for a long time.)

a. a college education, which generally increases a person's average annual earnings by $15,000 for the rest of their life

b. a license to be the monopoly provider of cable service in a local area that is expected to generate $5 million in profit per year

c. the current value of a thirty-year U.S. Treasury savings bond given to you five years ago by your grandmother—it will mature in another twenty-five years at a face value of $500

d. a machine that will last three years and generate net revenue of $5,000 at the end of each year

e. a rental property that generates net rental income of $300 per month (that is, $3,600 per year)

MULTIPLE CHOICE

1. The development and construction of machines that enhance our ability to produce goods and services in the future requires
   a. devoting more resources toward investment.
   b. devoting fewer resources toward current consumption.
   c. a negative rate of time preference.
   d. both *a* and *b*.

2. A positive rate of time preference implies that a person would value
   a. receiving $100 today more than receiving $100 one year from now.
   b. receiving $100 today less than receiving $100 one year from now.
   c. receiving $100 today equally to receiving $100 one year from now.
   d. any amount, no matter how small, today more than receiving $100 one year from now.

3. The net present value of $100, delivered one year from now, would
   a. fall if the rate of interest increased.
   b. fall if the rate of interest decreased.
   c. rise if the rate of interest increased.
   d. not change if the interest rate changed.

Harcourt Brace & Company

4. If the interest rate was 6 percent, the net present value of $100 to be received one year from now would be
   a. $94.34.
   b. $98.04.
   c. $100.00.
   d. $106.00.

5. If the interest rate was 6 percent, the net present value of $100 to be received two years from now would be
   a. $89.00.
   b. $94.34.
   c. $100.00.
   d. $112.00.

6. If the interest rate was 6 percent, the combined net present value of *two* payments of $100, one to be received one year from now and the other two years from now, would be
   a. $89.00.
   b. $94.34.
   c. $183.34.
   d. $200.00.

7. If the interest rate was 6 percent, the net present value of a contract or asset that generated a repeating payment of $100 each year forever would be
   a. $100.00.
   b. $666.67.
   c. $1,000.00.
   d. $1,666.67.

8. The net present value of $100 will
   a. increase if the interest rate rises.
   b. increase with the number of years until it is received.
   c. be greater than the net present value of $95 to be received one year from now.
   d. be greater than the value of having $95 now if the interest rate is 10 percent.

9. Use statements I and II to answer this question. (I) Discounting procedures apply to decisions to invest in physical capital but are not relevant to human capital investment decisions. (II) Nonmonetary considerations are usually more important in human capital investment decisions than in nonhuman capital investment decisions.
   a. I is true; II is false.
   b. I is false; II is true.
   c. Both I and II are true.
   d. Both I and II are false.

10. Some governments enact usury laws, which hold the interest rate below its equilibrium level. Economic analysis indicates that under such laws,
    a. saving would increase.
    b. borrowers would demand less from the loanable funds market.
    c. anyone who wanted to borrow would be happy with the lower interest rate.
    d. there would be a shortage of loanable funds, necessitating rationing by some means other than the price (interest rate).

11. A company that mines coal on federally owned land is about to be told by the federal government that, beginning in five years, it must abandon the mine it expected to operate for another twenty years. This will mean a reduction in accounting profits beginning in five years. If the announcement of this ruling was made tomorrow, the price of the firm's stock would
    a. fall in about five years, just before the reduction in accounting profits was to begin.
    b. fall gradually, as the reduction in the firm's accounting profit drew near.
    c. fall immediately by the full amount of the discounted value of the decrease in future profit.
    d. fall immediately since some investors would panic irrationally, whereas smart investors would put the same value on the stock as before, up to the time of the decline in accounting profit.

12. Use statements I and II when answering this question. (I) Countries with high rates of investment also tend to have high rates of growth. (II) A country with a high rate of investment but a poorly functioning capital market will tend to have a lower rate of growth than a country with a comparable rate of investment but a capital market that functions well.
    a. I is true; II is false.
    b. I is false; II is true.
    c. Both I and II are true.
    d. Both I and II are false.

13. Which of these are the major sources of economic profit?
    a. uncertainty, entrepreneurial alertness, and barriers to entry
    b. competition, perfect information, and elasticity of market demand
    c. size of firm, economies of scale, and freedom from unionism
    d. externalities, inflation, and size of firm

14. Which of the following would reduce the net present value of your college education?
    a. higher interest rates
    b. earlier retirement age
    c. higher wages for high school graduates
    d. all of the above

15. Economists refer to the desire of consumers for goods now rather than in the future as
    a. a positive rate of time preference.
    b. the rational expectations hypothesis.
    c. roundabout methods of production.
    d. the inflationary premium.

16. The real rate of interest is the
    a. money rate of interest plus the inflationary premium.
    b. money rate of interest minus the inflationary premium.
    c. yield one can expect to receive on loanable funds without taking significant risk.
    d. risk component associated with the ownership of real assets.

17. If the money rate of interest is 10 percent and the real rate of interest is 7 percent, the inflationary premium is
    a. 3 percent.
    b. 7 percent.
    c. 10 percent.
    d. 17 percent.

18. The yield that one can expect to receive on loanable funds without taking significant risk is called the
    a. risk premium.
    b. pure interest yield.
    c. inflationary premium.
    d. nominal interest yield.

19. If the interest rate was 5 percent and an investment project was expected to yield net revenue of $3,000 per year (to be received at year end) for each of the next three years, profit-maximizing decision makers would undertake the investment only as long as it cost less than
    a. $7,461.
    b. $8,170.
    c. $8,652.
    d. $9,000.

20. If an investment project costing $2,700 was expected to yield $1,000 (to be received at year end) for each of the next three years, a profit-maximizing entrepreneur would
    a. definitely undertake the project.
    b. never undertake the project.
    c. undertake the project if the interest rate exceeded 12 percent.
    d. undertake the project if the interest rate was 5 percent or less.

Harcourt Brace & Company

21. You are considering buying a business that currently earns $15,000 per year in after-tax profit. If these conditions are expected to continue into the future, and the interest rate is currently 10 percent, the current market value of this business is
   a. $1,500.
   b. $15,000.
   c. $150,000.
   d. $1,500,000.

DISCUSSION QUESTIONS

1. U.S. government bonds are considered risk-free in the sense that there is a negligible chance of default.
   a. What uncertainty is still involved in purchasing government bonds?
   b. How can you earn a profit from the purchase and resale of government bonds? How can you suffer a loss?

2.a. What are the components of the money interest rate? the real interest rate?
   b. Are risk premiums efficient since the result is that different borrowers pay different interest rates? Explain.
   c. From the self-interested viewpoint of a future generation responsible for interest payments, is it beneficial to use a positive, market-clearing interest rate for rationing loanable funds among competing investment opportunities? Why or why not?

3. If you were going to lend someone money, would the following events cause you to increase, decrease, or leave unchanged the nominal interest rate you were thinking of asking for?
   a. You hear a news report that causes you to increase the inflation rate you expect to exist over the life of the loan.
   b. You discover documents that cause you to think there is a reasonable chance that the loan might not be completely repaid. (Assume that you still want to loan the money.)
   c. You read in the newspaper that most major banks have lowered the interest rate they charge their prime customers.

4. "When a firm's total costs are less than its sales, the firm has increased the value of the resources it has used. Such firms will be rewarded with profits. In contrast, losses indicate that the resources used to produce a good were more valuable than the good that was produced. Profits are evidence of the wise utilization of resources, whereas losses are indicative of waste and inefficiency." Are these statements always true, never true, or sometimes true? Explain your answer.

5. A smoothly functioning capital market is necessary in order to channel available funds to their most profitable uses. However, with almost an infinite number of possible investment projects, it is the job of the entrepreneur to find the ones that are most beneficial to the economy. Discuss the role of the entrepreneur in a market economy and the role of uncertainty and profit in the job they perform.

Harcourt Brace & Company

PERSPECTIVES IN ECONOMICS

STATE'S LOTTERY "MILLIONAIRES" WILL BE SOMEWHAT LESS THAN

by Lee Dembart

[From the *Los Angeles Times*, August 16, 1985. Reprinted with permission.]

When the California lottery gets into full swing this fall, it will offer jackpots of $1 million, $2 million and $3 million. The lucky winners, therefore, will be "millionaires," according to common parlance.

Not so fast. There's a rub. "All million-dollar prizes will be awarded as annuities over a 20-year period," said an article in *The Times*. In other words, if you win, say, a million dollars, the Lottery Commission won't hand you a check for a million. It will pay you $50,000 now and promise to pay another $50,000 a year for 19 more years, for a total of $1 million.

Now, $50,000 a year for 20 years is not worth a million dollars by a long shot. In fact, according to Bill Seaton, spokesman for the Lottery Commission, if you win "a million dollars" in the lottery, what they actually will give you is not a million dollars but an annuity worth $400,000 today.

A $400,000 annuity winds up being worth $1 million over 20 years because of the miracle of compound interest. Think about it. Money that is put aside today earns interest and is worth more in the future. The longer the future is, the more it grows.

So if the state promises to pay you $50,000 nineteen years from now—the time of the last payment—how much does it have to put aside in order to have the $50,000 then? It depends, obviously, on the interest rate. The higher the interest rate, the less that has to be set aside initially. If it earns 8%, $11,585.60 will yield $50,000 in 19 years. At a 10% rate, $8,175.40 will grow to $50,000 in 19 years. And at 12%, it would take just $5,805.34 today to produce $50,000 in 2004.

This a well-known bit of straight-forward mathematics, which is called the present-value or present-worth calculation. It involves running the formula for compound interest backward, and it answers the question, "What is the present value of a future sum of money?" Everybody understands that if a person invested $1,000 today at 10% interest it would earn $100 in a year and then be worth $1,100. The question can be asked the other way: If you wind up with $1,100 in a year at 10% interest, how much did you start with? The answer is $1,000, and that is called the present value of $1,100 in a year at 10% interest.

Occasionally, when athletes sign multiyear, multimillion-dollar contracts, someone points out an owner who promises to pay $2 million 30 years from now can do it with much less than $2 million today.

How does the lottery figure the present value of $1 million doled out in 20-year installments of $50,000 a year? The same calculation is done for year 19—the last year—can also be done for years 18, 17, 16 and so on to determine the amount of money that must be set aside today to pay the $50,000 in each of the subsequent years. Then those present values can be added to yield the total present value of the state's "million dollar lottery." The following is a table showing the present values of 20 once-a-year payments of $50,000 each, assuming earnings of 12.8%:

Year	Payment	Present value
0	$50,000	$50,000.00
1	50,000	44,326.24
2	50,000	39,296.31
3	50,000	34,837.16
4	50,000	30,884.00
5	50,000	27,379.44
6	50,000	24,272.55
7	50,000	21,518.22
8	50,000	19,076.43
9	50,000	16,911.73
10	50,000	14,992.67
11	50,000	13,291.38
12	50,000	11,783.13
13	50,000	10,446.04
14	50,000	9,260.67
15	50,000	8,209.82
16	50,000	7,278.21
17	50,000	6,452.31
18	50,000	5,720.13
19	50,000	5,071.04

The total present value of $1 million handed out in $50,000 chunks over 20 years is $401,007.48.

So it is at least misleading to call $50,000 a year for 20 years "a million dollars." (This analysis ignores income tax, inflation, life expectancy and all other factors related to the question of which is a better deal, $400,000 today or $50,000 a year for 20 years.)

The Lottery Commission says further that, based on the same calculation, a winner of a $2-million jackpot will receive an $800,000 annuity. In addition, the commission says, the odds against winning a $2-million pot are 25 million to 1.

So a person who buys a $1 ticket will have a 25 million-to-1 shot at winning a "$2-million prize." That sounds like bad odds to begin with. The odds are made worse by the fact that the $2-million prize is really only $800,000.

DISCUSSION

1. After reading the article, a friend says, "It seems to me that a million dollars is a million dollars. As long as you get the money eventually, it's still worth the same amount!" How would you convince your friend that it matters quite a bit when you get the money? Be specific.

Harcourt Brace & Company

2. The article ignores the taxes that will be due on the prize winnings. Assuming a 50 percent tax rate (combined federal and state on prize winnings), what is the true after-tax present value of winning this advertised $2-million jackpot?

3. The present values in the article were calculated assuming earnings of 12.8 percent, but this might seem a bit high for today. Calculate the present value of $50,000 a year for twenty years if the interest rate (earnings) were only 6 percent a year. Does the total go up or down? Why?

4. How ethical is it of the state of California to advertise a $2-million prize when it knows the actual value is less than half of that? What could be done to change the lottery (or at least its advertising) to make the truth obvious? Many people have claimed that a private firm could not get away with this kind of deception in its advertising. Do you agree?

Harcourt Brace & Company

CHAPTER 15

Income Inequality and Poverty

TRUE OR FALSE

T F

☐ ☐ 1. Differences in the number of persons working per family are an important source of income inequality among families in the United States.

☐ ☐ 2. During the 1990s, income inequality in the United States has increased.

☐ ☐ 3. Most millionaires in the United States inherited their wealth.

☐ ☐ 4. Income mobility refers to the movement of individuals and families up and down the income distribution rankings.

☐ ☐ 5. Income and wealth are not a "fixed-size economic pie" to be divided among individuals but rather are created by individuals.

☐ ☐ 6. Families headed by workers in their prime working years (ages thirty-five to sixty-four) tend to have more income than families headed by either younger or older persons.

☐ ☐ 7. Households headed by either a single parent or an elderly person are more likely to be in poverty.

☐ ☐ 8. Unlike other transfer programs, the eligibility for means-tested income transfer programs does not depend upon income status.

☐ ☐ 9. The increasing gap between the wages earned by college graduates and those with less education has contributed to the rise in income inequality in the United States.

☐ ☐ 10. When deciding whether a family is officially counted in poverty, the value of all transfer and welfare benefits are counted in the family's income.

☐ ☐ 11. The Samaritan's dilemma refers to the negative effect that transfer programs have on the incentive to avoid choices leading to poverty.

☐ ☐ 12. When transfer programs have high take-back rates (implicit marginal tax rates), they reduce the incentive for poor families to work and earn.

T F

☐ ☐ 13. The experience from the last several decades shows that increased spending on transfer programs produces substantial reductions in poverty and income inequality.

☐ ☐ 14. Because large transfer programs lead to higher tax rates for taxpayers and also higher implicit tax rates for recipients, they tend to lower an economy's productivity and output.

PROBLEMS AND PROJECTS

1. When transfer programs have high implicit marginal tax rates (or "take-back rates"), it lowers the incentive for those receiving the transfer to work. Exhibit 1 shows data from a study prepared for the U.S. House of Representatives on how a family's disposable (spendable) income changed with earned income from work in 1983. This data is for a single mother with two children living in Pennsylvania.

EXHIBIT 1

	MINUS	PLUS	EQUALS
GROSS EARNINGS FROM WORK	INCOME AND EMPLOYMENT TAXES DUE	TRANSFER BENEFITS RECEIVED	DISPOSABLE INCOME
$ 0	$ 0	$7,568	_____
6,000	611	2,059	_____
10,000	1,469	698	_____

a. Disposable income is equal to earned income from work minus any taxes that must be paid on this income plus any transfer (welfare) benefits received. For the three levels of earned income shown, compute this family's disposable income.

b. Suppose this mother is currently not working (earned income is zero), but she has been offered a part-time job earning $6,000 per year. If she accepts the job, how many dollars worth of transfer benefits will she lose? Considering both the reduction in benefits and the taxes she will owe on this earned income, what will happen to her disposable income if she accepts the job?

c. Alternatively, suppose this nonworking mother has been offered a full-time job earning $10,000 per year. Taking the job will mean having to pay for transportation to and from work that totals $200 per year and for child care that will total $1,800 per year. After subtracting the expenses for transporta-

Harcourt Brace & Company

tion and child care, will the family have more or less spendable income if she accepts the job?

Between 1983 and 1994, welfare programs were changed to reduce the high implicit marginal tax rates faced by welfare recipients. Exhibit 2 compares the disposable income from 1983 (from Exhibit 1) to the disposable income at these same earned income levels in 1994.

| | EXHIBIT 2 | |
| | 1983 | 1994 |
GROSS EARNINGS FROM WORK	DISPOSABLE INCOME	DISPOSABLE INCOME
$ 0	$7,568	$7,548
6,000	7,448	9,657
10,000	9,229	10,937

d. In 1983, how much extra disposable income would the family have if the mother earned $6,000 per year instead of not working? How had this changed by 1994?

e. In 1983, how much extra disposable income would the family have if the mother earned $10,000 per year instead of not working? How had this changed by 1994?

f. How do you think the changes between 1983 and 1994 would have affected the incentive of this mother to take a job?

2. For each of the following pairs of countries, decide which country would tend to have the *higher* degree of income inequality among families as measured by traditional statistics.

_____ a. In country A, all husbands work and all wives stay at home. In country B, all husbands work and half of the wives work as well.

_____ b. In country C, half the population is college educated and half has only a high school education. In country D, all persons have only a high school education.

_____ c. In country E, all families have two parents. In country F, there is a substantial fraction of single-parent families.

_____ d. In country G, everyone is the same age. In country H, people differ in their ages.

_____ e. In country I, the poor stay poor and the rich stay rich, while in country J, there is substantial income mobility from year to year.

3. Income mobility refers to the degree to which individuals move up and down within the income distribution through time. Exhibit 3 on page 178 shows data regarding income mobility in the United States between 1968 and 1991.

EXHIBIT 3

INCOME MOBILITY—INCOME RANKING, 1968 AND 1991

INCOME STATUS OF HOUSEHOLD IN 1968	INCOME STATUS OF HOUSEHOLD IN 1991				
	TOP-PAID QUINTILE	NEXT-HIGHEST-PAID QUINTILE	MIDDLE QUINTILE	NEXT-LOWEST-PAID QUINTILE	LOWEST-PAID QUINTILE
Top-Paid Quintile	42.0	24.5	16.1	10.8	6.7
Next-Highest-Paid Quintile	27.6	26.2	20.4	16.7	9.2
Middle Quintile	18.2	26.2	20.2	21.8	13.6
Next-Lowest-Paid Quintile	9.6	14.3	26.4	26.2	23.6
Lowest-Paid Quintile	2.7	8.7	17.3	24.5	46.0

a. The data show that for the richest 20 percent of households in 1968 (the top paid quintile), only 42 percent remained among the richest 20 percent of households by 1991. Reading across the first row shows that 24.5 percent of these richest households in 1968 had fallen to the second highest quintile by 1991. What percent of these richest households in 1968 had fallen into the poorest 20 percent of households by 1991? On average, was it more likely that a household in the highest quintile in 1968 remained there, or that they moved down the income distribution?

b. Consider the poorest 20 percent of households in 1968 (the lowest quintile). What percent of these households remained in the poorest 20 percent by 1991? What percent had risen to the richest group by 1991? On average, was it more likely that a household in the lowest quintile in 1968 remained there, or that they moved up the income distribution?

c. For the middle quintile in 1968, what percent remained there by 1991? What total percent had risen up in the income distribution by 1991? What total percent had fallen down in the income distribution by 1991?

d. An alternative way to look at these data is to see where households in a given quintile in 1991 came from with respect to their position in 1968 (by reading down the columns, instead of across the rows). What percent of the top quintile of households in 1991 came from the lowest *two* quintiles in 1968 combined? What percent of the lowest quintile in 1991 came from the top *two* quintiles in 1968 combined?

e. Let's consider the top two quintiles the "top half" of the income distribution and the bottom two quintiles the "bottom half" of the income distribution. What percent of those in the bottom half of the income distribution in 1991 came from the top half of the income distribution in 1968? What percent of those in the top half of the income distribution in 1991 came from the bottom half of the income distribution in 1968?

MULTIPLE CHOICE

1. Over the past several decades, family incomes in the United States have
   a. become less equal.
   b. become more equal.
   c. maintained the same level of inequality.
   d. declined substantially for all families.

2. Which of the following is *false* about data on the inequality of annual family (or household) incomes?
   a. The degree of inequality is reduced when transfers and taxes are considered.
   b. The inequality in annual income data understates the true degree of inequality in lifetime income.
   c. Differences in age and family characteristics contribute to the degree of inequality.
   d. The inequality in consumption spending across households is smaller than the inequality in annual income.

3. The official definition of poverty in the United States does not account for
   a. Social Security income.
   b. cash income transfers.
   c. income earned by workers other than the head of a household.
   d. in-kind transfers.

4. Which of the following has contributed to the rising income inequality in the U.S.?
   a. The proportion of single-parent families has increased.
   b. The proportion of dual-earner families has increased.
   c. Earnings differentials between skilled and less-skilled workers have increased.
   d. All of the above.

5. Use the following two statements to answer this question. (I) In a market system, resource prices both provide incentives for the efficient allocation of resources *and* determine income distribution. (II) Income and wealth are neither created nor destroyed, they are just fixed-sized pies to be allocated among individuals.
   a. Both I and II are true.
   b. Both I and II are false.
   c. I is true; II is false.
   d. I is false; II is true.

Harcourt Brace & Company

6. (I) High implicit marginal tax rates reduce the incentive of the poor to earn. (II) The Samaritan's dilemma is that transfer programs lower the cost of activities that lead to poverty.
   a. Both I and II are true.
   b. Both I and II are false.
   c. I is true; II is false.
   d. II is true; I is false.

7. Even if lifetime incomes were equal, there still might be substantial inequality in annual income data because
   a. wage rates might differ substantially.
   b. some might have inherited their wealth.
   c. some might have retired, while others are prime-age earners.
   d. educational levels might differ substantially.

8. When deciding whether to classify a family as in poverty, official figures
   a. count all transfer and welfare benefits received by the family as income.
   b. do not count in-kind benefits in the calculation of the family's income.
   c. do not count cash benefits in the calculation of the family's income.
   d. do not count any transfer or welfare benefits as income.

9. (I) In 1997, a family of four making $16,000 would be considered living in poverty. (II) The poverty threshold level of income is adjusted for family size and for inflation (price level changes) through time.
   a. Both I and II are true.
   b. Both I and II are false.
   c. I is true; II is false.
   d. II is true; I is false.

10. Imagine two countries, Lebos and Egap, that have identical average annual incomes. In Lebos, the poorest families one year almost always end up as the richest families the next year and become middle-income families the year after that. In Egap, however, poor remain poor and rich remain rich. Which of the following is true about the two countries?
    a. The measured distribution of annual income in any given year is more equal in Lebos than in Egap.
    b. The measured distribution of annual income in any given year is more equal in Egap than in Lebos.
    c. The measured distribution of annual income in any given year will be the same in Lebos and Egap.
    d. The distribution of lifetime income is more equal in Egap than in Lebos.

11. In a market economy,
    a. there is not a fixed economic pie to be divided among individuals, but rather income is created by the individuals who earn it.
    b. differences in incomes provide individuals with an incentive to supply resources that are highly valued by others.
    c. a person's income is determined by the quantity and value of the resources that they supply to the market.
    d. all of the above are true.

12. Compared to low-income families, high-income families tend to
    a. have smaller family sizes (fewer persons per family).
    b. have more workers per family.
    c. be headed by a person who has not completed high school
    d. supply fewer weeks of work per year.

13. Since 1970, income inequality in the United States has
    a. decreased.
    b. increased.
    c. remained the same.
    d. increased throughout the 1970s and 1980s but has fallen in the 1990s.

14. Which of the following is true?
    a. The distribution of income after taxes and transfers is considered more equal than when they are excluded.
    b. The distribution of lifetime income tends to be more unequal than the distribution of annual income.
    c. The distribution of income has become more equal in recent years.
    d. Developed, industrialized countries generally tend to have higher income inequality than less developed countries.

15. Data on income inequality in the United States indicate that
    a. rich families stay rich and poor families stay poor through time.
    b. there is substantial movement among income groupings in the United States through time.
    c. most poor families never significantly rise above the poverty level, but rich families tend to become less wealthy over time.
    d. most rich families remain rich, but most poor families move up in the income distribution through time.

16. Which of the following is accurate regarding income statistics?
    a. Current annual income is also an accurate indicator of relative economic status over a longer period, such as a decade or lifetime.
    b. Inequalities of income observed at one point in time with annual income data overstate the degree of true income inequality in lifetime income.
    c. Recent studies indicate that the relative income position of a family generally determines the relative income position of their children and grandchildren.
    d. High-income earners generally maintain their status year after year, while those with low current incomes tend to stay poor year after year.

Harcourt Brace & Company

17. (I) Over the past several decades, the official poverty rate of *nonelderly* families has risen. (II) Over the past several decades, the official poverty rate of *elderly* families has declined.
    a. I is true; II is false.
    b. I is false; II is true.
    c. Both I and II are true.
    d. Both I and II are false.

18. How do the high implicit marginal tax rates that often occur when transfer payments are inversely linked to earnings affect the incentive of poor people to work and earn?
    a. A poor person's incentive to earn is increased.
    b. A poor person's incentive to earn is reduced.
    c. The incentive of the poor to earn is unaffected.
    d. The incentive of the poor to earn reported income is increased, but the incentive to earn unreported income is reduced.

19. If a family earned an additional $6,000 of income from work and as a result their welfare benefits were reduced by $3,000, the implicit marginal tax rate for this family would be
    a. zero.
    b. 30 percent.
    c. 50 percent.
    d. 100 percent.

20. The idea that transfer benefits to the poor encourage behavior that increases the risk of poverty is known as the
    a. Samaritan's dilemma.
    b. rule of inverse benefits.
    c. implicit marginal tax law.
    d. Smith paradox.

21. Data suggest that the large increase in government spending on income transfers over the past two decades has been accompanied by
    a. a reduced poverty rate for the nonelderly.
    b. a more equal distribution of income.
    c. fewer single-parent families because a married couple receives benefits twice as large.
    d. none of the above.

DISCUSSION QUESTIONS

1. Some people blamed the rising income inequality in the 1980s on "bad" economic policies. However, income inequality has continued to increase in the 1990s and, in fact, at a slightly higher rate than it did in the 1980s. What do you

think are the major factors contributing to rising income inequality in the United States in recent decades?

2. "The average poor person in the United States has three times as much annual income as the average middle-class person in most other countries in the world. If we really cared about helping the poor and reducing income inequality, we would be sending our money to other countries rather than giving it to people in the United States." Evaluate this statement. Does giving our welfare dollars to a "richer" person in the United States rather than a "poorer" person in another country imply that our main concern is not with helping the poor in general?

3. "When the government engages in large-scale redistribution from the rich to the poor, it results in a smaller total economic pie, reducing the income of all." Evaluate this statement. How does the tax rate on taxpayer income and the implicit tax rate on transfer programs alter the incentive to work and earn income for each group? What is the Samaritan's dilemma, and what does it imply about the validity of this statement?

4. What are some of the problems with annual income data at a given time as a measure of one's economic well-being? Do you think that, across individuals, lifetime earnings are more or less unequal than annual earnings? In the United States, is it typical for the vast majority of poor to remain poor and the rich to remain rich over long periods of time? Explain.

5. In a free market economy, a person's income is linked to their contribution to the nation's output. The traditional Marxist view is that a person's income should be determined by their need, while everyone should put forth maximum work effort regardless of the personal reward they get from working.
   a. Economist Milton Friedman has argued that a perfectly equal income distribution would thoroughly undermine our incentives to be productive. Do you agree or disagree?
   b. Is it fair that someone who produces more output receives more income independent of their needs? What, or who, determines exactly what a person's "needs" are?

6. How does income distribution in the United States compare with that of other developed nations? of less developed nations?

7. Do you think the official poverty statistics in the United States are misleading? If so, in what ways? How would you change the way poverty is measured? In your answer be sure to address how transfer benefits are considered in the calculations.

8. "If I were to take a job, my welfare benefits would fall by more than the amount of income I would earn. It is not that I do not want to work, but rather that I care about best supporting my family." Evaluate this statement. How do the implicit marginal tax rates of welfare programs affect the incentive of recipients to work?

Harcourt Brace & Company

CHAPTER 16

Gaining from International Trade

TRUE OR FALSE

T F

☐ ☐ 1. Economic theory suggests that free trade between two countries generally benefits only one country, the other is harmed.

☐ ☐ 2. Economic analysis shows that *every* individual within an economy gains from international free trade whenever it takes place.

☐ ☐ 3. The joint output of countries would be maximized if each country specialized in production of those commodities for which it is the low opportunity-cost producer, exchanging them for other commodities for which it is a high opportunity-cost producer.

☐ ☐ 4. In a sense, tariffs and quotas are identical in that they can be designed to produce the same exact outcome in terms of price and quantity of imports.

☐ ☐ 5. A secondary effect of policies that restrict imports is that they lower the demand for the nation's export products.

☐ ☐ 6. An import quota places a maximum limit on the amount of a product that can be imported during a specific time period.

☐ ☐ 7. A country that is rich in resources and an efficient producer will gain if it refuses to trade, although this action hurts the rest of the world.

☐ ☐ 8. Three popular arguments for imposing trade restrictions are to protect infant industries, to prevent dumping of goods below cost, and to keep in place certain industries essential for a country's national defense.

☐ ☐ 9. If all tariffs were removed in the United States, fewer jobs would be available to U.S. workers since wage rates are high in the United States.

☐ ☐ 10. The North American Free Trade Agreement (NAFTA) has caused widespread job losses in the United States and a large movement of U.S. companies to Mexico.

☐ ☐ 11. Canada, Japan, and Mexico are the major trading partners of the United States.

☐ ☐ 12. U.S. tariffs, in general, are much lower now than they were in 1930.

☐ ☐ 13. Because trade restrictions generate concentrated benefits to special interest groups at the expense of the general public, politicians find them attractive to implement.

PROBLEMS AND PROJECTS

1. Use Exhibit 1 when answering the following questions.
   a. In the space provided, plot the production possibilities curves for Lebos and Egap from the data given. Label the points in the graph with the corresponding letters and connect the points.
   b. Lebos is currently producing at point C (80 units of food and 80 units of clothing) but wishes to expand its production of food to 120 units. What point would Lebos move to? How many units of food has Lebos gained? How many units of clothing has Lebos had to give up to free the extra resources to produce this additional food? Write your answers in equation form such as *xx* F = *xx* C where *xx* F represents the number of units of food

EXHIBIT 1

Production Possibilities for Lebos and Egap

	LEBOS				EGAP	
	FOOD	CLOTHING			FOOD	CLOTHING
A	0	160		A	0	120
B	40	120		B	10	90
C	80	80		C	20	60
D	120	40		D	30	30
E	160	0		E	40	0

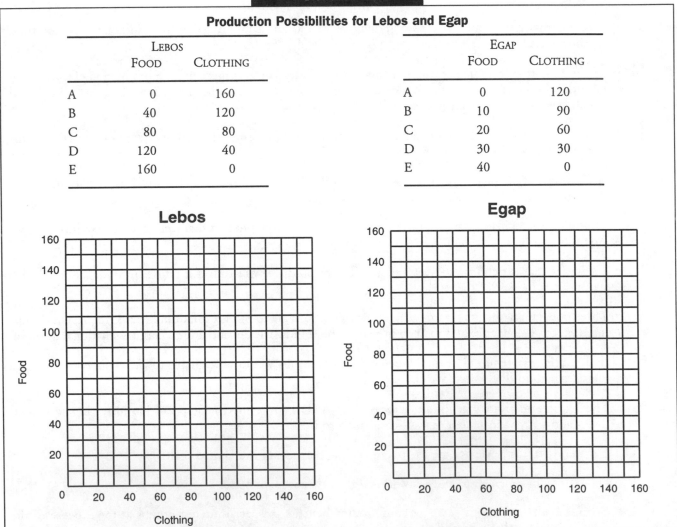

Harcourt Brace & Company

gained and *xx* C represents the number of units of clothing given up in your answers above.

c. Pick any two points (such as points A and B) for Egap. Between these two points, how many units of food are gained? How many units of clothing are given up? Write this in equation form similar to what you did in part b.

d. Take the equations you found above for each country and simplify them in terms of *one* unit of food. [Hint: As an example, for Lebos divide both sides by 40 to get 1F = 1C.] These equations now represent the opportunity cost of producing one unit of food in each country in terms of how much clothing must be given up. From these new equations, which country has to give up the *least* amount of clothing to produce one unit of food? Note that this country has the comparative advantage in food (because it has the lowest opportunity cost of producing food). Now, rewrite and simplify each equation in terms of one unit of *clothing*. Using this, which country has the comparative advantage in clothing?

e. For survival, Lebos needs to have 120 units of food and Egap needs 40. If these countries do not trade, how much clothing will the people of Lebos be able to produce and consume given the resources remaining after the required food is produced? Egap? Circle these points in the diagrams.

f. Suppose that Lebos and Egap agree to trade with each other at the rate of 1 unit of food for 2 units of clothing (1F = 2C). Lebos will specialize in producing all food and Egap all clothing. If Lebos produces only food, how much food can it produce? How many units of food will Lebos have left to trade after keeping 120 units for itself? Given the rate of exchange above, how many units of clothing will they acquire in trade from Egap for these extra units of food?

g. Carefully compare the amount of food and clothing Lebos has after specializing and trading with the amount it had when it was self sufficient in part e. Is Lebos better off?

h. After Egap specializes in clothing and trades with Lebos, how much food will it have acquired in trade? How much clothing will it have left after trading for this food? Compare the amount of food and clothing Egap has after trade with the amount it had when it was self sufficient in part e. Is Egap better off?

2. The country of Arcadia produces and consumes unique computers. Exhibit 2 on page 188 shows Arcadia's demand and supply curves for their computers along with the demand for Arcadian computers from the rest of the world (ROW). The final column in the table is the total demand for Arcadia's computers from both domestic citizens and foreigners combined.

a. In the space provided, graph Arcadia's domestic supply and Arcadia's domestic demand for computers in the absence of trade. What is the equilibrium price and quantity with no international trade?

b. With trade there will be additional demand for Arcadian computers. Fill in the missing values for the total demand column in the table. Now, graph the *total* demand with foreign trade in the diagram. What is the equilibrium price and quantity with trade?

c. What has happened to the price of Arcadian computers when they begin to trade? the quantity produced? What happened to Arcadia's productions of *other* goods and services as a result of international trade?

Harcourt Brace & Company

EXHIBIT 2

Price	Arcadia's Quantity Supplied	Arcadia's Quantity Demanded	ROW's Quantity Demanded	Total Quantity Demanded
$3,000	14,000	5,000	1,000	6,000
$2,500	12,000	6,000	2,000	____
$2,000	10,000	7,000	3,000	____
$1,500	8,000	8,000	4,000	____
$1,000	6,000	9,000	5,000	____
$500	4,000	10,000	6,000	____

d. With trade (and the new higher price), what is the new quantity of computers demanded only by the citizens of Arcadia? [Hint: not the total, just the amount demanded by Arcadia.] Compare the quantity of computers demanded in Arcadia without trade. What quantity of computers is exported by Arcadia?

e. Given your answers above, what can you say about how exporting a product affects a country's citizens? Does it benefit domestic producers?

3. Exhibit 3 depicts the domestic supply and demand for a product that the U.S. can import from the rest of the world at a fixed price of $500 per unit.

a. In the absence of international trade, what would be the price of this product in the United States? What quantities would be demanded and supplied?

b. Suppose this product can be imported into the United States without restriction at a price of $500. Draw a world supply curve in the diagram [Hint: It is a horizontal line at the world price.] Show in the diagram the new price, quantity demanded, the total quantity supplied, the quantity domestically supplied, and the quantity imported with trade.

EXHIBIT 3

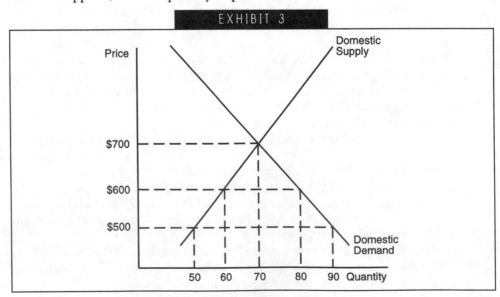

Harcourt Brace & Company

c. If a 20 percent tariff is imposed on the importation of the product, the price of the imported products will rise to $600. Show this new world supply with tariff in the diagram as a horizontal line at the new price with the tariff included. How will the price, amount demanded, the amount domestically produced, and the amount imported change as a result of the tariff?

d. Suppose that *instead* of the tariff of part c, government imposed a quota on imports of twenty units per year. How would the effects of this quota differ from the effects of the tariff on the price, quantity demanded, amount domestically supplied, and amount imported?

4. Consider the following hypothetical information about the United States and South Korea shown in Exhibit 4.

a. Which country has the absolute advantage in steel production? _____ absolute advantage in wheat production? _____ comparative advantage in steel production? _____ comparative advantage in wheat production? _____

EXHIBIT 4		
	OUTPUT PER WORKER PER DAY	
	UNITED STATES	SOUTH KOREA
Tons of steel	8	4
Bushels of wheat	80	8

b. If these countries trade steel and wheat with each other, which country will export steel and import wheat?

c. Suppose that the United States and South Korea agree to a daily trade of ten tons of steel for fifty bushels of wheat. One worker in the United States then switches from steel production to wheat production. At the same time, four workers in South Korea switch from wheat production to steel. Complete the following table to show that both countries end up with more steel and more wheat than they had initially.

UNITED STATES	TONS OF STEEL	BUSHELS OF WHEAT
Change in production	−8	+80
Trade	+10	−50
Change in consumption	_____	_____

SOUTH KOREA	TONS OF STEEL	BUSHELS OF WHEAT
Change in production	_____	_____
Trade	_____	_____
Change in consumption	_____	_____

Harcourt Brace & Company

MULTIPLE CHOICE

1. A tariff or quota that limits the entry of foreign goods to the U.S. market will
   a. benefit domestic producers in the protected industries and harm domestic consumers.
   b. increase the nation's real income by protecting domestic jobs from foreign competition.
   c. reduce the demand for U.S. export goods, lowering employment in export industries.
   d. do both a and c.

2. According to the law of comparative advantage, a nation will benefit from international trade when it
   a. imports more than it exports.
   b. exports more than it imports.
   c. imports goods for which it is a high opportunity-cost producer, while exporting goods for which it is a low opportunity-cost producer.
   d. exports goods for which it is a high opportunity-cost producer, while importing those goods for which it is a low opportunity-cost producer.

Exhibit 5 outlines the production possibilities of Italia and Slavia for food and clothing. Use it to answer questions 3 through 6.

EXHIBIT 5

ITALIA		SLAVIA	
FOOD	CLOTHING	FOOD	CLOTHING
0	16	0	8
2	12	2	6
4	8	4	4
6	4	6	2
8	0	8	0

3. Italia is currently producing 4 units of food and 8 units of clothing. If it increases its production of food by 2 units (up to a total of 6 units of food), its clothing production will
   a. fall by 2 units.
   b. fall by 4 units.
   c. increase by 2 units.
   d. increase by 4 units.

4. What is the opportunity cost of producing *one* unit of food in Italia?
   a. one-half of a unit of clothing
   b. 1 unit of clothing
   c. 2 units of clothing
   d. 5 units of clothing

Harcourt Brace & Company

5. Which of the following is true?
    a. Italia has the comparative advantage in producing food.
    b. Italia has the comparative advantage in producing clothing.
    c. Slavia has the comparative advantage in producing clothing.
    d. Slavia is the low opportunity cost producer of clothing.

6. The law of comparative advantage suggests that
    a. neither country would gain from trade.
    b. Only Slavia would gain from trade, Italia would be harmed.
    c. both countries could gain if Italia traded food for Slavia's clothing.
    d. both countries could gain if Slavia traded food for Italia's clothing.

7. If the United States were to adopt a policy of free trade with European countries and Japan, this policy would
    a. help the United States and hurt the other countries because the United States has a larger population.
    b. help all of the countries involved because every country would have a comparative advantage in the production of some good.
    c. hurt the United States and help the other countries involved because job opportunities in the U.S. would fall while they rose in other countries.
    d. help the United States and hurt the other countries because the U.S. has more natural resources than the other countries.

8. The theory of comparative advantage suggests that nations should produce a good if they
    a. have the lowest opportunity cost.
    b. have the lowest wages.
    c. have the most resources.
    d. can produce more of the good than any other nation.

9. A tariff differs from a quota in that a tariff is
    a. levied on imports, whereas a quota is imposed on exports.
    b. levied on exports, whereas a quota is imposed on imports.
    c. a tax levied on exports, whereas a quota is a limit on the number of units of a good that can be exported.
    d. a tax imposed on imports, whereas a quota is an absolute limit to the number of units of a good that can be imported.

10. An import quota on a product protects domestic industries by
    a. reducing the foreign supply to the domestic market and thereby raising the domestic price.
    b. increasing the foreign supply to the domestic market and thereby lowering the domestic price.
    c. increasing the domestic demand for the product and thereby increasing its price.
    d. providing the incentive for domestic producers to improve the efficiency of their operation and thereby reduce their per-unit costs of production.

Harcourt Brace & Company

11. Which of the following would be the most likely long-run effect if the United States increased its tariff rates and adopted stricter import quotas?
    a. a decrease in both U.S. imports and exports
    b. an increase in both U.S. imports and exports
    c. a decrease in U.S. imports and an increase in U.S. exports
    d. an increase in U.S. imports and a decrease in U.S. exports

12. Trade restrictions that limit the sale of low-price foreign goods in the U.S. market
    a. increase the real income of Americans.
    b. benefit domestic producers in the protected industries at the expense of consumers and domestic producers in export industries.
    c. help channel more of our resources into producing goods for which we are a low-cost producer.
    d. reduce unemployment and increase the productivity of American workers.

13. A basic flaw in the infant-industry argument is that
    a. most industries need protection when they are mature, not when they are first established.
    b. the amount of the tariff is unlikely to have much impact on the success of an infant industry.
    c. once a tariff is granted, political pressure will likely prevent the withdrawal of the tariff even when the industry matures.
    d. domestic consumers will continue to buy the foreign products anyway, regardless of the tariff.

14. Countries that impose high tariffs, exchange rate controls, and other barriers that restrict international trade have, on average,
    a. high rates of economic growth.
    b. low rates of economic growth.
    c. a large export sector.
    d. a large import sector.

15. If the United States imports low-cost goods produced in low-wage countries instead of producing the goods domestically,
    a. the United States will lose jobs.
    b. the United States will gain and domestic resources will be employed more productively.
    c. dollars that leave the United States will not return to buy goods produced by high-wage American workers.
    d. the availability consumption of goods in the United States will be reduced.

Harcourt Brace & Company

16. Suppose that the United States eliminated its tariff on automobiles, granting for-eign-produced automobiles free entry into the U.S. market. Which of the fol-lowing would be most likely to occur?
    a. The price of automobiles to U.S. consumers would decline, and the demand for U.S. export products would increase.
    b. The price of automobiles to U.S. consumers would increase, and the demand for U.S. export products would decline.
    c. The price of automobiles to U.S. consumers would decline, and the demand for U.S. export products would decline.
    d. The price of automobiles to U.S. consumers would increase, and the demand for U.S. export products would increase.

17. If Japan offered every U.S. citizen a new automobile for a price of only $1,
    a. the action would be considered "dumping."
    b. domestic automobile manufacturers and workers would likely favor impos-ing tariffs or quotas to restrict this action.
    c. domestic citizens would benefit from this action by Japan.
    d. all of the above are true.

18. Relative to a no-trade situation, what effect will importing a good from foreign nations have on the domestic market for the good?
    a. Equilibrium price will rise and total domestically produced output will fall.
    b. Equilibrium price will rise and total domestically produced output will rise.
    c. Equilibrium price will fall and total domestically produced output will fall.
    d. Equilibrium price will fall and total domestically produced output will rise.

19. Relative to a no-trade situation, what effect will exporting a good to foreign nations have on the domestic market for the good?
    a. Equilibrium price will rise, domestic production will fall, and domestic con-sumption will fall.
    b. Equilibrium price will rise, domestic production will rise, and domestic con-sumption will fall.
    c. Equilibrium price will fall, domestic production will fall, and domestic con-sumption will increase.
    d. Equilibrium price will fall, domestic production will rise, and domestic con-sumption will increase.

20. If all tariffs (and quotas) between countries on the North American continent were eliminated,
    a. small Central American countries would be hurt since they would be unable to compete with larger nations.
    b. the United States would gain at the expense of the less-developed North American countries.
    c. the combined wealth of the countries would increase since elimination of trade restrictions would permit greater gains from specialization.
    d. wage rates in the United States would decline to the average for the North American continent.

Harcourt Brace & Company

21. Which of the following is **not** an argument for adopting trade restrictions on imported goods?
    a. Antidumping argument.
    b. National-defense argument.
    c. Consumer-protection argument.
    d. Infant-industry argument.

Questions 22 through 25 refer to Exhibit 6, which shows the effect of a country imposing a tariff on an imported product.

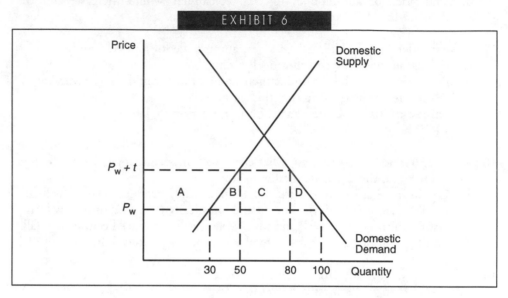

EXHIBIT 6

22. If the world price of this good is P_W and there are no restrictions on imports, domestic suppliers will produce _____ units, domestic demanders will consume _____ units, and total imports will be _____ units. (Fill in the blanks.)
    a. 30; 100; 70
    b. 50; 100; 50
    c. 30; 80; 80
    d. 100; 70; 30

23. Suppose that a tariff of t is imposed upon this good, raising the price to $P_W + t$. As a result,
    a. imports will fall to 30.
    b. domestic production will increase to 50.
    c. domestic consumption will fall to 80.
    d. all of the above are true.

24. Given the tariff described in the question above,
    a. the combined areas A + B + C + D represent the losses to domestic consumers from the tariff.
    b. area C represents the government's revenue from the tariff.
    c. area A represents the gain to domestic suppliers from the tariff.
    d. all of the above are true.

Harcourt Brace & Company

25. The same price and quantity outcomes under the tariff above could have also been produced by the imposition of a quota of
    a. 30 units.
    b. 50 units.
    c. 80 units.
    d. No quota can produce the same price and quantity outcomes.

DISCUSSION QUESTIONS

1. "We are not opposed to competition when it does not destroy jobs. But last year, while many American auto workers were idle, we exported a million jobs to foreigners by importing automobiles that could have been produced by domestic workers. An increase in the tariff on automobiles would strengthen our economy, provide jobs, and improve our standard of living." [Auto Workers' Union official]
    a. Do you agree that higher automobile tariffs would "provide jobs"? Why or why not?
    b. Do you agree that higher automobile tariffs would "improve our standard of living"? Why or why not?
    c. Prior to the 1970s, the United Auto Workers were an advocate of free trade. What do you think accounts for the reversal in their position?

2. All else constant, if the cost of Japanese laser printers is $2,300 in Japan, would you expect the cost of Japanese laser printers in the United States to be $2,300? more than $2,300? less than $2,300? If the Japanese are, in fact, selling laser printers in the United States for $1,575, what arguments for protection might U.S. manufacturers of laser printers make? Does selling the printers at prices lower than the cost of production benefit or harm U.S. consumers?

3. Describe each of the major, "partially valid," reasons for adopting trade restrictions. Discuss the pros and cons of each argument.

4. a. Montana encourages a local liquor-bottling industry by taxing bulk imports into the state at lower rates than bottled liquors. Does this make economic sense? Why or why not?
    b. Should Connecticut ban imports of bananas to promote a local banana industry? Explain.
    c. Should state governments adopt trade restrictions to target specific industries for promotions? If not, why not? If so, why and under what circumstances?

5. In the United States, the price of labor is relatively high and the price of capital is relatively low. In developing countries, the reverse is true.
    a. Based on these resource market conditions, what types of products would you expect the United States to import from developing countries? to export to them?
    b. Most U.S. trade is with other industrial high-wage nations. In light of the law of comparative advantage, is this surprising? If not, why not? If so, why and how can you account for this aspect of U.S. trade?

Harcourt Brace & Company

PERSPECTIVES IN ECONOMICS

THE ECONOMIC CASE FOR FREE TRADE

By Milton and Rose Friedman

[Reprinted with permission from Chapter 2 of *Free to Choose* (New York: Harcourt Brace Jovanovich, 1980) Abridged.]

Today, as always, there is much support for tariffs—euphemistically labeled "protection," a good label for a bad cause. Producers of steel and steelworkers' unions press for restrictions on steel imports from Japan. Producers of TV sets and their workers lobby for "voluntary agreements" to limit imports of TV sets or components from Japan, Taiwan, or Hong Kong. Producers of textiles, shoes, cattle, sugar—they and myriad others complain about "unfair" competition from abroad and demand that government do something to "protect" them. Of course, no group makes its claim on the basis of naked self-interest. Every group speaks of the "general interest," of the need to preserve jobs or to promote national security.

One voice that is hardly ever raised is the consumer's. The individual consumer's voice is drowned out in the cacophony of the "interested sophistry of merchants and manufacturers" and their employees. The result is a serious distortion of the issue. For example, the supporters of tariffs treat it as self-evident that the creation of jobs is a desirable end, in and of itself, regardless of what the persons employed do. That is clearly wrong. If all we want are jobs, we can create any number—for example, have people dig holes and then fill them up again, or perform other useless tasks. Work is sometimes its own reward. Mostly, however, it is the price we pay to get the things we want. Our real objective is not just jobs but productive jobs—jobs that will mean more goods and services to consume.

Another fallacy seldom contradicted is that exports are good, imports bad. The truth is very different. We cannot eat, wear, or enjoy the goods we send abroad. We eat bananas from Central America, wear Italian shoes, drive German automobiles, and enjoy programs we see on our Japanese TV sets. Our gain from foreign trade is what we import. Exports are the price we pay to get imports. As Adam Smith saw so clearly, the citizens of a nation benefit from getting as large a volume of imports as possible in return for its exports, or equivalently, from exporting as little as possible to pay for its imports.

The misleading terminology we use reflects these erroneous ideas. "Protection" really means exploiting the consumer. A "favorable balance of trade" really means exporting more than we import, sending abroad goods of greater total value than the goods we get from abroad. In your private household, you would surely prefer to pay less for more rather than the other way around, yet that would be termed an "unfavorable balance of payments" in foreign trade.

The argument in favor of tariffs that has the greatest emotional appeal to the public at large is the alleged need to protect the high standard of living of American workers from the "unfair" competition of workers in Japan or Korea or Hong Kong who are willing to work for a much lower wage. What is wrong with this argument? Don't we want to protect the high standard of living of our people?

The fallacy in this argument is the loose use of the terms "high" wage and "low" wage. What do high and low wages mean? American workers are paid in dollars; Japanese workers are paid in yen. How do we compare wages in dollars with wages in yen? How many yen equal a dollar? What determines that exchange rate?

It is simply not true that high-wage American workers are, as a group, threatened by "unfair" competition from low-wage foreign workers. Of course, particular workers may be harmed if a new or improved product is developed abroad, or if foreign producers become able to produce such products more cheaply. But that is no different from the effect on a particular group of workers of other American firms, developing new or improved products or discovering how to produce at lower costs. That is simply market competition in practice, the major source of the high standard of life of the American worker. If we want to benefit from a vital, dynamic, innovative economic system, we must accept the need for mobility and adjustment. It may be desirable to ease these adjustments, and we have adopted many arrangements, such as unemployment insurance, to do so, but we should try to achieve that objective without destroying the flexibility of the system—that would be to kill the goose that has been laying the golden eggs. In any event, whatever we do should be evenhanded with respect to foreign and domestic trade.

What determines the items it pays us to import and to export? An American worker is currently more productive than a Japanese worker. It is hard to determine just how much more productive—estimates differ. But suppose he is one and a half times as productive. Then, on average, the American's wages would buy about one and half times as much as a Japanese worker's wages. It is wasteful to use American workers to do anything at which they are less than one and a half times as efficient as their Japanese counterparts. In the economic jargon coined more than 150 years ago, that is the *principle of comparative advantage.* Even if we were more efficient than the Japanese at producing everything, it would not pay us to produce everything. We should concentrate on doing those things we do best, those things where our superiority is the greatest.

Another source of "unfair competition" is said to be subsidies by foreign governments to their producers that enable them to sell in the United States below cost. Suppose a foreign government gives such subsidies, as no doubt some do. Who is hurt and who benefits? To pay for the subsidies the foreign government must tax its citizens. They are the ones who pay for the subsidies. U.S. consumers benefit. They get cheap TV sets or automobiles or whatever it is that is subsidized. Should we complain about such a program of reverse foreign aid? Was it noble of the United States to send goods and services as gifts to other countries in the form of Marshall Plan aid or, later, foreign aid, but ignoble for foreign countries to send us gifts in the indirect form of goods and services sold to us below cost? The citizens of the foreign government might well complain. They must suffer a lower standard of living for the benefit of American consumers and of some of their fellow citizens who own or work in the industries that are subsidized. No doubt, if such subsidies are introduced suddenly or erratically, that will adversely affect owners and workers in U.S. industries producing the same products. However, that is one of the ordinary risks of doing business. Enterprises never complain about unusual or accidental events that confer windfall gains. The free enterprise system is a *profit* and *loss* system. As already noted, any measures to ease the adjustment to sudden changes should be applied evenhandedly to domestic and foreign trade.

We are a great nation, the leader of the free world. It ill behooves us to require Hong Kong and Taiwan to impose export quotas on textiles to "protect" our textile industry at the expense of U.S. consumers and of Chinese workers in Hong Kong and Taiwan. We speak glowingly of the virtues of free trade, while we use our political and economic power to induce Japan to restrict exports of steel and TV sets. We should move unilaterally to free trade, not instantaneously, but over a period of, say, five years, at a pace announced in advance.

Few measures that we could take would do more to promote the cause of freedom at home and abroad than complete free trade. Instead of making grants to foreign governments in the name of economic aid—thereby promoting socialism—while at the same time imposing restrictions on the products they produce—thereby hindering free enterprise—we could assume a consistent and principled stance. We could say to the rest of the world: we believe in freedom and intend to practice it. We cannot force you to be free. But we can offer full cooperation on equal terms to all. Our market is open to you without tariffs or other restrictions. Sell here what you can and wish to. Buy whatever you can and wish to. In that way cooperation among individuals can be worldwide and free.

DISCUSSION

1. When a politician speaks out in favor of protectionism against imports, how do you react? Is this debate a question of economic theory against political reality, or are there political and economic arguments on both sides? Explain.

2. As you read the article, you were probably impressed with the superb logic and internal consistency with which the Friedmans write. If you were going to attempt to refute their arguments, where would you start? Are there any major assumptions you could question? Are there secondary effects that they neglect to analyze? Explain.

3. The article points out that the harm done to consumers by restricting trade is usually ignored. Why do you think this is the case? Generally, even people who are "pro-consumer/antibusiness" are in favor of restricting imports, when economic theory tells us that it only helps producers while harming individual consumers. Can you explain this apparent contradiction?

Harcourt Brace & Company

CHAPTER *17*

International Finance and the Foreign Exchange Market

T F

☐ ☐ 1. Foreign exchange markets enable an individual to exchange the currency of one nation for the currency of another nation.

☐ ☐ 2. A nation's exports generate a demand for the currency of the exporting nation on the foreign exchange market.

☐ ☐ 3. Under a system of fixed exchange rates, a balance-of-payments equilibrium is automatic.

☐ ☐ 4. Under a system of flexible exchange rates, the government must use monetary policy to ensure a balance-of-payments equilibrium.

☐ ☐ 5. The economic analysis of foreign trade is unique in that supply-and-demand relationships do not usually determine equilibrium.

☐ ☐ 6. One problem with a system of flexible exchange rates is that black markets in foreign currencies are more likely to develop than with controlled rates of exchange.

☐ ☐ 7. When a country's balance of trade registers a deficit, both its current and capital accounts will also be in deficit.

☐ ☐ 8. If foreigners suddenly began investing more in the U.S., causing the capital account to run a larger surplus, the current account deficit would rise.

☐ ☐ 9. If imports consistently exceeded exports, U.S. consumers would be hurt as a result of an unfavorable balance of trade implied by such a situation.

☐ ☐ 10. If expansionary fiscal policy (a budget deficit) leads to higher interest rates, it will cause a nation's currency to appreciate and the current account to move toward a trade deficit.

☐ ☐ 11. A rapid U.S. monetary expansion would tend to reduce the number of German Marks it takes to buy a U.S. dollar, other things constant.

T F

☐ ☐ 12. For a common currency, such as the Euro, to be successful, each country must give up the independence of their monetary policy.

☐ ☐ 13. The International Monetary Fund (IMF) is the central bank of the world and is in charge of determining the world money supply with an eye toward controlling world inflation.

PROBLEMS AND PROJECTS

1. Exhibit 1 shows the exchange rate values of several major world currencies relative to the U.S. dollar as they were on June 7, 1999. The first column shows the number of units of the foreign currency that could be obtained by trading in one U.S. dollar. The second column shows the number of U.S. dollars that could be obtained by trading in one unit of the foreign currency. (Note: These are simply the reciprocals of the data in the first column.)

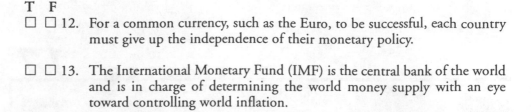

EXHIBIT 1

FOREIGN CURRENCY	UNITS OF FOREIGN CURRENCY PER U.S. DOLLAR	U.S. DOLLARS PER UNIT OF FOREIGN CURRENCY
French franc	6.3753	0.15686
German Mark	1.9009	0.52607
Japanese yen	120.6500	0.00829
English pound	0.6255	1.59880
European Euro	0.9719	1.02890

    a. If a German citizen wished to purchase a Ford automobile costing 20,000 U.S. dollars, how much would it cost in German Marks?

    b. If a U.S. citizen wished to purchase a bottle of French wine costing 150 francs, how much would it cost in U.S. dollars?

    c. If a French citizen wished to purchase a Japanese automobile costing 2,500,000 Japanese yen, how much would it cost in French francs? [Hint: With the data given, you must first convert from yen to dollars, then convert dollars to francs.]

    d. To carry out the transaction in part c, a French citizen could either convert francs to dollars, then dollars to yen, or she could simply convert francs directly to yen. From the data above, what would you expect the exchange rate to be between the franc and the yen?

    e. In 1990, one German Mark was equal to 0.619 U.S. dollars, one Japanese yen was equal to 0.0069 U.S. dollars, and one British pound was equal to 1.7841 U.S. dollars. Compare these values to the ones in Exhibit 1 and decide whether each of these currencies has either appreciated or depreciated over this period relative to the U.S. dollar.

2. Each of the diagrams below represents the U.S. demand for and supply of foreign exchange, here the English pound. For each of the events described below, diagram how the demand and/or supply of English pounds changes (use +, [minus], or 0 to show no change). Then fill in the blanks to the right of the diagram, indicating in the last blank whether the *English pound* has appreciated, depreciated, or undergone an indeterminate change as a result of the event(s). The first question has been answered as an example, and in the diagrams, price (P) is in dollars per English pound.

EVENTS	DIAGRAMS	D	S	CHANGE
a. As a result of recovering from a depression, U.S. incomes rise significantly.		+	0	depreciated
b. The United Kingdom experiences a serious recession, causing a decline in income.		___	___	_____
c. Restrictive monetary policy in the United States causes U.S. interest rates to rise relative to United Kingdom rates.		___	___	_____
d. The Chairman of the Fed is quoted as saying, "If the high value of the dollar is not soon corrected by market forces, the Fed will take corrective action."		___	___	_____

Harcourt Brace & Company

Events	Diagrams	D	S	Change
e. While the United States experiences stable price, prices in the United Kingdom rise by 15 percent.		—	—	—
f. In an effort to stimulate the economy, the United States embarks on an expansionary fiscal policy.		—	—	—
g. Both the United States and the United Kingdom experience inflation rates of 20 percent		—	—	—

EXHIBIT 2

Debit		Credit	
	(BILLIONS OF DOLLARS)		
CURRENT ACCOUNT			
Merchandise imports	249.3	Merchandise exports	224.0
Service imports	84.6	Service exports	120.7
Net unilateral transfers	7.1		
CAPITAL ACCOUNT			
U.S. investment abroad	18.5	Foreign investment in the United States	10.9
Loans to foreigners	58.1	Loans from foreigners	70.2

3. Exhibit 2 presents balance-of-payment data for the United States for 1980.
   a. Use the data in Exhibit 2 to calculate the balance on the (1) merchandise trade account, (2) services account, (3) current account, (4) capital account, and (5) combined current-and-capital accounts.

Harcourt Brace & Company

b. What has to happen in order for the combined current-and-capital accounts (number 5 in part a) to be different from zero?

c. Compare these balances to the ones for 1997 in Exhibit 5 in the text. What happened to U.S. international balances between those years? Why do you think this occurred?

MULTIPLE CHOICE

1. If the exchange rate value of one U.S. dollar changes from 120 Japanese yen to 140 yen,
   a. the U.S. dollar has appreciated relative to the yen.
   b. the Japanese yen has depreciated relative to the dollar.
   c. the U.S. dollar has depreciated relative to the yen.
   d. both a and b have occurred.

2. Under a flexible exchange rate system, which of the following will be most likely to cause a depreciation in the exchange rate value of the dollar (relative to the English pound)?
   a. An economic boom occurs in England, inducing English consumers to buy more American-made automobiles, trucks, and computer products.
   b. Real interest rates in the United States fall lower than real interest rates in England.
   c. Restrictive monetary policy in the United States causes inflation to be lower than in England.
   d. Attractive investment opportunities in the U.S. induce English investors to buy stock in U.S. firms.

3. If the exchange rate between the U.S. dollar and the French franc were such that one U.S. dollar equals 6 francs, what would be the price in dollars of a French automobile that cost 120,000 Marks?
   a. $6,000
   b. $20,000
   c. $120,000
   d. $720,000

4. Other things constant, which of the following will most likely cause the dollar to appreciate on the exchange rate market?
   a. higher interest rates in the U.S.
   b. the U.S. Fed pursuing restrictive monetary policy
   c. high rates of income growth in Europe
   d. all of the above

5. If the U.S. dollar depreciates, then U.S. exports become _____ expensive to foreigners and foreign goods become _____ expensive to U.S. citizens. (Fill in the blanks.)
   a. less; less
   b. less; more
   c. more; less
   d. more; more

6. An unanticipated shift to a more expansionary monetary policy will most likely cause the nation's currency to _____ and its current account to move toward a _____. (Fill in the blanks.)
   a. depreciate; deficit
   b. depreciate; surplus
   c. appreciate; deficit
   d. appreciate; surplus

7. Under a pure flexible exchange rate system, the rate that equates demand and supply in the exchange rate market will also lead to a balance of
   a. merchandise exports and merchandise imports.
   b. current account transactions.
   c. capital account transactions.
   d. current and capital account transactions.

8. If the value of a nation's merchandise imports exceeds merchandise exports, the nation is running a
   a. balance of payments deficit.
   b. balance of payments surplus.
   c. merchandise trade deficit.
   d. merchandise trade surplus.

9. Which one of the following would supply dollars to the foreign exchange market?
   a. the spending of U.S. tourists in France
   b. the purchase of U.S. automobiles by Japanese consumers
   c. the sale of U.S. automobiles to French consumers
   d. the purchase of an American electronics factory by a Japanese investor

10. During the early 1980s, the United States shifted to a more restrictive monetary policy that resulted in a deceleration in inflation and a more expansionary fiscal policy, which placed upward pressure on interest rates in the United States. This macroeconomic policy combination resulted in capital
    a. inflow and a depreciation in the exchange rate of the dollar.
    b. outflow and an appreciation in the exchange rate of the dollar.
    c. outflow and a depreciation in the exchange rate of the dollar.
    d. inflow and an appreciation in the exchange rate of the dollar.

11. (I) The U.S. trade deficit is a financial obligation of the federal government, and if it is not paid off, foreigners will be reluctant to loan money to the U.S. government. (II) When a nation runs a current account deficit due to a merchandise trade deficit, it must also be true that the nation has a surplus on its capital account due to an inflow of foreign capital.
    a. I is true; II is false.
    b. I is false; II is true.
    c. Both I and II are true.
    d. Both I and II are false.

12. For a country to successfully maintain a fixed exchange rate value of its currency relative to another currency (for example, as is done when currencies are unified or pegged), it must
    a. maintain a relatively high rate of inflation.
    b. balance the government budget each year.
    c. give up the independence of its monetary policy.
    d. run a trade deficit.

13. An appreciation in the value of the U.S. dollar would
    a. encourage foreigners to make more investments in the United States.
    b. encourage U.S. consumers to purchase more foreign-produced goods.
    c. increase the number of dollars that could be purchased with the Mexican peso.
    d. discourage U.S. consumers from traveling abroad.

14. Which of the following would be likely to cause a nation's currency to depreciate?
    a. an increase in foreign demand for the nation's products
    b. a lower domestic rate of inflation than that of the nation's trading partners
    c. higher domestic interest rates
    d. higher foreign interest rates

15. Under a system of flexible exchange rates, transactions that increase the supply of the nation's currency to the foreign exchange market will cause the nation's
    a. currency to depreciate in value.
    b. currency to appreciate in value.
    c. trade deficit to increase.
    d. products to become more expensive to foreigners.

16. With time, a depreciation in the value of a nation's currency in the foreign market will cause the nation's
    a. imports to increase and exports to decline.
    b. exports to increase and imports to decline.
    c. imports and exports to decline.
    d. imports and exports to rise.

Harcourt Brace & Company

17. "Wine experts are discovering that California wines of several varieties and vintages are comparable to many of the best French wines. The result is an increased demand, here and abroad, for California wines." With regard to the U.S. balance on current account, this trend will
    a. increase the U.S. deficit because of the rise in the price of California wine.
    b. decrease the U.S. deficit because of increased shipments of California wines abroad.
    c. decrease the demand for U.S. dollars.
    d. increase the U.S. demand for French francs.

18. The major impact of a restrictive monetary policy on the domestic exchange rate would be
    a. an increase in the foreign exchange value of the domestic currency.
    b. a decrease in the foreign exchange value of the domestic currency.
    c. no change in the foreign exchange value of the domestic currency.
    d. impossible to predict the impact on the foreign exchange value of the domestic currency.

19. Under a system of flexible exchange rates, which of the following will cause the nation's currency to depreciate in the exchange market?
    a. an increase in foreign incomes
    b. a domestic inflation rate of 10 percent while the nation's trading partners are experiencing stable prices
    c. an increase in domestic interest rates
    d. a reduction in interest rates abroad

20. Expansionary fiscal policy exerts upward pressure on prices, output, and interest rates. As a result, expansionary fiscal policy tends to cause
    a. an appreciation of the exchange rate and a deficit in the current account.
    b. a depreciation of the exchange rate and a surplus in the current account.
    c. an uncertain effect on the exchange rate and a deficit in the current account.
    d. uncertain effects on both the exchange rate and the current account.

DISCUSSION QUESTIONS

1. "Exports pay for a nation's imports. Other countries will not continue shipping us their goods if they lose interest in the goods, services, and financial assets we export to them in exchange." Do you agree? Explain.

2. "No patriotic American wants the value of the dollar to fall on the foreign exchange market." Whether or not this quote is true, it is fair to say that Americans seem to like a strong dollar and a trade surplus.
    a. What are the advantages of a strong dollar? the disadvantages?
    b. What are the advantages of a trade surplus? the disadvantages?
    c. Why is it difficult to have both a strong dollar and a trade surplus at the same time?

3. In today's world of flexible exchange rates and mobile financial assets, a country's domestic macroeconomic policies and its foreign sector are closely interrelated. Economists focus especially on the interaction between domestic policies, interest rates, exchange rates, and international capital flows.
   a. How can a budget deficit contribute to capital inflows and an offsetting current account deficit?
   b. With flexible exchange rates, why does trade protection tend to be ineffective as a cure for a current account deficit?
   c. Some economists have recommended that a tax be imposed on international capital flows to reduce their volume. Would you favor such a tax? Why or why not?

4. "A nation's balance of payments must always be in balance." In what sense is this true? What is a "balance-of-payments deficit"? Under a flexible exchange system, will a balance-of-payments deficit automatically be corrected? Explain.

5. "A system of flexible exchange rates is advantageous because it enables a nation to stabilize domestic employment and prices without regard to the foreign sector and insulates a country from the effects of foreign macroeconomic policies." Do you agree or not? Explain.

6. Discuss the role of time in balance-of-payments adjustments. Why might the current account of a country with a depreciating currency deteriorate in the short run and improve in the long run? Why would the opposite scenario for the capital account be surprising?

PERSPECTIVES IN ECONOMICS

DON'T WORRY ABOUT THE TRADE DEFICIT

By Herbert Stein

[From *The Wall Street Journal*, May 16, 1989. Reprinted with permission from *The Wall Street Journal*. Copyright © Dow Jones & Co., Inc. All Rights Reserved.]

There seems to be a conspiracy against telling even the simplest truth.

This somber thought was brought home to me by an experience on a recent Tuesday afternoon. I'm goofing off, staying at home and watching daytime TV. I have a choice of 16 channels. On 15 of them beautiful women and handsome men are working out the complications of their love-lives, mostly in hospital rooms. I know that at my age I cannot expect any of these complications to be resolved during my lifetime, so I settle for C-SPAN and the U.S. Senate at "work."

I'm hearing a senator carrying on about how terrible it is that other countries insist on selling us more stuff than they buy from us. He demands that we let these countries know in no uncertain terms that we are not going to put up with that kind of thing any longer.

Excuses for Economists. At first I am shocked. Is there no limit to what can be put over the air, even in the daytime when children may

be listening? But then I get over it and become more philosophical. I know that this senator has an undergraduate degree from one of our leading liberal arts colleges and another degree from one of our most eminent law schools. He is, however, a senator and may be forgiven for committing nonsense on the public airwaves.

But what about the trained staffs of international financial institutions who write serious reports about the need to correct "imbalances"—which is polite language for eliminating or reducing the U.S. trade deficit? What about the finance ministers from the industrial countries who meet every six months or so to cook up plans for correcting these "imbalances"—again meaning the U.S. trade deficit? And what about my sophisticated economist friends who talk about the need to eliminate the trade deficit? What are they all talking about?

I say to my economist friends that the trade deficit is not hurting the U.S., but, on the contrary, is helping us, and I ask them why we should be concerned about reducing the trade deficit. The more candid among them answer as follows: "We know that the trade deficit is not hurting us. But there are a lot of people out there—including presidents, senators, and congressmen—who think that the trade deficit is a bad thing and as long as it persists they will feel driven to protectionist measures, which would be very bad. In order to restrain the protectionist movement the trade deficit must be reduced."

What this comes down to is an argument for reducing the budget deficit as a way to reduce the trade deficit and thereby head off

Harcourt Brace & Company

protectionism, even though we all know that the trade deficit is not hurting us and does not constitute a valid reason for protectionism.

Readers of this page may know that I am more willing than most people to pay more taxes and give up some of my Social Security and Medicare benefits in order to balance the federal budget and run a surplus. There are good reasons for wanting to do that. But I would hate to pay anything in the hope of thereby heading off protectionism.

Some people have good reason to be protectionist; they have immediate interests at stake. No economist, however much devoted to free trade, ever denied that. These "knowing" protectionists will not be dissuaded by seeing the trade deficit disappear. But most people have no good reason to be protectionist. They support or tolerate protectionism out of ignorance. There should be a more efficient way to convert them to the virtues of free trade than by eliminating the trade deficit. Or, to put the case more modestly, it is worth trying to convert them by telling the truth. That is what economists are for. If some more "devious" ways of avoiding protectionism have to be found, let some one else do it.

Let's remember a few simple propositions.

1. The U.S. has a trade deficit because people in the rest of the world invest their savings here. This inflow of capital is voluntary on both sides—foreigners are seeking the best place to put their money and American governments and companies are seeking the best place to obtain money. Foreigners seeking to invest here have to obtain dollars. Their demand for dollars keep the exchange rate of the dollar at a level where U.S. imports exceed U.S. exports.

2. As a result of the capital inflow—and the accompanying trade deficit—over the past eight years, the stock of productive capital in the U.S. is now about $700 billion higher than it would otherwise have been. This fact is commonly misunderstood because people think the capital inflow is financing the budget deficit. It is true that foreigners have bought a large amount of U.S. Treasury securities. But if foreigners had not bought them they would have had to be bought by Americans, who would have had less of their own savings to invest in productive assets.

3. This inflow of capital has been mainly of benefit to American workers, who as a result of it, work with a larger capital stock and have higher productivity and real incomes. It has also increased the U.S. tax base.

4. Large and persistent trade deficits have not prevented an unusually long recovery and the achievement of an unusually high level of total output.

5. Continuation of the capital inflow-trade deficit combination will increase the amount of interest and dividends that American governments and corporations have to pay to foreigners. But it will also increase the amount of capital in this country that would not otherwise be here, and that additional capital will generate the income to pay for foreigners. That income will not come out of income that Americans would otherwise have earned.

6. The inflow of capital and ownership of assets in the U.S. by foreigners is not a cause of dangerous dependence that is a political or security danger to us. What may be politically dangerous is the effort of governments to manipulate this relationship—an effort to which we are the leaders, unfortunately.

7. The inflow of goods and capital may not go on forever, but it is unlikely to stop so abruptly as to create difficulties for us. The two-sided inflow is an adaptation to basic conditions—propensities to save and investment opportunities at home and abroad—that will change only gradually. The most serious qualification is that government efforts to manage exchange rates may cause such great uncertainties about the future of those rates that international capital flows dry up for a time.

Exchange Rates Everything

8. Protectionist measures imposed by government, ours and others, impair efficiency but do not cause the trade deficit. Trying to eliminate these measures would be worthwhile whether we have a deficit or a surplus, but success would not change the deficit.

9. Having a trade deficit is not a sign of low productivity or economy weakness. Poor, weak countries—like Brazil—can have trade surpluses. Rich, strong countries like us can have trade deficits. Everything depends on prices and exchange rates.

10. Let's forget about the trade deficit. We have plenty of real deficits to worry about—including the education deficit, the defense deficit, the poverty deficit and the investment deficit.

DISCUSSION

1. Do you agree with Stein? Should we worry about the trade deficit? Why or why not?

2. If Stein is right that "rich, strong countries like us can have trade deficits," then why are Congress and the media so concerned with avoiding the current U.S. trade deficit?

3. If the trade deficit isn't hurting the U.S. but policy makers think it is and are considering protectionist policies that *will* hurt the country, which would be easier, fixing the trade deficit or educating the policy makers? Explain your reasoning.

Harcourt Brace & Company

Labor Markets and Unemployment Rates: A Cross-Country Analysis

TRUE OR FALSE

T F

☐ ☐ 1. Unemployment rates in Europe, Canada, and Australia are substantially higher than in the United States and Japan.

☐ ☐ 2. The high rates of unemployment in Europe are due to recessionary economic conditions and high rates of inflation.

☐ ☐ 3. Key differences in unionization, government regulation, and the level of unemployment benefits exist between Europe, Australia, and Canada versus the United States and Japan.

☐ ☐ 4. Countries with the higher rates of unemployment tend to also have a high proportion of employees whose wages are set by collective bargaining agreements.

☐ ☐ 5. The presence of high rates of unionization and collective bargaining allow market-determined wages to better allocate an economy's labor resources.

☐ ☐ 6. Severance pay is a payment that must be made to a worker when he or she is terminated from their employment.

☐ ☐ 7. Regulations requiring companies to pay workers dismissal (or severance) pay generally increase the cost of hiring and firing workers, making capital a more attractive resource for firms.

☐ ☐ 8. The "replacement rate" is the share of previous earnings replaced by unemployment benefits when a worker is unemployed.

☐ ☐ 9. Higher rates of unemployment benefits tend to encourage shorter spells of unemployment and shorter periods of job search among unemployed workers.

☐ ☐ 10. Countries with higher unemployment benefits tend to have higher rates of unemployment.

☐ ☐ 11. Solid labor market reforms, such as those in New Zealand and the United Kingdom, have resulted in lower rates of unemployment.

PROBLEMS AND PROJECTS

1. For each of the following factors, decide whether it would tend to increase (+) or decrease (–) the unemployment rate in the United States.

_____ a. The U.S. federal government passes a new law forcing employers to pay each employee severance pay equal to two months regular wages when the employee is terminated.

_____ b. The dollar value of unemployment benefits are reduced from their current levels.

_____ c. The share of employees whose wages are determined by collective bargaining agreements falls because of declining unionization.

2. Exhibit 1 shows data on the unemployment rates and key indicators of the labor markets in the countries discussed in this application. Use the data to answer the following questions.

EXHIBIT 1

	AUSTRALIA	CANADA	JAPAN	UNITED STATES	FRANCE	GERMANY	ITALY	SPAIN	UNITED KINGDOM
Unemployment Rate (1991–1998)	9.6	10.0	3.0	5.9	11.6	8.0	10.6	20.9	8.7
Percent of employees whose wages are determined by collective bargaining (1995)	80.0	36.0	21.0	18.0	95.0	92.0	82.0	78.0	47.0
Restrictiveness of government dismissal regulations (1995)	1.5	0.6	0.5	0.0	2.1	1.4	11.6	5.2	3.6
Replacement rate of unemployment benefits (1995)	27.0	27.0	10.0	12.0	38.0	26.0	20.0	32.0	18.0

a. Which two countries have the lowest unemployment rates?
b. Which two countries have the lowest percent of employees whose wages are determined by collective bargaining agreements?
c. Which two countries have the lowest government restrictions on dismissal?
d. Which two countries have the lowest rate of unemployment benefits?
e. How do your answers to b, c, and d compare with your answer to a?
f. Which two countries have the highest unemployment rates?
g. Which two countries have the highest percent of employees whose wages are determined by collective bargaining agreements?
h. Which two countries have the highest government restrictions on dismissal?
i. Which two countries have the highest rate of unemployment benefits?
j. How do your answers to g, h, and i compare with your answer to f? Which factors do you think are most highly related to causing high unemployment rates?

MULTIPLE CHOICE

1. Which of the following countries had the lowest unemployment rate over the 1991 through 1998 period?
    a. Spain
    b. Germany
    c. United States
    d. Italy

2. Which of the following helps explain the higher unemployment rates in Europe than in the United States over the past two decades?
    a. Europe was in recession throughout this period, while the United States was not.
    b. Europe had high and variable inflation, while the United States did not.
    c. Europe was consistently above its natural unemployment rate, so this difference is simply a temporary phenomenon.
    d. None of the above.

3. Which of the following countries had a higher unemployment rate than the United States over the 1991 through 1998 period?
    a. Australia
    b. Germany
    c. France
    d. all of the above

4. In Germany and France, collective bargaining agreements set the wages of approximately _____ percent of employees. (Fill in the blank.)
    a. 10
    b. 20
    c. 30
    d. 90

5. Which of the following countries has the lowest share of employees whose wages are set by collective bargaining?
    a. Australia
    b. Canada
    c. Japan
    d. United States

6. Which of the following countries has the most generous unemployment benefits?
    a. France
    b. United Kingdom
    c. Japan
    d. United States

Harcourt Brace & Company

7. (I) Centralized wage setting will have smaller adverse effects in small countries with labor forces that are quite similar in skill levels. (II) Countries with more centralized wage setting tend to have a lower overall unemployment rate.
   a. Both I and II are true.
   b. Both I and II are false.
   c. I is true; II is false.
   d. I is false; II is true.

8. For which age group of workers do restrictive employee dismissal policies increase the unemployment rate the most?
   a. young workers
   b. middle-aged workers
   c. older workers
   d. The policies impact all workers the same.

9. Countries with higher unemployment rates tend to have _____ centralized wage setting, _____ restrictive employee dismissal policies, and _____ generous unemployment benefits. (Fill in the blanks.)
   a. less; more; more
   b. more; less; less
   c. less; less; less
   d. more; more; more

10. If an unemployed worker previously earned $1,000 per week at his job and is now receiving unemployment benefits of $600, the replacement rate of the unemployment benefits is
    a. 6 percent.
    b. 40 percent.
    c. 60 percent.
    d. 100 percent.

11. Compared to the United States and Japan, the labor markets in Europe, Canada, and Australia have
    a. higher unionization and collective bargaining.
    b. more generous unemployment benefits.
    c. more regulations about hiring and firing workers.
    d. all of the above.

12. Since 1980, the United Kingdom has _____ the generosity of its unemployment benefit program and the unemployment rate has _____. (Fill in the blanks.)
    a. decreased; decreased
    b. increased; increased
    c. increased; decreased
    d. decreased; increased

DISCUSSION QUESTIONS

1. Are the higher rates of unemployment in Europe, Canada, and Australia the result of short-run, temporary factors (such as a recession) or the result of bigger underlying problems that are raising the long-run natural rate of unemployment?

2. How does the generosity of unemployment benefits affect the rate of unemployment? Carefully discuss the linkage between job search time and the rate of unemployment in a country.

3. Why does centralized collective bargaining tend to raise the rate of unemployment? Does it make labor markets better or less able to adjust to changing economic conditions.

4. What is severance pay? How does it affect the cost of hiring new workers? the cost of terminating workers? the unemployment rate among which age groups are most affected by such policies?

5. Summarize the main reasons why Europe, Australia, and Canada have higher rates of unemployment than the United States and Japan. What reforms could these countries adopt to lower their unemployment rates?

Harcourt Brace & Company

Social Security: The Nature of the Problem and Alternatives for Dealing with It

TRUE OR FALSE

T F

☐ ☐ 1. The Social Security program in the United States takes the taxes collected from present workers and saves this money for their retirement.

☐ ☐ 2. When a current worker pays Social Security taxes, the majority of that money is directly paid out to current retirees rather than being saved.

☐ ☐ 3. The downward trend in the number of workers per retiree requires that higher social security tax rates be used just to maintain a constant level of benefits for retirees.

☐ ☐ 4. In terms of benefits received relative to taxes paid, today's workers will fare much better than workers have in the past.

☐ ☐ 5. For a worker aged thirty-five or younger, the rate of return they will receive on their Social Security contributions exceeds what could have been earned if they had invested the money personally.

☐ ☐ 6. The share of the population aged seventy or over will continue to rise as the baby boom generation ages.

☐ ☐ 7. Essentially, the surplus of the Social Security system exists only on paper. The federal government used this money to finance current government spending by issuing U.S. Treasury bonds.

☐ ☐ 8. For Social Security to spend its trust fund will require the federal government to either raise taxes or cut other spending to repay the trust fund money it has borrowed.

☐ ☐ 9. Investing the Social Security trust fund in the stock market might delay the financial problems for several years, but many concerns exist about whether the government might abuse its ability to manipulate the stock prices of one or many corporations.

☐ ☐ 10. In Chile, when workers were given an option to switch to a private investment fund, most decided to stay with the government program and have since earned more money for their retirement than they would have in the private funds.

T F

☐ ☐ 11. The average worker in the baby boom generation would have had at least $200,000 of additional retirement dollars had their money been invested in a private investment rather than Social Security.

☐ ☐ 12. The benefits a person receives from Social Security rise in direct proportion to his or her average annual earnings.

☐ ☐ 13. Most married women who work will receive virtually no additional benefits relative to if they had not worked (and not paid Social Security taxes) at all.

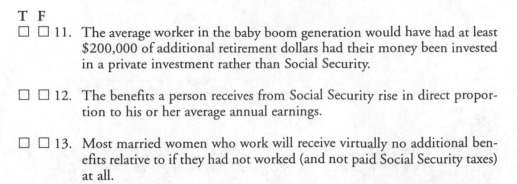

PROBLEMS AND PROJECTS

1. Social Security is a "pay-as-you-go" system, so the money paid out in benefits to current retirees comes from tax collections on current workers. One of the main problems facing Social Security is the declining number of workers per retiree in the United States. Suppose that Social Security wishes to pay benefits of $15,000 per year to each retiree. If there were ten workers per retiree, this would mean each current worker would have to pay, on average, $1,500 in taxes per year to support this level of benefits for each retired person.
   a. In the 1950s, there were approximately fifteen workers per retiree. How much would each worker in the 1950s have to pay in taxes each year to support a level of benefits equal to $15,000 per year per retiree?
   b. By 1998, this ratio had fallen such that there were approximately three workers per retiree. How much would each worker in 1998 have to pay in taxes each year to support a level of benefits equal to $15,000 per year per retiree?
   c. By 2025, this ratio will fall to approximately two workers per retiree. How much will each worker in 2025 have to pay in taxes each year to support a level of benefits equal to $15,000 per year per retiree?
   d. As this ratio falls in the future, the alternative to increasing taxes is to cut benefits. If the amount of *taxes* per worker is held constant between 1998 and 2025, by how much will benefits to each retiree have to be reduced?

2. Suppose you have been saving for a new boat by putting cash in an old shoe box in your house. So far you have saved $5,000. Your spouse, however, has been running a "deficit" and has borrowed all of the money and left IOUs (notes promising to repay the money) in the box.
   a. Technically do you have $5,000 saved for your boat?
   b. If you went to buy the boat and needed the money, what would it require your spouse do?
   c. How does this example differ from the Social Security trust fund, which has been "invested" in U.S. Treasury bonds?

3. Workers born between 1945 and 1964 will earn a real rate of return of about 1.8 percent from their Social Security contributions. This same money, if invested in

the stock market, would have given approximately a 7 percent rate of return. A frequently used tool in finance is the "rule of 72," which states that the number of years it will take for an investment to double (with compound interest) is equal to 72 divided by the rate of return. With a rate of return of 1.8 percent, this implies that a given amount of money invested would double every forty years. On the other hand, at a rate of return of 7 percent, the money would double almost every ten years.

a. Using these values, if you placed $20,000 in a retirement account invested in the stock market at age twenty-five, it would grow to $40,000 by the time you were thirty-five, to $80,000 by the time you were forty-five, to $160,000 by the time you were fifty-five, and to $320,000 by the time you retired at age sixty-five. How does this compare to the amount you would have at age sixty-five had you earned the 1.8 percent offered by the Social Security program?

b. If a worker selected a private retirement plan that was safer than the stock market and so only earned a 3.6 percent rate of return, how much additional money would they have at age sixty-five than at the 1.8 percent rate?

c. Because Social Security pays current tax revenue out to current recipients ("pay-as-you-go" system), there is no real savings involved in the program. Many economists believe that the structure of the system has lowered the savings rate in our economy, which in turn lowers investment and economic growth. The system is approximately seventy-two years old. Suppose that it has lowered our rate of economic growth by 1 percentage point per year. If these numbers were accurate, how much larger would our economy be today if Social Security had not been adopted?

d. You may have heard that it is much better to save a little bit when you are younger than to save a lot when you are older. Use a 7.2 percent rate of return (so the money doubles every ten years) to figure out the following amounts. If you placed $10,000 in an account when you were twenty-five, how much would you have in the account when you turned sixty-five? How much would you have at age sixty-five if you had put $15,000 in when you were twenty-five? Suppose you waited until age thirty-five to put money in an account. How much would you have to deposit at age thirty-five to have the same amount at age sixty-five as if you placed $10,000 in when you were twenty-five? if you waited until age forty-five?

MULTIPLE CHOICE

1. Social Security
   a. collects taxes from current workers and invests this money to repay the workers when they retire.
   b. is based on the same principles as private insurance programs.
   c. is an intergenerational transfer program that takes money from current workers and transfers it to current retirees.
   d. is designed so that administrative decisions can be made independent of political concerns.

Harcourt Brace & Company

2. Which of the following best explains why the Social Security system is expected to face financial difficulties in the near future?
   a. Too much Social Security revenue was invested in the private sector rather than in government bonds.
   b. The federal government does not pay interest on the money it borrows from the Social Security system.
   c. The funds in the Social Security trust fund were invested in high-risk ventures that failed to pay off.
   d. The number of workers paying into the system is expected to decline relative to the number of retirees collecting benefits.

3. When the Social Security system enters its deficit years and the bonds held in the trust funds are drawn down,
   a. overall taxes will be reduced as the trust funds are used to pay benefits to retirees.
   b. the payroll taxes used to finance Social Security benefits can be reduced because the trust funds will be sufficient to pay the retirement benefits of the baby boom generation.
   c. income and other federal taxes will have to be raised (or additional funds will have to be borrowed) in order to redeem the bonds held by the trust fund.
   d. income taxes will have to be reduced in order to keep the revenues and expenditures of the Social Security system in balance.

4. In approximately what year will Social Security outlays begin to exceed revenues?
   a. 1999
   b. 2014
   c. 2050
   d. 3030

5. In approximately what year will the Social Security trust fund be depleted?
   a. 1999
   b. 2032
   c. 2050
   d. 3030

6. (I) Current Social Security retirees typically receive real benefits that are equal to three or four times the amount of their contributions into the system. (II) Current young workers can expect to receive real benefits less than their contributions into the system.
   a. I is true; II is false.
   b. I is false; II is true.
   c. Both I and II are false.
   d. Both I and II are true.

7. The surplus in the Social Security retirement system is currently held in the form of
    a. U.S. Treasury bonds.
    b. gold.
    c. U.S. corporate stock.
    d. cash reserves in major U.S. banks.

8. The Social Security system is currently generating tax revenues that exceed the benefits paid to recipients. This surplus is
    a. being invested in foreign bonds, which will provide Americans with a source of income when the baby boom generation retires.
    b. being invested in government bonds, which will require an increase in general tax revenues when the bonds come due.
    c. separated from other government revenue so politicians will not spend the money during the current period.
    d. being channeled into earmarked private savings accounts.

9. As the baby boom generation retires in the future, Social Security will have to
    a. reduce benefits to retirees.
    b. increase taxes on workers.
    c. borrow money.
    d. Some combination of a, b, and c will be utilized.

10. The Social Security payroll tax does not apply to annual income above
    a. $15,000.
    b. $32,000.
    c. $65,400.
    d. $100,000.

11. Jim earns an average of $40,000 per year, while Bob earns an average of $50,000 per year. When they retire, Bob can expect to receive annual Social Security benefits that are
    a. equal to what Jim receives.
    b. $1,500 more than Jim receives.
    c. $10,000 more than Jim receives.
    d. $20,000 more than Jim receives.

12. Most married women who choose to work can expect to receive
    a. substantially higher Social Security benefits than if they had not worked and thus not paid into the system.
    b. substantially lower Social Security benefits than if they had not worked and thus not paid into the system.
    c. approximately the same Social Security benefits than if they had not worked and thus not paid into the system.
    d. benefits equal to their husbands salary plus 50 percent of their own salary.

13. Which of the following is a concern if the government is allowed to invest Social Security funds in the stock market?
    a. When the stock market fluctuates, government may be tempted to use its policy to intervene with so much money at stake.
    b. As the government withdraws its money in large amounts, stock prices might fall substantially.
    c. The government may be tempted to favor some firms over others, perhaps because they have provided campaign contributions.
    d. All of the above.

14. Which of the following countries has not taken steps to privatize its Social Security system?
    a. United States
    b. Mexico
    c. United Kingdom
    d. Argentina

15. Which of the following is true regarding Chile's privatized Social Security program?
    a. The majority of workers chose to remain in the government system when offered the choice to switch to private investment funds.
    b. Those who switched to private investment funds will generally have less for their retirement than if they had stayed in the government program.
    c. As a result of privatization, the overall rate of savings has risen, stimulating investment and a higher rate of economic growth in Chile.
    d. When workers left the government system, they lost all of the money they had previously contributed.

DISCUSSION QUESTIONS

1. If given a choice between remaining in the government Social Security program or switching to a private investment fund, which would you choose? What factors would be the most important in your decision?

2. The two most frequently discussed reform options for Social Security are to (1) allow the government to invest money in the stock market or (2) either partially or fully privatize the Social Security program.
    a. What potential drawbacks are there of allowing the government to invest Social Security money in the stock market? What would be the advantages?
    b. What potential drawbacks are there of privatizing Social Security? What would be the advantages?

3. What is the difference between a "fully-funded" system and a "pay-as-you-go" Social Security system? How would the problems facing the Social Security system have been different if the system had been fully funded from the beginning?

Harcourt Brace & Company

The Stock Market: What Does It Do and How Has It Performed?

TRUE OR FALSE

T F

☐ ☐ 1. During the 1980s and 1990s, the real returns from stock market investment have been far worse than the long-term average of 7 percent.

☐ ☐ 2. An investor may lower the risk of his or her portfolio by holding shares of many different firms in unconnected industries.

☐ ☐ 3. While the stock market may vary substantially from day to day, if stocks are held over long periods of time the variation in return is relatively small.

☐ ☐ 4. More than 40 percent of all households in the U.S. now own stock either directly or through investment in a mutual fund.

☐ ☐ 5. Periods of low inflation and low interest rates will generally be accompanied by a poorly performing stock market.

☐ ☐ 6. The random walk theory of the stock market suggests that current stock prices already reflect the best-known information about the future values of stocks.

☐ ☐ 7. The highest return and lowest risk can generally be earned by an investor who is willing to frequently buy and sell large quantities of individual stocks for quick profit.

☐ ☐ 8. The general consensus among all forecasters is that stock prices must fall because the Dow Jones Industrial Average cannot sustain a value above 10,000.

☐ ☐ 9. Mutual funds allow small investors with limited investment budgets to obtain lower risk and more diversity in their portfolios than if the investors had to purchase individual stocks.

☐ ☐ 10. When a corporation originally issues stock, this is done in the primary market. The more familiar secondary markets are where investors trade the ownership rights embodied in stocks that were previously issued.

☐ ☐ 11. When a person purchases a stock, they are effectively lending a corporation money, which will be repaid to the stockholder at a future date.

Harcourt Brace & Company

PROBLEMS AND PROJECTS

1. Underlying the current price of a firm's stock is the present value of the firm's expected future net earnings or profit. For each of the following, indicate whether the change would result in an increase or decrease in the present value of a firm's future net earnings.
   _____ a. The interest rate increases.
   _____ b. There is an increase in the annual dividend the corporation is expected to pay.
   _____ c. The corporation withholds this year's dividend and uses the money to make an investment that is expected to be extremely profitable in the future.

2. Use the present value formula in the text to compute the current value of each of the following streams of future income.
   a. a payment of $100 one year from now and a payment of $100 two years from now, when the interest rate is 10 percent
   b. a payment of $100 one year from now and a payment of $100 two years from now, when the interest rate is 5 percent
   c. a payment of $150 one year from now and a payment of $50 two years from now, when the interest rate is 10 percent
   d. a payment of $100 one year from now and a payment of $150 two years from now, when the interest rate is 10 percent
   e. a payment of $150 one year from now and a payment of $150 two years from now, when the interest rate is 10 percent

MULTIPLE CHOICE

1. Investors can make their investments in corporate stocks less risky by
   a. purchasing shares of a mutual fund, which holds the stocks of many diverse corporations.
   b. buying stocks and holding them each for only for short periods of time.
   c. investing in firms that are in the same, rather than different, industries.
   d. none of the above.

2. Which of the following would reduce the risk of an investment in the stock market?
   a. investing in a portfolio of diverse firms
   b. holding the investment for a long period of time
   c. both a and b
   d. neither a nor b

Harcourt Brace & Company

3. Historically, when a diverse set of stocks are held over a lengthy time period, stocks have yielded a _____ rate of return and the variation in the rate of return has been _____. (Fill in the blanks.)
   a. low; low
   b. low; high
   c. high; low
   d. high; high

4. (I) The market for new issues of stock is called the primary market. (II) The New York Stock Exchange is an example of a secondary market in which previously issued shares are traded between investors.
   a. I is true; II is false.
   b. I is false; II is true.
   c. Both I and II are true.
   d. Both I and II are false.

5. An increase in interest rates coupled with higher inflation would tend to
   a. result in higher stock prices.
   b. result in lower stock prices.
   c. have a mixed result on stock prices as higher interest rates lower prices, while higher inflation raises prices.
   d. increase stock prices if corporate earnings were falling but decrease stock prices if corporate earnings were rising.

6. Because it is based on the present value of future earnings and dividends, the current price of stock would
   a. decline if interest rates fell.
   b. increase if expected future profits were to increase.
   c. increase if the time until a future dividend payment was suddenly delayed farther into the future.
   d. decrease if next year's expected dividend was larger.

7. A lower and more stable inflation rate results in
   a. a higher tax burden on capital gains.
   b. less uncertainty on investment and other long-term contracts.
   c. lower stock prices.
   d. all of the above.

8. According to the random walk theory, which of the following is true?
   a. Stock prices reflect all available information about factors that affect stock prices.
   b. Future movements of stock prices are unpredictable.
   c. Changes in stock prices are driven by surprise occurrences.
   d. All of the above.

9. Which of the following is true?
   a. Lower corporate earnings would tend to cause an increase in stock prices.
   b. If baby boomers begin to withdraw their money from the stock market to pay for their retirement, the stock market should surge upward.
   c. Because the profitability of U.S. corporations underlies the stock market, changes in the wealth and prosperity of foreign nations generally do not affect U.S. stock prices.
   d. If inflation in the U.S. was to rise and become more unstable, stock prices would fall.

10. The real returns from stock market investment over the past twenty years have been
   a. roughly equal to the long-term average of 7 percent.
   b. higher than the long-term average.
   c. lower than the long-term average.
   d. negative in each year except 1991.

DISCUSSION QUESTIONS

1. A friend of yours just inherited $100,000 and asks your opinion on the best way to invest the money for her retirement. She wants to earn the highest return possible but also wants to have a relatively low-risk investment. What advice would you give her? Would your advice depend on her current age?

2. What factors have contributed to the relatively high performance of the stock market over the past twenty years? Based upon what might happen to these same factors in the future, how do you expect the stock market to perform in the near future?

3. The random walk theory holds that all available information is already reflected in stock prices. Therefore, stock prices change due to new, surprise information. The result is that stock prices move in a random, unpredictable, fashion. What does this theory imply about
   a. how well a person who picks stocks by throwing darts at the newspaper will do relative to someone who spends hours picking their stocks based upon detailed research.
   b. how well someone will do who holds on to one portfolio of stocks for many years relative to someone who buys and sells stocks frequently.
   c. the current price of the stock of XYZ corporation relative to the price of ABC corporation stock if XYZ is expected to earn more profits in the future than ABC.

Harcourt Brace & Company

How Does Government Regulation Affect Your Life?

TRUE OR FALSE

T F

☐ ☐ 1. Traditional economic regulation of product price or industrial structure is a relatively recent phenomenon beginning in the 1960s.

☐ ☐ 2. The demand for regulation often stems from the desire of special interest groups to increase their wealth at the expense of others, rather than the pursuit of economic efficiency.

☐ ☐ 3. Because specific regulations are set by agencies that are knowledgeable about the industries they regulate, the rules and regulations imposed tend to be very flexible and change relatively quickly in response to changes in market conditions.

☐ ☐ 4. One of the shortcomings of regulatory agencies is that with the passage of time they tend to represent broad groups such as workers and consumers at the expense of the businesses they regulate.

☐ ☐ 5. Economic theory suggests that the added production costs required to meet government regulations are generally not passed on to consumers.

☐ ☐ 6. The full cost of government regulation is reflected in the government budget because the government must compensate consumers and businesses for the added costs created by government regulations.

☐ ☐ 7. Some regulations are much more cost effective at saving lives than are others. Thus, a reallocation of money could result in more lives being saved for the same amount of total cost to society.

☐ ☐ 8. Health and safety regulation is designed to improve the health, safety, and environmental conditions available to workers and/or consumers.

☐ ☐ 9. In recent decades, regulatory policy has shifted heavily toward traditional economic regulation and away from health and safety regulation.

☐ ☐ 10. American cars are approximately five hundred pounds heavier than they would have been without the CAFE standards, making them more sturdy and safe for occupants when in an accident.

☐ ☐ 11. Because the deaths caused by delaying the approval of new drugs onto the market are less visible than deaths that occur from the approval of unsafe drugs, regulatory agencies have a tendency to be too cautious in allowing new drugs into the marketplace.

PROBLEMS AND PROJECTS

1. Reproduced below in Exhibit 1 is the data on the median cost per life year saved for various regulatory agencies from the text. These values represent the cost per *single year of life saved* by the policies of the agency. Use this data when answering the following questions.

EXHIBIT 1

REGULATIONS AND DIFFERENCES IN THE COST OF SAVING LIVES

AGENCY	MEDIAN COST PER LIFE YEAR SAVED
Federal Aviation Administration	$23,000
Consumer Product Safety Commission	$68,000
National Highway Transportation Safety Administration	$78,000
Occupational Safety and Health Administration	$88,000
Environmental Protection Agency	$7,600,000

   a. For every life year saved by Environmental Protection Agency (EPA) regulations, approximately how many life years are lost as the result of this money not alternatively being devoted toward Federal Aviation Administration (FAA) regulations?

   b. Suppose you were given $10,000,000 and were asked to allocate it across the agencies listed in the table. If your goal was to maximize the number of lives saved with this additional money, how would you allocate it?

   c. If the government was attempting to maximize the number of lives saved by regulations, how might you expect these numbers to differ? (Hint: We might expect the law of diminishing returns to apply, in that the cost per life year saved increases as the budget size increases.)

2. For each of the following regulations, decide whether you would expect the variable listed to increase (+), decrease (–), or remain unchanged (0) if the regulation was to be imposed.

	Variable	Regulation
_____ a.	Price of new cars	All new cars must have airbags in the rear seats.
_____ b.	Price of airline tickets	All airplanes must install new fire barriers in the cargo (luggage) area.
_____ c.	Number of AIDS deaths	New AIDS medicines must be tested for fifteen years before being sold on the market.
_____ d.	Rental rate for housing	Landlords must provide smoke detectors, carbon monoxide detectors, and fire extinguishers in each rental property.

Harcourt Brace & Company

_____ e. Pollution   All new cars sold after December 31, must emit zero pollution. (Hint: Think about the cost of producing these new cars, and how it would change the incentive to purchase a new car.)

MULTIPLE CHOICE

1. The concept of economic regulation typically involves
   a. the regulation of product price.
   b. the regulation of production processes.
   c. the regulation of industrial structure.
   d. both *a* and *c*, but not *b*.

2. Regulations covering health and safety
   a. act like a subsidy to consumers, shifting out demand and lowering prices.
   b. act like a price ceiling, creating a shortage of the good regulated.
   c. act like a tax on producers, shifting in supply and raising prices.
   d. cannot be shown in a supply and demand diagram.

3. Use statements I and II to answer this question. (I) Regulation tends to be inflexible; it often fails to adjust very rapidly to dynamic changes in competitive markets. (II) The demand for regulation often stems from organized groups seeking to gain personal profit from the regulation, rather than from forces seeking an economically efficient solution.
   a. I is true; II is false.
   b. I is false; II is true.
   c. Both I and II are true.
   d. Both I and II are false.

4. Which of the following would be most likely to be supported by workers and executives in the natural gas industry?
   a. a law requiring all firms that now get more than 90 percent of their energy from electricity to reduce their reliance on electricity and find alternative energy sources
   b. a law requiring all homes that use natural gas to undergo expensive annual inspections for potentially dangerous natural gas leaks
   c. a regulation that requires firms producing electricity to install expensive antipollution devices
   d. The natural gas industry would likely support both *a* and *c*, but not *b*.

Harcourt Brace & Company

5. Regulation that requires the producers of a product to adopt more costly production techniques will
    a. increase supply and lead to a lower market price of the product.
    b. decrease supply and lead to a higher market price of the product.
    c. increase demand and lead to a higher market price of the product.
    d. leave the market price unchanged since producers are forced to bear the burden of regulatory costs.

6. During the last few decades, health and safety regulations have increased in the U.S. economy. Economic theory suggests that
    a. the expansion of health and safety regulations have improved the efficiency of the market since the value of each life saved by such regulations is infinite.
    b. the net benefits of health and safety regulation are difficult to determine. Information problems in the market reduce the efficiency of the market but also make it difficult to craft effective regulations.
    c. the expansion of health and safety regulations have substantially reduced the efficiency of the market.
    d. none of the above. Health and safety regulations are imposed for noneconomic reasons and are beyond the scope of economic analysis.

7. Homeowners in a housing development have successfully induced the local government to restrict the future building of homes (and apartments) in surrounding areas for environmental reasons. The long-run economic impact of this policy will be to
    a. increase the selling price of homes already built in the development.
    b. reduce the rental price of existing apartments in the area.
    c. decrease the demand for homes in the development.
    d. lower the wealth of persons who currently own housing in the development.

8. Which of the following statements is true?
    a. Recent trends have been toward imposing less traditional economic regulation but more health and safety regulation.
    b. The compliance costs for regulations generally far exceed the budget sizes of the agencies imposing the regulations.
    c. Agencies involved in health and safety regulation usually have regulatory power over more industries than those agencies conducting traditional economic regulation.
    d. All of the above are true.

9. Public choice analysis indicates that
    a. the demand for regulation often stems from the special interest effect rather than from the pursuit of economic efficiency.
    b. with the passage of time, regulatory agencies will often adopt the views of the business interests they are supposed to regulate.
    c. the demand for regulation often stems from the efforts of some businesses to limit the intensity of competition.
    d. all of the above are true.

Harcourt Brace & Company

10. When regulatory approval is required before a new product can be introduced, economic analysis indicates that the regulatory agency
    a. will generally approve new products too rapidly from the viewpoint of economic efficiency.
    b. will generally approve new products too slowly from the viewpoint of economic efficiency.
    c. will generally approve new products at exactly the rate consistent with economic efficiency.
    d. None of the above.

11. Whenever regulations are imposed on how a product must be produced, these added regulatory costs will
    a. reduce the supply of the product, causing the price of the product to rise to consumers.
    b. result in an increase in the supply of the product and lower a product price.
    c. drive all firms in the industry out of business in the long run.
    d. generally come out of the profits of the firms and not be passed on to consumers in the form of higher prices.

12. If a new regulation was passed requiring all new automobiles to get ninety miles per gallon of fuel, this would most likely cause
    a. higher auto prices and higher producer profits in the long run.
    b. higher auto prices and leave producer profits unchanged in the long run.
    c. higher auto prices and lower producer profits in the long run.
    d. no change in auto prices and lower producer profits in the long run.

13. Evidence shows that the imposition of CAFE standards requiring car makers to build cars that get more miles per gallon of fuel
    a. increased the number of lives lost due to auto accidents.
    b. resulted in manufacturers building cars with more heavy metals.
    c. lowered the price of cars.
    d. resulted in lower total fuel consumption.

14. The cost per life year saved by the Environmental Protection Agency (EPA) is
    a. approximately $7,600,000.
    b. more than 330 times the cost per life year saved for the Federal Aviation Administration (FAA).
    c. so high that more lives could be saved for the same total cost by shifting resources toward other agencies.
    d. all of the above.

DISCUSSION QUESTIONS

1. How does social regulation differ from economic regulation? Why is social regulation more difficult to administer than economic regulation? Do the higher

costs of social regulation make it less desirable than economic regulation? Explain.

2. Suppose the government uses licensing to limit the number of firms in the retail liquor industry. Thus, ignoring the cost of a license, firms in the industry make substantial economic profit.
    a. Analyze the price, costs, and profits of firms when the limited number of licenses (good for five years) is auctioned off to the highest bidders. Assume that ownership of the licenses is widespread, so there is no problem in collusion.
    b. Analyze the price, costs, and profits of firms when the limited number of licenses is granted "free" to persons approved by a committee appointed by the legislature (or governor).
    c. When choosing between these two, state legislatures have almost exclusively chosen the alternative in part b. Can you explain why?

3. Would a business be willing to make their product safer if customers valued the improved safety enough to pay a higher price for the product? If businesses are out for profit, which safety improvements will they undertake (with respect to cost of production versus benefit to the consumer)? If customers are not willing to pay enough to cover the added cost of the safety improvement, but the government mandates it through regulation anyway, how will this affect consumer welfare? Explain.

4. Economists have argued that some regulatory agencies are more efficient than others, when efficiency is measured as the number of dollars spent per life saved by the regulatory activities of a given agency. Noneconomists are often repulsed by the willingness of economists to attach a dollar value to human life. Can human life be measured by a dollar value? Can you think of ways that individuals place a dollar value on their own lives, by making choices about how much to spend to preserve their lives? If someone died in an accident, how would you go about placing a value on their life if you were on a jury that had to decide upon a specific dollar amount for the settlement to the family of the person killed?

5. Do you think that government decisions about regulation are subject to the same political pressures as other decisions made by government? If so, what inherent conflicts do you expect to see between economically efficient regulation and the regulations adopted through the political process?

Harcourt Brace & Company

Income Inequality, Transfers, and the Role of Government

TRUE OR FALSE

T F

☐ ☐ 1. There has been virtually no significant change in the poverty rate in the United States since 1970.

☐ ☐ 2. As a percent of GDP, government spending on transfer programs and health care have more than doubled since 1960.

☐ ☐ 3. The percent of children living in poverty has fallen over the past twenty years.

☐ ☐ 4. Opponents of government action to correct income inequality argue that the pattern of economic outcomes (such as the observed distribution of income) is not nearly as important as the fairness of the process that generates the outcome.

☐ ☐ 5. The high implicit marginal tax rates in the transfer system greatly lower the incentive of welfare recipients to earn income.

☐ ☐ 6. When people remain out of the workforce for long periods of time, their productivity generally increases, making them more employable.

☐ ☐ 7. Recent federal and state welfare reforms have resulted in significant increases in welfare caseloads in the United States.

☐ ☐ 8. Because there will always be competition to obtain subsidies and transfers from government, recipients generally receive a net gain significantly lower than the value of the subsidy or transfer obtained.

☐ ☐ 9. When a subsidy is tied to the ownership of an asset (such as taxicab medallions), the value of the asset will rise until it reflects the full value of the subsidy.

☐ ☐ 10. Government actions to reduce poverty and income inequality generally have harmful secondary effects (such as lower economic growth, reductions in available jobs, or the creation of adverse incentives) that can either partially or fully offset the intended outcome of the actions taken.

PROBLEMS AND PROJECTS

1. Exhibit 1 shows data on how the 1994 net transfer benefits a representative mother with two children living in Pennsylvania would change as her earned income rises. Follow the questions below to fill in the missing values in the table.

EXHIBIT 1

GROSS ANNUAL EARNED INCOME FROM WORK		NET TRANSFER BENEFITS		DISPOSABLE INCOME	CHANGE IN EARNED INCOME	CHANGE IN NET TRANSFER BENEFITS	IMPLICIT MARGINAL TAX RATE
$0	+	$7,548	=	$7,548	N/A	N/A	N/A
2,000	+	6,923	=	8,923	$2,000	−$625	31.3%
4,000	+	5,290	=	9,290			
6,000	+	3,657	=	9,657			
8,000	+	1,956	=	9,956			
10,000	+	937	=	10,937			

a. When the mother does not work and thus has no earned income, she receives $7,548 in transfer benefits. In this case her disposable (spendable) income is $7,548. Whenever her income from work rises to $2,000, her transfer benefits (net of taxes) fall to $6,923. Her new level of disposable income is $8,923. The change columns show that between these two cases, her earned income increased by $2,000 (the new level of $2,000 minus the old level of $0). However, the change in her transfer benefits was a decrease of $625 (the new level of $6,923 minus the old level of $7,548). In this range she faces an implicit marginal tax rate of 31.3 percent ($625 ÷ $2,000). What this means is that for every dollar of earned income she received, her disposable income rose by only 68.7 cents (100 − 31.3). Using this example, fill in the missing values in the table.

b. Between which two levels of income do her net transfer benefits fall by the most? In that range, how much additional disposable income (in dollars) does she receive when she earns the additional $2,000 of earned income?

c. Suppose this mother is not currently working but is offered a full-time job making $10,000 per year. By how much would her family's disposable income increase if she takes the job? Can you think of any offsetting costs that might be larger than the additional income?

d. Suppose this mother had no reported income but could find a way to earn $3,500 of unreported income (perhaps in the black market or by doing unreported small jobs). Would she have more disposable income than if she took a full-time job earning $10,000 per year?

2. Exhibit 2 shows data on the income distribution in a three-person economy. Before working the following questions, calculate the percent of total income

Harcourt Brace & Company

earned by each individual in the economy for cases two, three, and four. Case one is already done as an example.

EXHIBIT 2							
	CASE 1		CASE 2		CASE 3		CASE 4	
PERSON	INCOME	PERCENT OF TOTAL INCOME	INCOME	PERCENT OF TOTAL INCOME	INCOME	PERCENT OF TOTAL INCOME	INCOME	PERCENT OF TOTAL INCOME
Ann Rich	$100	50%	$200	_____	$45	_____	$330	_____
Mike Middle	60	30	120	_____	30	_____	180	_____
Rob Low	40	20	80	_____	25	_____	90	_____
Totals	$200	100%	$400	100%	$100	100%	$600	100%

a. Compare the percent of income earned by the richest person and the poorest person in each case. Which case would you say has the most *unequal* distribution of income? Which case has the most *equal* distribution of income?

b. Suppose through time this economy originally began with case one and moved to case two. Has the distribution of income become more or less equal or has it stayed the same? Who is better or worse off in case two relative to case one in terms of the money income they have?

c. Suppose instead that the economy moved from case one to case three. Here, has the distribution of income become more or less equal or has it stayed the same? Who is better or worse off in case three relative to case one in terms of the money income they have?

d. Suppose instead that the economy moved from case one to case four. Here, has the distribution of income become more or less equal or has it stayed the same? Who is better or worse off in case three relative to case one in terms of the money income they have?

e. Finally, assume that beginning from case one, these individuals could choose between which government policy they would prefer, one leading to case two, one leading to case three, and the other to case four. Which do you think Ann would prefer? Mike? Rob?

f. Over the past thirty years, average real income in the United States has doubled, but at the same time, the distribution of income has become more unequal. Based upon your answers above, has this increase in inequality necessarily made someone worse off?

3. Consider a case in which there are two neighboring states, State A and State B, with equal average income levels and equal distributions of income. Suppose that State A decides to declare a "war on poverty" and adopts legislation that substantially raises the income taxes on upper-income individuals in order to provide rather generous benefits to lower-income individuals living in the state.

a. If people could easily move between the two states, what do you think would happen to the relative number of poor and rich people in the two states?

Harcourt Brace & Company

b. If the movement you found in part a happens, how will this influence the ability of State A to provide benefits to lower-income individuals?

c. Will the resulting distributions of income within States A and B be more or less unequal than they were before? Explain.

d. Suppose instead of moving to State B, the richer people in State A simply decide to work less at the higher tax rates. How will this influence the ability of State A to provide benefits to lower income individuals?

MULTIPLE CHOICE

1. During the 1965 through 1997 period, expenditures on income transfers (including means-tested transfers directed toward those with low incomes) have _____ as a share of GDP. Since 1970, the overall official poverty rate in the United States has _____. (Fill in the blanks.)
    a. declined; increased
    b. increased; changed very little
    c. increased; declined
    d. declined; changed very little

2. In 1997, the overall official poverty rate was approximately
    a. 5 percent.
    b. 8 percent.
    c. 13 percent.
    d. 40 percent.

3. Between 1965 and 1997, real income per person in the United States
    a. fell in half.
    b. fell but only slightly.
    c. remained about the same.
    d. about doubled.

4. (I) The high implicit marginal tax rates that accompany the current transfer system substantially reduce the incentive of low-income families to earn more and thereby escape poverty. (II) When the poor opt out of the labor force, declining skills further limit their ability to escape poverty in the future.
    a. Both I and II are true.
    b. Both I and II are false.
    c. I is true; II is false.
    d. I is false; II is true.

5. (I) The collapse of the two-parent family has resulted in higher poverty rates and more income inequality. (II) The poverty rate of children has been steadily declining in the United States for the past several decades.
    a. Both I and II are true.
    b. Both I and II are false.
    c. I is true; II is false.
    d. I is false; II is true.

6. Which of the following was a feature of the 1996 welfare reform legislation?
   a. Limits were placed on the length of time recipients could receive welfare benefits.
   b. Most heads of families drawing benefits must begin to work within two years.
   c. All welfare payments are now loans and must be repaid within twenty years.
   d. Both a and b were part of the 1996 legislation; c was not.

7. Since the passage of the 1996 welfare reform legislation, welfare caseloads have
   a. risen substantially.
   b. risen slightly.
   c. stayed about the same.
   d. fallen substantially.

8. Which of the following is true?
   a. Governments establish a qualification criterion to limit spending on transfer programs.
   b. Potential recipients for transfer programs will incur costs seeking to qualify for the program.
   c. The net gain to beneficiaries of transfer programs is less than the cost of supply of the transfers.
   d. All of the above are true.

9. Some cities issue a limited number of taxicab medallions in an attempt to raise the profitability of taxicab driving. Which of the following best explains the effect of these policies on the profitability of the taxicab driving industry?
   a. The profitability of the industry is the same as without the medallions because the market price of purchasing a medallion has risen to offset the gain from the limit on the number of taxicabs.
   b. The profitability of the industry has risen substantially because the limited number of taxicabs has resulted in higher taxicab fares, while the medallions are free to anyone who wants them.
   c. The profitability of the industry has fallen because drivers have to pay for the medallions but are not getting to charge higher taxicab fares.
   d. None of the above.

10. Proponents of government action to reduce income inequality have proposed
    a. restricting immigration to prevent the entry of more unskilled workers.
    b. erecting higher trade barriers to keep out foreign-made goods.
    c. raising the minimum wage.
    d. all of the above.

11. (I) Opponents to government action to reduce income inequality argue that the pattern of economic outcomes is more important than the process that generates the outcomes. (II) Opponents of government action to reduce income inequality argue that the proposed solutions will retard economic growth.
    a. Both I and II are true.
    b. Both I and II are false.
    c. I is true; II is false.
    d. I is false; II is true.

DISCUSSION QUESTIONS

1   Outcome: Joe has $1,000,000 and Steve has $200 of annual income this year. Below are several possible cases of how this outcome arose (the "process" that generated this outcome). In each case, judge whether you think the outcome and/or process is fair. Does your judgment about the fairness of the outcome depend upon how fair you consider the process?

  a.   Process: Joe and Steve both used to have $201 and both spent $1 on a lottery ticket. Joe won the lottery.

  b.   Process: Steve owns his own business and made $1,000,200, but Joe came in and robbed the business at gun point and took $1,000,000.

  c.   Process: Joe owns his own business and made $1,000,200, but Steve came in and robbed the business at gun point and took $200.

  d.   Process: Joe made the money from his new business that he purchased from Steve in exchange for a house and a yacht. Steve is now sailing the oceans on his new boat and made $200 of interest income this year on the little money he left in his savings account back home.

  e.   Process: Joe and Steve are both retirees who invested their money in the stock market. Joe did well this year, but Steve did not.

  f.   Process: Joe owns his own business and made $1,000,200, but he had to pay $200 in taxes to the government, which were then paid out to Steve in the form of welfare benefits.

2.   Do you believe that rising income inequality is a serious problem? Why or why not? Do you believe that our economic process, the market system, is "fair"? Why or why not? How do you define "fair"?

3.   What are the greater social consequences of intervening in the market in order to force greater equality of outcomes? What benefits are there from intervening? Do you think the benefits outweigh the costs?

APPLICATION *6*

Do Labor Unions Increase the Wages of Workers?

TRUE OR FALSE

T F

☐ ☐ 1. Union membership as a percentage of the labor force has steadily increased since 1960.

☐ ☐ 2. The bargaining power of a union is limited by competition from other firms selling similar products.

☐ ☐ 3. A right-to-work law prohibits union shop provisions that require employees to join a union as a condition of employment.

☐ ☐ 4. The increased competition and lower prices caused by deregulation in the transportation and communication industries have lowered union strength in these industries.

☐ ☐ 5. A union will be more successful in raising wages when it is able to organize all firms in an industry rather than only one.

☐ ☐ 6. Men and women are about equally represented in union membership.

☐ ☐ 7. Of all sectors of the economy, the service sector tends to be the most unionized.

☐ ☐ 8. The greater the ability of management to substitute machines and nonunion labor for union labor, the weaker the bargaining power of a union.

☐ ☐ 9. Southern states tend to have higher rates of union membership than other parts of the United States.

☐ ☐ 10. Evidence shows that unions have increased the wages of all workers, including nonunion workers.

PROBLEMS AND PROJECTS

1. If the professors at a university form a union and successfully increase their salaries, indicate whether you would expect each of the following to (+) increase or (−) decrease as a result.
   ____ a. the tuition rate charged by the university
   ____ b. the number of students attending the university

     ___ c. the average number of students per class (i.e., the size of classes)
     ___ d. the number of professors employed by the university
     e.   Explain how your answers to b and c help explain your answer to d.

2.   According to the text, unions can raise wages three ways:

     (1) Supply restrictions on competitive labor.

     (2) Bargaining power (resulting in a wage floor above the equilibrium level).

     (3) Increase in the demand for union workers.

     For each of the following union strategies, list the number given above for the type of effect the strategy illustrates, and indicate whether employment in the unionized industry rises (+) or falls (−) as a result. The first case is completed as an example.

Type Of Effect	Change in Employment	Union Strategy
3	+	a. In a practice called featherbedding, railroad unions require that all trains carry firemen, even though modern locomotives pose little fire danger.
_____	_____	b. The American Medical Association restricts accreditation of medical schools.
_____	_____	c. Garment workers run an ad campaign with the jingle, "Look for the union label."
_____	_____	d. Unions comonly bargain for wage increases indexed to inflation plus a negotiated premium.
_____	_____	e. Auto workers lobby for domestic content legislation stipulating that at least 90 percent of each car sold in the United States be constructed from U.S.-made parts.
_____	_____	f. To become Certified Public Accountants, candidates must pass an industry-administered exam that over three-fourths of all applicants fail.

Harcourt Brace & Company

MULTIPLE CHOICE

1. Which of the following is true?
   a. The proportion of female workers who are union members is higher than the proportion of male workers.
   b. The proportion of government employees who are union members is higher than the proportion of private sector workers.
   c. The proportion of workers in southern states who are union members is higher than the proportion in northern states.
   d. The proportion of white workers who are union members is higher than the proportion of black workers.

2. Which of the following is **not** a cause of the decline in unionization in the United States.
   a. deregulation in transportation and communication industries
   b. increased foreign competition
   c. growth in the number of smaller firms
   d. an increase in the number of workers wishing to be union members

3. Which of the following is **not** one of the channels through which a union may raise wages?
   a. supply restrictions
   b. increasing the demand for union labor
   c. more competitive product pricing
   d. bargaining power

4. A worker living in a state with a right-to-work law
   a. cannot be employed at a union firm until he has joined the union.
   b. cannot be required to join a union as a condition of employment.
   c. must agree when he is hired never to join a union.
   d. is guaranteed a job in government if he cannot find a private sector job.

5. Because the demand for a broadly defined product line (automobiles, for example) is less elastic than the demand for a more narrow product category (Fords, for example), a union will be better able to raise wages without large unemployment effects when
   a. it has organized an entire industry, rather than only one firm.
   b. it organizes only a few firms in each industry.
   c. it bargains with all firms in a narrow product line but ignores the rest of the industry.
   d. only a small part of the industry that makes the broadly defined product is unionized.

6. By raising their wages, unions typically
   a. increase total productivity, which must rise proportionally with the wage rate.
   b. encourage employers to find substitutes for union labor.
   c. raise the wages of nonunion workers as well.
   d. lower the prices consumers pay for the products produced by union firms.

7. In 1998, approximately what percent of the nonagricultural workforce belonged to a union?
   a. 2 percent
   b. 14 percent
   c. 35 percent
   d. 98 percent

8. The percent of workers belonging to a union in the United States
   a. has been continuously declining since the 1950s.
   b. has been continuously increasing since the 1950s.
   c. has remained fairly constant since the 1950s.
   d. rose sharply from 1950 to 1970 but has declined since.

9. The experience of the Teamsters in the late 1970s and early 1980s suggests that
   a. there are few restraints on the ability of a strong union to increase the wages of its members.
   b. product market competition with goods made from (or services provided by) nonunion labor significantly limits the ability of a union to get increased wages for its members.
   c. higher wages tend to stimulate aggregate demand, which makes it easier for a union to gain still higher wages.
   d. wages are established by the relative skill of union and management negotiators, independent of market conditions.

10. From the 1950s to the 1990s, union membership has declined from more than 30 percent of the workforce to less than 15 percent. Over this period, the share of national income going to labor
    a. declined substantially.
    b. increased substantially.
    c. remained approximately the same.
    d. initially increased but has fallen recently.

11. A union representing a group of workers will tend to be stronger when
    a. there are no good substitutes for the labor services of the unionized workers.
    b. the domestic producers of the good produced by the unionized workers face intense competition from foreign suppliers of the good.
    c. the cost of employing the unionized workers is a large part of the total cost of the product that they produce.
    d. the demand for the good produced by the unionized workers is highly elastic.

Harcourt Brace & Company

12. Which of the following statements is true for the U.S. economy?
    a. Higher wages in the unionized sectors of the economy push up wages in the nonunion sectors as well.
    b. Inflation tends to accelerate when the proportion of the labor force that is unionized increases.
    c. Union workers currently receive wages that are 15 to 20 percent higher, on average, than similar nonunion workers.
    d. When we compare similar union and nonunion workers, we find virtually no difference in the wages they receive.

DISCUSSION QUESTIONS

1. "The wages of union workers are higher than the wages of nonunion workers." Which of the following can we conclude from this observation? Explain your decision in each case.
    a. Unions raise the wage rates of union members.
    b. Unions generally organize high-wage workers.
    c. Unions lower wages for nonunion labor.

2. It is sometimes argued that the largest factor limiting the ability of unions to raise wages is the unwillingness of consumers to pay higher prices for the goods they consume. Evaluate this statement and explain how it relates to the idea that a union will be more successful if it organizes all firms in an industry instead of only one.

3. For each item below, discuss how if affects the ability of unions to raise the wages of their members. Explain your reasoning in each case.
    a. right-to-work laws
    b. competition from foreign firms
    c. organizing only one firm in an industry instead of all firms in the industry

4. Business decision makers can sometimes argue that they cannot make a profit because of the excessive wage demands of unions. Suppose that a strong union in a highly competitive industry obtains for its members a 15 percent increase in wages.
    a. Will the higher wage rates reduce the industry's rate of profit in the short run? in the long run?
    b. How much of the higher wage rates do you think will be passed on to consumers in the long run?

5. "Every union knows that an airline is more vulnerable to strikes than most other businesses. Airlines have high fixed costs regardless of whether their planes are flying. They can neither stockpile seats during a strike nor sell from inventory afterward. Strike losses cannot be recovered. The strong impulse is to avoid a strike, even if that means settling on an unsatisfactory basis." [From an airline newsletter.]

Harcourt Brace & Company

a. Do you think the airline industry is particularly vulnerable to union demands? Why or why not?

b. If the airlines are vulnerable, who would pay for an "unsatisfactory" labor settlement in the short run? in the long run? Explain.

c. Many economists have concluded that, in the absence of regulation, barriers to entry are pretty low in the airline industry. How does this affect your answer to part a?

d. Do you think unions would favor or oppose a return to government regulation of airlines? Why or why not?

Harcourt Brace & Company

APPLICATION 7

Natural Resources and the Future

T F

☐ ☐ 1. When property rights are clearly defined and enforced, resource markets promote resource conservation.

☐ ☐ 2. According to the economic way of thinking, consumers will adjust more completely to a rise in the price of energy products when more time is allowed for the adjustment.

☐ ☐ 3. Because resources are privately owned and resource prices are market determined in market economies, market economies tend to have much higher energy usage than socialist economies.

☐ ☐ 4. The economic way of thinking suggests that unlike in other decisions, opportunity costs are not relevant when making decisions involving energy or natural resource usage.

☐ ☐ 5. Studies and evidence suggest that resource scarcity is growing rapidly and that the relative price of most resources is rising as a result.

☐ ☐ 6. The energy crisis of the 1970s showed that the energy needs of consumers are far greater than the absolute reserves of crude oil.

☐ ☐ 7. One benefit of private property rights is that they provide incentives for maximizing the long-term value of a resource, even for owners whose personal outlook is short term.

☐ ☐ 8. By weakening private property rights and altering incentives, the Endangered Species Act has created harmful secondary effects that have been detrimental to the species the act was trying to protect.

☐ ☐ 9. An increase in the price of a resource will encourage people to conserve on their use of the resource.

☐ ☐ 10. An increase in the price of a an energy source (such as oil) will encourage more effort to be put into finding and using substitute (alternative) energy sources.

PROBLEMS AND PROJECTS

1. Exhibit 1 shows data on natural gas reserves, consumption, and prices in the United States from 1950 to 1995. Use this data when answering the following questions.

EXHIBIT 1

NATURAL GAS RESERVES, CONSUMPTION, AND PRICE: 1950–1995

YEAR	PROVED RESERVES	ANNUAL CONSUMPTION	PRICE
1950	185.6	6.0	$0.44
1960	246.6	10.3	0.60
1970	291.0	21.1	0.67
1980	199.0	19.9	2.94
1990	169.3	18.7	1.99
1995	165.1	21.6	1.55

Notes: Quantities in trillions of cubic feet. Price in constant 1995 dollars per 1,000 cubic feet.

a. In 1950, the proved reserves of natural gasoline were 185.6 trillion cubic feet and the rate of natural gas consumption was 6.0 trillion cubit feet per year. If the reserve data really reflected the remaining amount of natural gas, and if annual consumption rates continued into the future, how many years worth of natural gas remained in 1950? If someone had presented you with this data in 1950, and had asked you when we were going to run out of natural gas, what year would you have told them based upon your calculation?

b. Given your answer to part a, why have we not run out of natural gas? Between 1950 and 1960 and again between 1960 and 1970, proved reserves of natural gas increased. Does this explain part of the answer? How is it possible for reserves to increase despite continued consumption?

c. Is the trend of increasing reserves you found in part b continuing? Between 1990 and 1995, proved reserves fell by 4.2 trillion cubic feet (from 169.3 to 165.1). However, based upon the data given, we should have consumed about 100 trillion cubic feet over these five years (five years at a usage rate of about 20 trillion cubic feet). What does this suggest about the rate of growth in proved reserves relative to the rate of consumption?

d. What happened to the price of natural gas between 1970 and 1980? How did the annual consumption of natural gasoline change in response? Given that it takes time for consumption to fully adjust, is it surprising that consumption continued to fall between 1980 and 1990?

Harcourt Brace & Company

e. What happened to the price of natural gas between 1990 and 1995? How did consumption respond? Overall, since 1970, what has happened to the price of natural gas? Based on this, do you think the relative scarcity of natural gas has been rising or falling since 1970?

f. Based upon the proved reserves and rate of consumption in 1995, in what year do you *really* think we will run out of natural gas?

2. Exhibit 2 shows data on the usage of natural gas by residential homes and commercial buildings in 1990. These data show how many trillions of BTU were used by homes and businesses depending upon the age of the building (i.e., the year the building was constructed).

EXHIBIT 2

1990 NATURAL GAS USAGE (TRILLIONS BTU PER YEAR)

YEAR BUILT	RESIDENTIAL HOMES	COMMERCIAL BUILDINGS
Prior to 1960	1,570	522
1960s	770	501
1970s	780	528
1980s	240	196

a. Homes built prior to 1960 use twice as much natural gas as homes built since. In addition, while there is only a slight difference between homes constructed in the 1960s and 1970s, homes constructed in the 1980s use significantly less natural gas. How well do these changes in usage correspond to changes in the price of natural gas? (Hint: You will need to look back up to Exhibit 1 in problem 1 for the price data.)

b. Usage of natural gasoline by homes built in the 1980s is very low relative to homes built earlier (only about 15 percent). While some of the reduction in natural gasoline consumption could be accounted for by rising use of other fuels, overall, household energy consumption for homes built in the 1980s is only one-fourth of the usage of old homes. How can this be explained?

c. How much of the reduced consumption do you think is explained by people becoming aware of energy problems in society versus how much is simply due to a reaction to higher natural gas prices? Which is more effective at creating incentives to conserve?

d. Is the trend for commercial buildings similar to the trend for residential homes?

3. Exhibit 3 shows how a decrease in supply affects the market for gasoline. Included in the diagram is both the short-run and long-run demand curves for gasoline. Use the exhibit to answer the following questions.

Harcourt Brace & Company

a. In the short run, how did the decrease in supply (from S_1 to S_2) affect the price of gasoline and the quantity consumed?

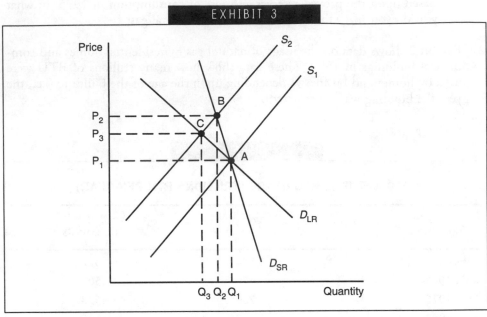

EXHIBIT 3

b. In the long run, how did the decrease in supply (from S_1 to S_2) affect the price of gasoline and the quantity consumed relative to its original level? relative to the short-run level?

c. Based upon your answers to a and b, would you say that the conservation that results from higher prices is greater in the short run or in the long run? Why is there a difference?

4. Suppose that the blue-eyed fillow was in danger of extinction because its natural habitat has been declining. The bird is very particular and will only nest in red sipe trees (which require special care and added fertilizer to grow well). For each of the following, decide whether the government regulation or policy stated would increase (+) or decrease (–) your incentive to keep, plant, and have red sipe trees on your property.

____ a. a law that if a blue-eyed fillow is found nesting on your property, the government will fence off a fifty-foot circle around the tree, remove all buildings from the area, and place the property under public control without compensation to you

____ b. a law that requires each person owning a red sipe tree to purchase a new, very expensive fertilizer that increases growth and longevity and apply it to the trees ten times a month.

____ c. a law that provides for a $100 cash payment to any property owner finding a blue-eyed fillow nesting on their property

____ d. a new tax provision that exempts any property with more than ten red sipe trees per acre from any local, state, and federal property taxes.

Harcourt Brace & Company

MULTIPLE CHOICE

1. As we move from the short run to the long run in the energy market,
   a. supply tends to become more elastic, while demand tends to become more inelastic.
   b. supply tends to become more inelastic, while demand tends to become more elastic.
   c. supply and demand both tend to become more elastic.
   d. supply and demand both tend to become more inelastic.

2. "Doomsday" predictions about the imminent depletion of one or more of our vital natural resources usually are
   a. correct but are not reflected by relative price changes within our market economy.
   b. overstated because of arithmetic calculation mistakes.
   c. overstated because they disregard human responses to relative price changes.
   d. understated because substitutes for such natural resources are also becoming less available.

3. Given the past relationship between conservation in the capitalist nations and conservation in socialist nations, the recent move toward market economies of the former Soviet Union and other previously communist nations seems likely to
   a. improve conservation in the newly market-oriented economies.
   b. worsen conservation in the newly market-oriented economies.
   c. have no effect on conservation in the newly market-oriented economies.
   d. improve conservation in the short run but worsen conservation in the long run as their rate of economic growth speeds up under a market system.

4. The amount of an energy source consumed depends on
   a. the price of the energy source.
   b. consumer income.
   c. the price of substitute energy sources.
   d. all of the above.

5. If the prices of energy products rise sharply, consumers will most likely
   a. sharply reduce their consumption of these products in both the short run and the long run.
   b. reduce their consumption of these products slightly in the short run and more sharply in the long run.
   c. reduce their consumption of these products sharply in the short run, but in the long run, consumption will fall by only a small amount.
   d. increase their consumption of these products slightly in the short run and more sharply in the long run.

Harcourt Brace & Company

6. In natural resource markets, transferable private property rights
   a. prevent most citizens from influencing what happens to a privately owned resource.
   b. allow citizens to exercise an impact on resource use through their influence on market prices.
   c. allow only resource owners to influence resource conservation and utilization.
   d. guarantee that all owned resources will be properly protected; there will be no regrets later that all relevant resources were not preserved.

7. Private property rights and resource markets provide owners with the incentive to
   a. share (sell to others) resource access.
   b. conserve resources.
   c. exercise good stewardship.
   d. All of the above are correct.

8. Economic analysis implies that one of the most effective ways to deal with potential damages from environmental pollution is to
   a. declare the relevant resources as public goods.
   b. establish property rights for the resources that are being damaged.
   c. allow the government to take over and control all resources.
   d. enact legislation that makes all environmental pollution illegal.

9. (I) The U.S. Fisheries and Wildlife Service does not provide compensation to landowners affected by the Endangered Species Act land use regulations. (II) The Endangered Species Act reduced landowner willingness to help preserve declining wildlife.
   a. I is true; II is false.
   b. I is false; II is true.
   c. Both I and II are true.
   d. Both I and II are false.

10. The concept of "proved reserves" refers to the amount of a resource that can be produced
    a. in one year's time.
    b. in the next ten years.
    c. before it runs out.
    d. at current levels of price and technology.

11. Predictions that natural resources such as oil will be essentially used up in the next few decades have
    a. been frequently made for the past century but have always proven to be false.
    b. usually been based on the quantity of proved reserves.
    c. ignored the role of price in governing the quantities demanded and supplied.
    d. All of the above answers are correct.

Harcourt Brace & Company

12. Suppose that new demands greatly reduce the proved reserves of titanium to unexpectedly low levels, and it appears that the new demands will continue. If the market price is unregulated, we should expect that the price will rise and
    a. increase exploration and encourage more effective (and more costly) recovery methods, resulting in additional new supplies of titanium.
    b. encourage consumers and manufacturers to conserve titanium and to find substitutes for it.
    c. increase the current consumption of titanium sharply as people seek to use the resource before it is depleted.
    d. Both *a* and *b* are true.

13. Empirical evidence suggests that the relative scarcity of most resources is
    a. declining.
    b. increasing slowly.
    c. increasing rapidly.
    d. largely unchanged over the past four decades.

14. The Endangered Species Act has had the unintended consequence of leading some private property owners to deliberately make their properties uninhabitable by endangered species. We can conclude that
    a. the market left to itself will provide the proper amount of habitat for endangered species.
    b. the market will provide the proper amount of habitat for endangered species only if private property owners have enforceable property rights.
    c. the Endangered Species Act is an example of well-intentioned government policy making that has not thought carefully about the incentives created by the policy.
    d. none of the above.

DISCUSSION QUESTIONS

1. Why are the reactions on both the demand and supply sides of resource markets greater in the long run than in the short run? What does this imply about the elasticities of demand and supply in the long run versus the short run?

2. Has the Endangered Species Act had secondary effects that have harmed the habitats of the animals the act was trying to protect? Discuss some of the poor incentives created by the act and how they could be improved.

3. "With only a fixed amount of natural resources available, it is impossible for the quantity supplied to increase as price rises." Evaluate this statement.

4. "Allowing natural resources to be privately owned results in the owners using the resources selfishly. This selfish usage results in lower conservation efforts and owners not caring about the wishes of others when they use their resources." Carefully evaluate both of the above statements.

Harcourt Brace & Company

Economics and the Environment

T F

☐ ☐ 1. As an economy grows and becomes richer, the condition of the environment generally falls.

☐ ☐ 2. Because fishing streams in England are privately owned, while they are publicly owned in the U.S., the fishing streams in England generally have much lower environmental quality.

☐ ☐ 3. In decisions about the environment, secondary effects that result from changes in the incentive structure are very important to consider.

☐ ☐ 4. In Zimbabwe, where partial-private ownership rights to the African elephants have been established, herds have expanded rapidly and the threat of extinction is no longer a major concern.

☐ ☐ 5. Because environmental quality is important to everyone, its value is objective.

☐ ☐ 6. Private ownership and market institutions work to protect the environment to a greater degree than public ownership and socialist institutions.

☐ ☐ 7. Studies have now unquestionably concluded that disastrous effects from global warming are inevitable.

☐ ☐ 8. Private ownership of many environmentally threatened areas is the major threat that we face in attempting to protect the environment.

☐ ☐ 9. Generally, government regulation is just as effective at protecting the environment as adopting solutions based upon establishing private property rights.

☐ ☐ 10. In poor nations, environmental quality concerns generally have very low priority over the more important concerns for food and clothing and other necessities.

Harcourt Brace & Company

PROBLEMS AND PROJECTS

1. Consider the animals listed in the following table.

Column 1	Column 2
Cows	African elephants
Pigs	American bison
Chicken	Spotted owl
Cats	Blue whale
Dogs	Bald eagle

   a. Which column of animals above is either extinct or is currently threatened with extinction?
   b. Which column of animals above is allowed to be privately owned?
   c. What, if any, correlation is there between your answers to *a* and *b* above?
   d. People generally believe that the reason why animals go extinct is because they are killed at a very high rate solely for human consumption. Based upon your best guess, which specific animals listed above do you believe are killed in the highest numbers each year for human consumption? What correlation is there between the ones being killed in the highest numbers and the ones going extinct?
   e. Generally, cows are everywhere in the United States, they are far from going extinct. Who owns these cows, the environmental groups or the people who will eventually kill them? Based upon your answer, do you think that African elephants would be doomed for extinction if the private property rights to the animals were given to the ivory poachers in Africa? (Note: Ivory poachers are persons who kill the elephants to get their ivory to sell.)

2. The Audubon Society is a private organization that uses money from contributors to purchase the private property rights to land that they wish to preserve. In several cases, the Audubon Society has sold the mineral rights to allow companies to drill oil on their properties.
   a. Explain what incentive there would be for the Audubon Society to sell oil companies the right to drill oil on their property. Are both parties (the oil company and the Audubon Society) made better off by this voluntary transaction?
   b. When making a decision as to whether to allow oil drilling, what factors do you think the Audubon Society considers?
   c. Rumors have it that the U.S. government allowed a timber company to harvest trees in a government-owned forest and built a government-financed road into the forest for the company to use. However, the money the company received from selling the timber was not even as much as it cost the government to build the road into the forest. If this has been a property of Audubon, and the company would have had to buy the rights and pay for

the building of the road themselves, would the timber company have found it profitable to do so?

d. Suppose environmental groups currently spend $35 million each year lobbying to buy the votes of politicians to ensure they do not grant access to a U.S. government-owned forest for drilling oil. If a private oil company owned the forest, and could make $25 million in profit if they drilled, would they be willing to sell the property to the environmental group for $30 million instead? Would the environmental group be better off than under the current system?

3. The relationship between economic growth and environmental quality generally takes one of three forms, they are shown in Exhibit 1, parts a through c. Use the exhibits to **fill in the blanks** in the sentences below.

EXHIBIT 1

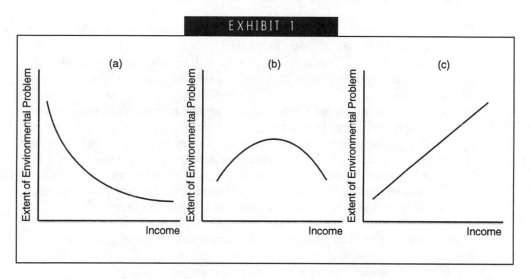

a. Part a of Exhibit 1 shows that some types of environmental problems, such as a lack of safe drinking water, continuously _____ as income increases because of economic growth.

b. Part b of Exhibit 1 shows that some types of environmental problems, such as pollutant particles in the air, originally _____ as income begins to increase because of economic growth, but then begin to _____ when income expands further.

c. Part c of Exhibit 1 shows that some types of environmental problems, such as the generation of solid waste, continuously _____ as income increases because of economic growth.

Harcourt Brace & Company

MULTIPLE CHOICE

1. When economists say that environmental quality has a high income elasticity, they mean that
   a. people are very sensitive to the price of environmental protection.
   b. when there is economic growth, the higher incomes generated produce relatively large percentage increases in the demand for environmental protection.
   c. spending on environmental protection is highest for those countries with the lowest income.
   d. spending on environmental protection generally falls as income expands but only up to a point where demand becomes elastic.

2. Which of the following actions by a major lumber corporation would cause the price of the stock of that corporation to rise?
   a. The corporation voluntarily abstains from harvesting ten thousand acres, which have recently proven to be one of the last homes of the endangered spotted owls.
   b. The corporation adopts a new, more expensive milling technology in order to comply with air pollution regulations.
   c. The corporation adopts a new harvesting policy, which will slightly reduce current output, but which will guarantee that the forests owned by the corporations will be able to sustain harvesting indefinitely into the future.
   d. The corporation adopts a long-available milling technology that economizes on energy usage in response to a dramatic increase in energy prices.

3. In the analysis of markets for natural resources, such as minerals, land, and access to sport fishing opportunities, we find that
   a. incentives matter, as they do in other markets.
   b. values for the goods are subjective, varying widely among individuals.
   c. changes in government policy can have important secondary, unwanted impacts.
   d. all of the above answers are correct.

4. The forces that encourage economic growth, such as market institutions and technological advance,
   a. generally both also harm the environment.
   b. can also both help to improve the environment.
   c. generally lead back to a socialist system, thus destroying the environment.
   d. lower per capita income, which usually reduces the willingness of people to pay for environmental quality.

5. Wealthy countries tend to have
   a. better environmental quality than poor countries.
   b. worse environmental quality as poor countries.
   c. a lower demand for environmental quality than poor countries.
   d. both b and c of the above.

6. Most of our environmental problems exist because of
   a. a lack of property rights.
   b. consumer ignorance.
   c. profit maximization on the part of business firms.
   d. the failure of political officials to regulate business activities.

7. If government control of pollution was largely replaced by transferable private property rights that are more extensive and more easily defended than before, we could expect that pollution would
   a. be greater, as private firms maximized profit by spending less on pollution control.
   b. rise, as well-funded polluters always prefer to purchase pollution rights rather than reduce emissions.
   c. fall in cases where property owners became able to defend their rights not to be bombarded with harmful pollution.
   d. be reduced in cases where it had previously been forbidden but where it would cause little damage.

8. Economic analysis implies that one of the most effective ways to deal with potential damages from environmental pollution is to
   a. declare the relevant resources as public goods.
   b. establish property rights for the resources that are being damaged.
   c. allow the government to take over and control all resources.
   d. enact legislation that makes all environmental pollution illegal.

9. With regard to environmental programs and regulations, economic analysis indicates that
   a. environmental quality is something that people value, and therefore, they are willing to pay for it.
   b. people also value many other things, and therefore, they are unwilling to pay an unlimited amount for environmental quality.
   c. increases in income are an important source of improvement in and support for environmental quality.
   d. all of the above are true.

10. Empirical evidence indicates that
    a. changes in the earth's cloud cover will clearly enhance the warming effects of carbon dioxide.
    b. the increase in carbon dioxide, over thousands of years, is definitely the cause of global warming.
    c. if global warming continues, the sea levels will definitely rise.
    d. none of the above are true.

Harcourt Brace & Company

DISCUSSION QUESTIONS

1. Suppose the government installed a monitor in your car that measured the pollutants in the car's exhaust. Further suppose that you received a monthly bill of $1.00 for every pound your car polluted the air. Would you change the amount of your driving because of it? If you were charged only for those pollutants that were emitted during heavy driving times (like rush hour), would you change the times of your driving?

2. Discuss the possible relationships between economic growth and environmental quality. Does the relationship differ for different types of environmental problems? What role does the rising incomes of people that economic growth brings have in the overall relationship?

3. "In nearly every case, environmental problems stem from insecure, unenforceable, or nonexistent property rights." Evaluate this statement made by Jane Shaw.

Harcourt Brace & Company

CHAPTER ONE

TRUE OR FALSE

The following are true: 1, 3, 5, 7, 9, 11, 13, 15

The following are false:

2. The opportunity cost is the value of the next best alternative that you forgo to attend class that day (such as the value of sleeping later, or watching television).

4. The value of a good is subjective; it differs across individuals. Some people like liver, while others hate it.

6. The resources devoted to education have alternative uses, thus public education is not free to society. It is a scarce or economic good.

8. Economizing behavior suggests you will purchase whichever is the *least* expensive.

10. *Ceteris paribus* means everything else is held constant.

12. This is a normative statement because it is an opinion.

14. Association is *not* causation.

PROBLEMS AND PROJECTS

1. a. (6) The lost manufacturing jobs were a secondary effect of the tax.
    b. (3) Incentives matter; as the benefits rise, the incentive to take the time to pick it up does as well. However, one could also relate this to guidepost (4) in a similar manner.
    c. (2) Economizing behavior suggests you will attempt to get the most out of your limited budget.
    d. (5) The deaths are the cost of waiting to acquire more information about the drug.
    e. (7) Value is subjective; the tomato and onion are worth different amounts to the husband and wife. This is what creates the opportunity for trade.
    f. (1) Bill Gates has a very high opportunity cost of his time spent making the wine, thus the wine is very costly to produce.
    g. (8) The test of a theory (and its eventual acceptance) is dependent upon its ability to predict real-world events.
    h. (4) The marginal cost of the trip to the beach is lower from the grandmother's house. However, one could also relate this to guidepost (3) in a similar manner.

2. a. (5) Only information worth the cost of acquiring should be collected.
    b. (6) This would cause secondary effects that would harm the poor. For example, those making less than $10,000 per year would have trouble finding someone who would rent housing to them.
    c. (1) While it becomes free to the student, it is still costly to society in terms of other forgone activities (other things that could have been produced with those resources).
    d. (2) You would prefer the one that is the least expensive.
    e. (3) Incentives matter—they predictably influence behavior, even for criminals.
    f. (4) The tuition and books are expenses that are not relevant for the current decision to attend class—they are not *marginal* costs.
    g. (7) Value is subjective.

h. (8) If it predicts well, the theory should be considered accurate.

3. a. (3) What is true for one individual is not necessarily true for the group. In fact, probably no one would play if the top prize was winning your $1 back!

    b. (1) The advent and popularity of computers is an event which is affecting the relationship; we have not held all else constant.

    c. (2) Better students tend to ask more questions. This does not imply that asking more questions will *cause* you to be a better student.

4. b. There is a direct (or positive) relationship.

    c. 1/15 is the slope; the car gets 15 miles per gallon; the slope is 1 divided by miles per gallon.

5. b. Inversely (or negatively) related.

    d. Increase by 200 thousand tons (from 600 to 800).

    e. Decrease by 100 thousand tons (from 600 to 500).

MULTIPLE CHOICE

1. b. Scarcity and poverty are not the same thing.

2. a. Economics is about the choices people make because of scarcity.

3. c. This is the definition of scarcity.

4. d. Again, this is a definition. Economizing behavior extends to a broad range of human activity.

5. a. The statement concerns what the government *ought* to do.

6. c. Choices a and b are violations of guideposts; choice d misunderstands what economists mean by the term scarce.

7. a. Scarcity prompts competitive behavior regardless of what allocation system is adopted.

8. b. Someone must incur the cost of producing a scarce good, regardless of who actually consumes it.

9. d. Goods will always be scarce regardless of whether there is poverty. Scarcity and poverty are not the same.

10. b. There is as much air freely available from nature as we would like to consume.

11. d. This is an example of thinking at the margin.

12. c. All other answers are characteristics of both micro and macro.

13. a. This is the definition of opportunity cost.

14. d. In all three, individuals are acting in accord with the incentives.

15. b. The total cost of 9 gallons plus the car wash is $14.50 (9 × $1.50 = $13.50 for the gas plus $1 for the car wash), while the total for 10 gallons plus the car wash is $15.00 (10 × $1.50 = $15.00 for the gas, and the car wash is free). Thus, buying the extra gallon only adds $0.50 ($15.00 − $14.50) to her total cost.

16. b. Both positive and normative economics deal with costs, benefits, and theory.

17. c. This is a subjective opinion.

18 a. The other answers are counter to the economic way of thinking.

19. c. This is the only statement that could be tested with data.

20. c. This is the definition of *ceteris paribus*.

21. b. This is the definition of utility.

CHAPTER TWO

True or False

The following are true: 2, 3, 5, 7, 9, 10, 11, 13

The following are false:

1. Opportunity cost is the value of the highest valued alternative forgone as the result of washing your car (say an afternoon at the movies with friends), *not* the undesirable non-money aspects of the choice.

4. As long as trade is voluntary, both parties gain from trade.

6. The value of property is determined by how much it is valued by others not by the owner. Thus, private property rights create an incentive for owners to use their property in ways that are most highly valued by others.

8. Middlemen play an important role in coordinating the economic activities of others. By bringing buyers and sellers together, they help create economic value by providing a service.

12. Capitalism is the use of unregulated market prices and the decentralized decisions of private property owners to allocate resources. Socialism uses the political process and government planning to allocate resources.

14. Increased technology increases a country's productive capacity, and thus shifts the production possibilities curve outward.

Problems and Projects

1. a. Because Susan will have to quit her job, she will forgo earning $20,000 per year, or a total of $80,000 over the four years. This is her opportunity cost of attending college and should be added to the table.

   b. Because room and board and transportation are costs that she will have regardless of whether she keeps working or goes to college, they are not relevant in the decision. They are not marginal costs of college because they do not change with her decision. If the drive to the university was longer than to her current job, her transportation expenses might increase and this is relevant, however, we do not have the information to know this here.

   c. For the per-year amounts, adding $20,000 and subtracting transportation ($557) and room and board ($4,434) yields a new per-year total of $22,743. For four years, this is a total of $90,972 ($22,743 × 4)

   d. Her forgone earnings account for 87.9 percent of her cost of going to college ($20,000 ÷ $22,743).

   e. Because earnings rise with age, the cost of college (the opportunity cost component of forgone earnings) rises with age. College is thus more expensive for older students.

2. a. (1) They are attempting to make the home more attractive to others to increase its market value.

   b. (4) You are held accountable for the damages you cause.

   c. (2) Commonly owned property is not taken care of as well as private property.

   d. (3) Commonly owned property is not conserved as well as private property. It is generally used up much more quickly.

   e. (2) or (3) Cows, pigs, and chicken are privately owned, while whales and elephants are not. Thus, they are better managed and better conserved through breeding to maintain future stocks.

   f. (2) Rented property is given less care because the occupant does not own the property and will not bear the full cost of the reductions in the value of the property from misuse and damage.

   g. (1) The selling value of the automobile is determined by how much others value the car. When Sam does things to his property that are not valued by others, he bears the cost.

3. a. The plane cost $450, the bus $200, so the plane is $250 more than the bus ($450 – $200).

   b. The plane takes 6 hours, the bus 56 hours, so the plane saves 50 hours of Bob's time.

   c. For 50 hours to be worth $250 requires that each hour be valued at $5 per hour ($5 = $250 ÷ 50).

   d. Fly. In fact, if Bob values his time at any rate more than $5 per hour he should fly.

4. b. 4; 3; 1

c. 10; 8; 2
d. Larry
e. Larry's is 1, Sam's is 1/2 (Hint: For Sam, you must divide both sides by two to get this answer from the exhibit which shows that 2 chairs = 1 table.); Sam
f. If Larry specializes in tables, he produces 4 tables and no chairs. Sam specializes and produces 10 chairs and no tables. Together they have produced 10 chairs and 4 tables, which is one more table *and* one more chair than if they do not specialize.

5. a. 3
    b. 2
    c. Brazil
    d. United States
    e. The United States should specialize in producing coffee, Brazil in tobacco, and the two countries should trade. As a result, both countries will be better off.

6. a. yes; yes; no
    b. 900 million bushels; 200 million bushels
    c. 100 million bushels; 1 bushel of wheat (Hint: 100 corn = 100 wheat, so dividing both sides by 100 gives 1 corn = 1 wheat.)
    d. No, point E is unattainable because the country does not have enough resources to simultaneously produce this much of both goods.

7. a. (3)
    b. (1)
    c. (5)
    d. (4)
    e. (2)

8. a. (1) C = 3, I = 5; (2) C = 5, I = 3
    b. Any of the points on the curve between C = 3, I = 5 to C = 5, I = 3 (the portion that includes C = 4, I = 4).

MULTIPLE CHOICE

1. c. Opportunity cost is the value (or utility) of the highest valued forgone alternative (such as, building more interstate highways).

2. c. The opportunity cost of time spent not working is the wage forgone.

3. a. For saving 20 hours of time to be worth $200 requires that each hour be valued at at least $10 ($10 = $200/20).

4. a. Specialization by comparative advantage raises available output.

5. d. The rational choice is the alternative that is most highly valued.

6. d. Answers *a* through *c* are the three basic questions listed in the text.

7. b. Private property rights allow an owner to gain when they use their property in ways that others value.

8. a. Ken gains $2,000 ($7,000 – $5,000) and Monica gains $1,000 ($8,000 – $7,000).

9. b. When the political process replaces market forces in allocating resources, political influence will be the primary determinant of allocations.

10. a. Specialization and trade result in gains at all levels from individuals to nations.

11. c. Points inside the curve represent output possibilities when resources are not being fully utilized.

12. c. Transaction costs are the costs of searching out and conducting a transaction.

13. a. Middlemen specialize in providing information and arranging trades, so you will not have to.

14. d. These are simply the three characteristics of private property rights given in the text.

15. b. Only if all resources are currently being used does it require taking resources away from the production of another good to expand production in another area.

16. d. All of these items shift the production the possibilities curve outward.

17. b. The alternative to the date is to have $10 worth of other goods and play tennis.

18. d.   Point A is efficient because it is on the curve, meaning all resources are employed; point B is inefficient because it is inside the curve, meaning the country is not using all of its resources; while point C is unattainable because the country does not have enough resources to produce this much of both goods.

19. d.   The extra cost of driving is = $200 (4 hours × $50 per hour)

20. b.   Specialization according to comparative advantage maximizes total output.

21. a.   One party of an exchange benefiting does not imply that others lose.

22. a.   Speaking out is considered the voice option, while leaving is exit.

23. a.   Exit and voice are similar methods of showing displeasure in both markets and the public sector.

CHAPTER THREE

TRUE OR FALSE

The following are true: 1, 2, 3, 5, 7, 8, 9, 13

The following are false:

4. Relatively inelastic refers to when consumer purchases are not very responsive. The correct answer is relatively *elastic*.

6. A decrease in supply results in a higher price.

10. The first two will shift the supply curve for wine to the left; higher prices for the wine will cause producers to move down *along* the supply curve.

11. A change in the cost of production results in a shift in the supply curve, not just a movement along the curve. Thus, it results in a change in supply, not just a change in quantity supplied.

12. The higher lumber prices would cause a decrease in the supply of new housing. This would result in higher prices, but only a reduction in *quantity* demanded, not demand (in other words, the demand curve does not shift).

14. The market is able to coordinate complex economic activity through the use of price signals. This is the "invisible hand."

PROBLEMS AND PROJECTS

1. c. $12
    e. $15
    f. There has been a change (an increase) in demand (a shift to the right of the demand curve), showing that consumers are willing to buy more shoes at all prices.
    g. There has been a change (an increase) in quantity supplied (a movement along the original supply curve) as producers expand output at the higher price.

2. a. 40 cents; 10
    b. 70 cents; 12

c. Yes, lower bun prices would also cause the demand for hot dogs to increase.

3. a. increase
    b. increase
    c. decrease
    d. increase
    e. increase: increase
    f. increase
    g. increase

4. b. 0; $-$; $+$; $-$
    c. $-$; 0; $-$; $-$
    d. $+$; 0; $+$; $+$
    e. 0; $+$; $-$; $+$

5. a. Quantity will fall by 5 (from 25 to 20) along demand curve D_1.
    b. Quantity will fall by 15 (from 25 to 10) along demand curve D_2.
    c. Demand curve D_2 shows a demand more responsive to price.
    d. Demand curve D_2 is relatively elastic; demand curve D_1 is relatively inelastic.

MULTIPLE CHOICE

1. d. A below-equilibrium price results in an excess of quantity demanded relative to quantity supplied.

2. d. Higher income would increase the demand for automobiles, causing an increase in price.

3. a. Consumer surplus arises when a consumer purchases an item for a price lower than the maximum price they would be willing to pay.

4. a. When cigar prices rise, smokers will substitute cigarettes for cigars.

5. d. If consumers expected the price to fall in the near future, they would hold off their purchases until later, causing the *current* demand to decline.

6. a. Because Budweiser is a substitute for Miller, higher Budweiser prices will cause people to substitute to Miller beer.

7. d. These are true statements of what the height of both the demand and supply curves represent.

8. a. Travelers will substitute bus, train, and air travel for auto travel.

9. b. Lower coffee prices will cause consumers to buy more coffee and, thus, more cream. The demand for cream will increase (shift to the right).

10. b. As price falls toward equilibrium, quantity demanded rises and quantity supplied falls.

11. d. This is the law of supply, which relates to the actions of sellers not buyers.

12. c. He is the seller, so it is producer surplus of the difference between the actual selling price and the minimum price he would accept. Thus, $2,600 − $2,000 = $600.

13. d. This is the definition of economic efficiency along with the second part that no activity generating more cost than benefit be undertaken.

14. c. A shift to the right of the demand curve results in a higher price and a higher quantity.

15. a. The area below the demand curve and above the price is consumer surplus, while the area above the supply curve and below the price is producer surplus.

16. b. Lower consumer income has caused a decrease in the demand for new cars. As a result, the price of new cars has fallen, which has caused a reduction in quantity supplied by producers.

17. c. The tax raises price causing *quantity demanded* (not demand) to fall.

18. c. Response *a* would lower price; *b* lowers quantity; *d* raises quantity but results in little change in the price.

19. c. A decrease in supply results in a higher price (which reduces quantity demanded, not demand).

20. a. Lower cattle feed prices reduce the cost of producing beef, causing an increase in supply and a lower price.

21. a. The demand for a good is generally more elastic in the long run than in the short run. Purchases will fall by more in the long run as consumers find additional substitutes.

22. b. The invisible hand shows that markets direct self-interested individuals to pursue activities that are beneficial to society.

23. d. The existing supply of plywood is now not sufficient to meet the increased demand to rebuild homes, so the price rises due to the higher demand.

24. c. An increase in demand results in a higher price and a movement upward along the given supply curve. This is an increase in quantity supplied, not an increase in supply.

CHAPTER FOUR

TRUE OR FALSE

The following are true: 1, 4, 5, 9, 10, 12, 13, 15

The following are false:

2. Higher demand for housing would increase (not decrease) the demand for lumber.

3. Interest rates would fall as the market would need to induce more individuals to borrow the excess money now available for loans.

6. A depreciation of the dollar would make U.S. products less expensive to foreigners, causing U.S. exports to increase. However, note that it would make foreign products more expensive to U.S. citizens, causing U.S. imports to fall.

7. A price ceiling that sets the price below equilibrium causes a shortage, not a surplus.

8. Shortages are caused by prices being set below equilibrium.

11. Because market prices will change, the burden of a tax can be shifted to other parties. The actual burden of a tax, in fact, will not depend on whether the tax is legally imposed on the buyer or seller.

14. A proportional tax is one in which everyone pays the same percent of their income in taxes. A tax that took the same dollar amount from everyone would instead be regressive because it would take a smaller percentage of a rich person's income.

PROBLEMS AND PROJECTS

1. a(i). An increase in the supply of accountants (shift to the right of the supply curve) would lower the equilibrium wage and raise equilibrium employment.
    a(ii). This would decrease the demand for accountants, lowering the equilibrium wage and equilibrium employment.

b(i). This would decrease the demand for loanable funds, lowering the equilibrium interest rate and quantity of loanable funds.

b(ii). This would increase the supply of loanable funds, causing the interest rate to fall, and the equilibrium quantity to rise.

c(i). This would increase the demand for the Mexican peso, causing the peso to appreciate (increase in value), and increasing the quantity traded.

c(ii). This would increase the supply of pesos onto the foreign exchange market, causing the peso to depreciate (decrease in value), and increasing the quantity traded.

2. a. $250; 500
    b. fall to 200, rise to 800, a shortage of 600 units of rental housing
    c. it would fall
    d. it would fall
    e. other non-price factors (such as discrimination) would become more important

3. a. $4; 5,000
    b. rise to 7,000; fall to 3,000
    c. a surplus of labor, a situation also known as unemployment
    d. better off as they retain their jobs at a higher wage rate
    e. worse off as they are no longer able to find jobs, not only lowering their current income but also reducing job training opportunities, which will reduce their future employment prospects

4. a. $1.50
    b. $2.25, risen by $.75
    c. $1.25 ($2.25 − $1.00), fallen by $.25 from the pretax level of $1.50
    d. Buyers are now paying $.75 more, while sellers receive $.25 less, so buyers bear the larger burden of the tax.
    e. Tax revenue is $200 ($1 × 200) which is the rectangle from $1.25 to $2.25 in price and 0 to 200 in quantity.
    f. Consumption falls by 50 units (250 − 200), and the deadweight loss is the triangular area to the right of the tax revenue box.
    g. Had the tax been imposed on buyers, the price would have fallen to $1.25. Sellers would receive

$1.25 from each sale, but buyers would pay $1.25 plus the tax of $1, or $2.25.

h. The burden is identical to when the tax is imposed on sellers.

5. a. 20 percent ($10,000 ÷ $50,000)
   b. 15 percent ($15,000 ÷ $100,000)
   10 percent [($15,000 − $10,000) ÷ ($100,000 − $50,000) = ($5,000 ÷ $50,000)]
   90 percent [100 percent − MTR = 100 percent − 10 percent]
   regressive because the ATR falls with income (15 percent now versus 20 percent before)
   c. A regressive tax means the average tax rate (the percent of income paid in taxes) falls with income, not that the dollar amount of tax paid falls.
   d. 20 percent ($20,000 ÷ $100,000)
   20 percent [($20,000 − $10,000) ÷ ($100,000 − $50,000) = ($10,000 ÷ $50,000)]
   80 percent [100 percent − MTR = 100 percent −20 percent]
   proportional because the ATR stays the same (still 20 percent)
   e. 35 percent ($35,000 ÷ $100,000)
   50 percent [($35,000 − $10,000) ÷ ($100,000 − $50,000) = ($25,000 ÷ $50,000)]
   50 percent [100 percent − MTR = 100 percent − 50 percent]
   progressive because the ATR rises with income (35 percent now versus 20 percent before)
   f. 60 percent ($60,000 ÷ $100,000)
   100 percent [($60,000 − $10,000) ÷ ($100,000 − $50,000) = ($50,000 ÷ $50,000)]
   0 percent [100 percent − MTR = 100 percent − 100 percent]
   progressive because the ATR rises with income (60 percent now versus 20 percent before)
   No, she will earn no additional take home pay because taxes take all of her raise.

6. a. $0, 500, 800, 900, 800, 500, 0
   c. $3
   d. lowering the tax to $3 would increase revenue from $500 to $900.

MULTIPLE CHOICE

1. a. The demand for resources will increase when the demand for the product rises.

2. a. A higher demand for loans will increase the interest rate.

3. a. When the peso appreciates, foreign goods become less expensive to Mexicans (thus Mexican imports will rise), but Mexican goods become more expensive to foreigners (so Mexican exports will fall).

4. a. Markets eliminate shortages by price rising to ration the available gasoline among the consumers desiring it.

5. d. Price floors create a surplus, also known as unemployment in this context.

6. c. This is kind of a trick question. A price ceiling sets a maximum legal price, so when it is set above equilibrium it has no effect on the market. The market will remain in equilibrium as long as the equilibrium price remains less than the legal maximum. A price ceiling set below the equilibrium price creates a shortage, while a price floor (a minimum legal price) set above equilibrium creates a surplus.

7. d. There will be a reduction in the future supply of rental housing.

8. d. All of the other answers are false statements and show the harmful secondary effects of making a market illegal.

9. c. The price is now $.40 higher to consumers than in the absence of the tax, while sellers are receiving $.05 less from each gallon sold (they now receive $1.20 minus the $.45 tax, or $.75).

10. b. The deadweight loss (or excess burden) is the lost gains from trade when market quantity falls.

11. a. A relatively inelastic demand means that most of the tax will be borne by consumers as the sellers pass the tax along to buyers in the form of higher prices.

12. d. A regressive tax requires that the percentage of income paid in taxes falls with income, not the dollar amount of taxes paid.

13. b.   The average tax rate is 10 percent at all income levels shown. Since it remains the same as income rises, the tax is proportional.

14. a.   The Laffer curve shows that revenue can rise when high tax rates are reduced.

15. a.   When tax rates are high, lowering them will increase revenue, but when tax rates are already low, lowering them further will reduce revenue.

16. d.   The marginal tax rate is the change in tax liability ($12,000 − $5,000 = $7,000) divided by the change in income ($30,000 − $20,000 = $10,000), so $7,000 ÷ $10,000 = 70 percent.

17. b.   The minimum wage is a minimum legal price, thus a price floor. A price ceiling is a maximum legal price (for example, a cap on the maximum professional sports players' salaries).

18. d.   Under both, the quantity traded falls as the quantity traded is determined by the lower of quantity demanded or quantity supplied.

19. a.   The tax would increase price and lower the amount purchased.

20. b.   The tax is borne less heavily by the elastic side of the market and more heavily by the inelastic side of the market.

CHAPTER FIVE

TRUE OR FALSE

The following are true: 1, 2, 3, 5, 6, 8, 9, 11, 12

The following are false:

4. Public goods are goods that have two characteristics: joint-in-consumption and nonexcludable. The government provides both public goods and private goods as do private markets. Mail delivery, for example, is a private good provided by government.

7. Poor information is present in many real-world markets.

10. This is an example of a private market providing a solution to the information problem.

13. The free rider problem happens when nonpaying customers *cannot* be excluded.

14. This is true for private markets, but the public sector breaks this link. Some people get more benefits from government than they pay for in terms of taxes, while others pay more than they receive.

15. There is always an opportunity cost associated with the government use of resources. Scarcity remains as someone must bear the cost of the government-provided goods.

PROBLEMS AND PROJECTS

1. a. yes, yes, public
   b. yes, no, private
   c. no, no, private
   d. no, no, private
   e. yes, yes, public
   f. yes, no, private
   g. no, no, private
   h. yes, no, private

2. a. P = $120; Q = 4,000 tons/year
   b. P = $130; Q = 3,000 tons/year (*Hint:* Add $20 to each price and graph the new supply curve. It will appear parallel to the original supply curve but shifted upward by $20. Find the efficient point at the intersection of the new supply curve and the original demand curve.)
   c. When producers and consumers do not bear the full cost of their actions, they will tend to overproduce (and overconsume) the good relative to what would be efficient.
   d. A tax of $20 per ton would shift the original supply curve upward (see Chapter 4), and it would match the supply curve reflecting the true social cost of production. The resulting private market equilibrium would match economic efficiency.

3. a. P = 50; Q = 26
   b. 32
   c. a subsidy of $24 million to a team locating in the city
   d. No, it will result in a number of teams exceeding the efficient amount.

4. a. efficient, rule 1
   b. inefficient, rule 2
   c. efficient, rule 1
   d. inefficient, rule 2
   e. inefficient, rule 2
   f. efficient, rule 1
   g. inefficient, rule 2
   h. inefficient, rule 2
   i. efficient, rule 1

MULTIPLE CHOICE

1. d. Government mandated price ceilings reduce efficiency.

2. b. The inability of private firms to exclude nonpaying customers creates a free rider problem. The firm will not be able to generate enough revenue to produce the good efficiently.

3. a. Competition over scarce resources is present in both sectors.

4. d. Scarcity implies that opportunity costs are always present when a good is produced either in the private or public sectors.

5. d. Your purchasing a hamburger is not likely to affect other third parties.

6. a. Externalities are costs that you impose on others such as pollution and congestion for which you do not have to pay compensation.

7. a. These are the two rules for efficiency listed in the book.

8. b. National defense is the only one meeting both criterion for a public good.

9. a. When private markets do not fully reflect the social costs, the good or service will be overprovided.

10. c. All externalities are the result of poorly defined or poorly enforced private property rights.

11. d. These are the two characteristics of a good that make it a public good.

12. d. Brand names are one way private markets attempt to overcome information problems.

13. c. The ability to legally use coercive force is a unique feature of government.

14. c. The external benefit is the benefit that goes to others in the form of a reduced likelihood of catching the flu.

15. a. National defense is under the protective function.

16. d. Markets underprovide goods that generate external benefits and overprovide goods that generate external costs.

17. a. All externalities are the result of poorly defined or poorly enforced private property rights.

18. b. Nonexcludability gives individuals an incentive to free ride, that is to consume without paying.

19. d. These are the primary functions of government listed in the book.

CHAPTER SIX

TRUE OR FALSE

The following are true: 1, 2, 4, 6, 7, 10, 11, 12, 14, 15

The following are false:

3. These are methods legislators use to get the special interest issues for their district passed in the legislature by gaining the votes of other members of the legislature.

5. Information is costly to acquire. With little personal benefit from being informed, voters will generally gather little information and be rationally ignorant.

8. The costs to any one individual are small, so they will not devote resources to fighting it.

9. Only one-sixth of all transfer dollars go to programs that are "means-tested," the rest are directed toward people who qualify based on criteria other than poverty. Transfers are directed to those interest groups with the most political power.

13. It is called logrolling. Pork-barrel legislation is combining many separate special interest issues together on a single bill.

PROBLEMS AND PROJECTS

1. a. A is efficient (benefits of $200 exceed costs of $150); B is inefficient (costs of $120 exceed benefits of $100).
   b. Under the equal tax plan, Adam would vote for proposal A because his benefit is $140 while his tax is only $50. Bob and Cathy would vote against proposal A. So, proposal A would fail to gain a majority and would not pass. Proposal B would pass as both Bob and Cathy would vote in favor of it, while Adam votes against it.
   c. No. The efficient proposal A fails, while the inefficient proposal B passes.
   d. Proposal A would now pass unanimously (all three in favor), while proposal B would now fail unanimously (all three against).
   e. Yes. When taxes are divided in proportion to benefits received, all voters will benefit from an effi-

cient project and will all be opposed to an inefficient project.

2. a. Only the new dam for district C is efficient (the total is positive). The totals for the other two are negative (the costs outweigh the benefits), so they are inefficient.
   b. In all three cases, only one representative gains from each project. Thus, each would receive one yes vote and two no votes. All three would fail.
   c. You gain $10 from the road in district A and lose only $5 from paying for B's park. You would be better off ($10 − $5 = +$5). Similarly, the representative from B gains $9 from the park and loses only $6 from your road. B would agree to the trade because $9 − $6 = +$3. With both you and B voting for these projects, they would both pass by a majority (2 to 1).
   d. A bill containing all three would give each representative the total that can be found by summing each row. Representative A would value the total bill at +$3 (+ $10 − $5 − $2), B would value it at +$1 (−$6 + $9 − $2) and C at +$2 (−$6 − $5 + $13). All three would vote unanimously in favor of the pork-barrel bill, and it would pass.

3. a. (2); b. (3); c. (1); d. (3); e. (1)

4. a. Types 1 and 3 where the costs and benefits are either both widespread or are both concentrated. This is the most similar to benefits-received principle of taxation.
   b. Type 2
   c. Type 4
   d. Type 2
   e. Type 4
   f. Type 1
   g. Type 2
   h. Type 4
   i. Type 2
   j. Type 3

MULTIPLE CHOICE

1. d. This is the special interest effect described in this chapter.

2. c. Of these groups, the remainder are large and unorganized.

3. a. The effect says politicians count the current more than the future and are best off for reelection purposes giving easy-to-see current benefits financed by uncertain future costs.

4. c. The costs of gathering information are worthwhile only if there are direct personal benefits.

5. b. Only one-sixth of all transfer dollars go to programs that are "means-tested," the rest are directed toward people who qualify based on criteria other than poverty. Transfers are directed to those interest groups with the most political power.

6. d. The ability of individuals to move from one local area to another effectively creates competition among localities that leads them to be more efficient.

7. a. Remember only voters from your district get to vote for your reelection.

8. d. Public choice theory applies basic economic principles to the individuals involved in the public sector decision-making process.

9. a. Incentives matter—it is the basic postulate of economics and is the key premise economists use in analyzing the behavior of individuals in the public sector.

10. d. A politician must win votes to get elected.

11. a. This is demonstrated in the problem and projects section in problem number 1.

12. c   In this way it most closely resembles taxes reflecting benefits received.

13. a. The political process has a bias toward adopting projects with concentrated benefits and widespread costs even when they are unproductive.

14. d. This is the definition of pork-barrel legislation.

15. a. This is the definition of logrolling.

16. d. When the government begins giving away more money, more resources will be devoted by individuals to capture this additional money that is now "up for grabs."

17. d. This is the definition of the shortsightedness effect.

18. b. Just like markets, governments can be inefficient. When special interests gain the upper hand in the political process, government action will retard our welfare.

CHAPTER SEVEN

TRUE OR FALSE

The following are true: 2, 3, 4, 5, 7, 9, 12, 14, 16

The following are false:

1. Market prices reflect consumers' valuation of an additional unit of the good, not the total valuation. Total value would need to include any consumer surplus on the units consumed.

6. Consumer surplus is the difference between the maximum price a consumer would be willing to pay (their marginal benefit) and the price.

8. If demand is elastic, total revenue will rise when price is decreased.

10. Marginal benefit is a reflection of marginal utility and thus diminishes with the rate of consumption due to the law of diminishing marginal utility.

11. A risk-averse person would be more likely to purchase insurance.

13. If demand is inelastic, total revenue will rise when price is increased.

15. Because consumers have more time to adjust and find substitutes, demand in the long run is more elastic.

PROBLEMS AND PROJECTS

1. a. Sign is always negative; 0.5 or 1/2.
    b. Cigarettes inelastic, oranges elastic; apples less elastic than oranges.
    c. Percent change in price is −0.25 or −1/4 [(7 − 9) ÷ ((7 + 9) ÷ 2) = −2 ÷ 8 = −1/4].
        Percent change in quantity is 0.5 or 1/2 [(50 − 30) ÷ ((50 + 30) ÷ 2) = 20 ÷ 40 = 1/2].
        Price elasticity is −2.0 [0.5 ÷ −0.25 or 1/2 ÷ −1/4]; demand is elastic.

2. a. Yes, because MB declines with quantity consumed.
    b. 4, 3, 2, 1

    c. They would be identical. Keri's demand curve is her marginal benefit curve.
    d. $40, 60, 60, 40
    e. increases; inelastic
    f. it stays the same; unitary elastic
    g. decreases; elastic
    h. 0.43 (or 3/7); 1; 2.33 (or 7/3); yes

3. b. 3, 6, 9, 12
    c. 4, 5, 9
    d. Ann's purchases will fall from 4 to 3; Bob's purchases will fall from 5 to 3; Bob's purchases are more responsive to price; Bob has the more elastic demand.

4. a. $600, 800, 600
    b. rises; inelastic; 0.6 or 3/5
    c. falls; elastic; 1.67 or 5/3
    d. It depends. If price is currently $3, lowering it to $2 will increase revenue. If price is currently $2, lowering it to $1 will decrease revenue.
    e. A price of $2 maximizes the total dollars spent and thus would maximize total tip revenue as well if tips are given as a percent of sales.
    f. No, revenue would have increased to $900.
    g. No, revenue would have increased to $900.

5. a. Fall from 70 to 60; fall from 70 to 50; D_2; D_1
    b. Rise from 70 to 80; rise from 70 to 90; D_2; D_1
    c. Answers are the same in either direction.

6. a. $20
    b. No; 3 new customers at $4 each is a gain of only $12 in new customer revenue, not enough to make up for the loss of $20 on his regular customers. His total revenue will fall by $8 ($12 − $20) from $100 to $92.
    c. Yes, exactly enough; 5 new customers at $4 each is a gain of $20 in new customer revenue, exactly what he will be losing on his regular customers. His total revenue will remain unchanged at $100.
    d. Yes, more than enough; 10 new customers at $4 each is a gain of $40 in new customer revenue. His total revenue will rise by $20 ($40 − $20) to $120.
    e. Yes; In part b demand was inelastic so total revenue fell, in part c demand was unitary elastic so total revenue remained the same, in part d demand was elastic so total revenue increased as a result of the price reduction.

f. If John loses 10 regular customers, he loses the $50 they used to spend. However, 10 customers keep coming and they are each paying $5 more (for a total of $50). The gains exactly equal the losses, so John's total revenue will remain unchanged. If only 5 customers left, his revenue would rise (lose $25 on the 5 who leave, gain $75 on the 15 who stay, so the net is $50 more total revenue). If 15 customers left, his revenue would fall (lose $75 on the 15 who leave, gain $25 on the 5 who stay, so the net is a loss of $50 in revenue). When 5 leave, demand is inelastic so revenue rises; when 10 leave, demand is unitary elastic so revenue remains unchanged; when 15 leave, demand is elastic so revenue falls.

7. Price elasticity: 1.0
    Change in price: up; up
    Change in total revenue: down; no change; up

MULTIPLE CHOICE

1. b. Price elasticity is 30 ÷ 15 = 2, which is greater than one, so demand is elastic. If demand is elastic, a price increase lowers total expenditure (or total revenue).

2. d. All of these are true statements about marginal benefit.

3. d. Income elasticity is +20 percent ÷ +10 percent = +2. This is positive, so jewelry is a normal good (her purchases rise with higher income). It is also greater than one, which means jewelry is a luxury good for Jane.

4. d. An inferior good is one for which purchases fall when *income* (not price) rises and vice versa. This inverse relationship shows up as a negative income elasticity.

5. a. Wine purchases rise with income so wine is a normal good, but fast food purchases fall with income so fast food is an inferior good.

6. d. As the rate of consumption increases, the additional (or marginal) utility derived from additional units falls.

7. b. The demand is elastic because the value is greater than one. It is larger than the value for bananas so it shows more responsiveness. If demand is elastic, an increase in price lowers total expenditures (or total revenue).

8. d. 10 ÷ 50 = 0.2, which is less than one so demand is inelastic.

9. c. For a higher price to increase total revenue, demand must be inelastic.

10. c. A risk-loving person would prefer the game, a risk-averse person would prefer the $100 certain cash, and a risk-neutral person would be indifferent.

11. a. Demand elasticity always increases with price along a linear demand curve.

12. d. This is why lowering price can either lower revenue, leave it unchanged, or raise revenue. In answer *a* demand is inelastic, in answer *b* demand is unitary elastic, and in answer *c* demand is elastic.

13. a. The issue is not *whether* more people will come or not, but *how many* more people will come. This is answered by elasticity. If demand is elastic, revenue will rise when price is lowered. If demand is inelastic, revenue will fall. The previous question (question 12) gives a numerical example to illustrate this point.

14. b. The numbers here are irrelevant. If an increase in price increases total revenue, demand must be inelastic. Remember, total revenue is *not* the same as quantity so these numbers cannot be directly used in the elasticity formula.

15. d. Consumers generally have incomplete information. This is why we sometimes make mistakes in our purchases, but we learn from these mistakes and make future choices more wisely.

16. c. To maximize utility, she should equate MU/P for both goods. Currently MU/P for hamburgers is 10/2 = 5, while MU/P for shirts is 50/25 = 2. Hamburgers are giving her more utility per dollar

than are shirts, so she should buy fewer shirts and more hamburgers to maximize her utility.

17. c.   The *marginal* cost of flying is $450 ($600 – $150), while the *marginal* benefit of flying is the 45 hours (50 – 5) of time saved. It is only worth spending the extra $450 to save 45 hours if you value your time at $10 per hour or more.

18. b.   A demand curve with a steeper (more negative) slope shows less responsiveness to price so it is relatively more inelastic.

19. a.   Total expenditures will be increased by a higher price if demand is inelastic.

20. b.   (90 – 70)/((90 + 70)/2) ÷ (10 – 6)/((10 + 6)/2) = 20/80 ÷ 4/8 = 1/4 ÷ 1/2 = 1/2.

21. c.   Greater than one is elastic. When a fraction is greater than one, it means the numerator (the percent change in quantity) is greater than the denominator (the percent change in price).

22. b.   Consumer surplus is equal to the difference between the maximum a consumer would be willing to pay ($100) and the price actually paid ($40), so $100 – $40 = $60.

23. a.   The total amount purchased in the market at a given price is the sum of the amounts purchased by all individuals at that price.

24. a.   He *substitutes* away from the place whose prices have risen, and the reduction in his *real income* will cause him to cut back on eating out.

25. a.   It measures how the quantity purchased by buyers responds to a price change.

26. d.   All of these are true regarding demand elasticity.

CHAPTER EIGHT

TRUE OR FALSE

The following are true: 1, 3, 4, 5, 6, 7, 10, 11, 13

The following are false:

2. Economic profit calculations differ because they *include* opportunity costs. Thus, economic profit calculations generally have higher levels of cost, and thus lower levels of profit.

8. It is called marginal cost. Average variable cost is total variable cost divided by output.

9. Average cost will always increase when marginal cost is *above* average cost. It does not matter whether the marginal cost is increasing, decreasing, or remaining constant.

12. Total cost may be found by *adding* total variable cost and total fixed cost.

14. It is experiencing economies of scale. Diseconomies of scale are when per unit costs rise with increased plant size in the long run.

15. It would shift the cost curves downward because the cost of production would decline.

16. A good decision maker ignores sunk costs when making decisions.

PROBLEMS AND PROJECTS

1. a. $9,000
   b. the opportunity cost of his equity capital, which is the forgone interest he could have earned on the $30,000 and the opportunity cost of his labor, which is the forgone wages he could have earned working for someone else (here given as $10,000)
   c. $3,000
   d. His total cost would be $48,000 + $3,000 + $10,000 = $61,000.
   e. He is making an economic loss of $4,000, which shows that he could make more money in his next best alternative. If he shut down, put his money back in the bank, and worked for the other person, he would make $4,000 more income per year. He is making $9,000 in accounting profit now but could make $3,000 of interest income plus $10,000 of regular wage income for a total of $13,000 in his next best alternative.

2. a. MP: 8, 16, 12, 8, 6, 4, 2, 0 (calculated as the change in total product)
   AP: 8, 12, 12, 11, 10, 9, 8, 7 (calculated total product divided by units of labor)
   c. After the second unit of labor, because this is the point after which MP begins to fall. You could say that diminishing returns begins on the third unit of labor, but we generally say that diminishing returns begin after the second unit because some firms can employ fractions of units of inputs (such as pounds of steel).

3. a. TFC: $50, 50, 50, 50, 50, 50, 50 (Remember TFC stays the same at all levels of output.)
   TVC: $50, 90, 127, 166, 215, 274, 349, 446 (equal to TC minus TFC)
   ATC: $100, 70, 59, 54, 53, 54, 57, 62 (equal to TC divided by output)
   AVC: $50, 45, 42.33, 41.50, 43, 45.67, 49.86, 55.75 (equal to TVC divided by output)
   MC: $50, 40, 37, 39, 49, 59, 75, 97 (equal to the change in TC from before; to find MC for the first unit, remember that the total cost of producing zero units of output is equal to total fixed cost [$50] because total variable cost is zero when no units are produced)
   b. 5 because this is the output level were the number in the ATC column is the smallest.
   c. after the third unit because MC is at its minimum at 3 units of output. See the answer for 2c above about the terminology.

4. ATC: $120, 100; AVC: $70, 75; MC: $60, 100
   a. $360 (equal to ATC times Q), 210 (AVC times Q), and 150 (equal to either AFC times Q or TC minus TVC)
   b. $600, 450, 150
   c. $500 (total cost of six units is $600 and the MC of the sixth unit was $100, so $600 minus $100 was the total cost of five units)
   d. $150 (it is the same at all output levels)

e. $50, 25 (either TFC divided by output or ATC minus AVC)

f.   Total cost is the rectangle with the corners: 0, $120, the ATC curve at three units, and the quantity 3. This rectangle has a bottom of length three and a side of length $120, so its area is $120 times 3 or $360, which is the total cost of producing 3 units. If the rectangle is divided into upper and lower parts at a value of $70 (by the AVC curve), the upper portion is TFC and the lower portion is TVC.

5. a.   5; (35 − 30)
    b.   150; (300 ÷ 2)
    c. $10; (TC is $100 + $200 = $300, so ATC is $300 ÷ 30)
    d. $3; (5 − 2)
    e. $100; (5 × 20)
    f. $5; (45 − 40)
    g. $350; (TFC same at all levels of output)
    h. $4; (200 ÷ 50)
    i. $700; (TVC is $100 × 5 = $500, so TC is $500 + $200)
    j. $2; (50 ÷ 25)
    k. $6,000; ($5,000,000 + $1,000,000 = $6,000,000 is TC, so ATC is $6,000,000 ÷ 1,000)

MULTIPLE CHOICE

1. d.   The marginal cost curve is a reflection of the marginal product curve.

2. c.   These are the "fixed" factors of production. They take the most time to change.

3. b.   This is the definition of sunk cost.

4. d.   Both of these are advantages.

5. c.   AFC, which is the difference between ATC and AVC, declines with output.

6. d.   This productivity or technological advance would lower costs.

7. d.   MC crosses ATC at the minimum of ATC.

8. d.   It can be stated either way. They mean the same thing.

9. d.   Find 10 on the horizontal (quantity) axis, then go up to the ATC curve.

10. a.   AFC = ATC − AVC = 12 − 8.

11. d.   Equal to ATC times quantity (13 × 10).

12. b.   AFC times quantity. AFC is ATC minus AVC or 13 − 7 = 6, so 6 × 10 = 60.

13. a.   Find 10 on the horizontal (quantity) axis, then go up to the MC curve.

14. c.   This is where the ATC curve is at its minimum.

15. a.   This is where the MC curve is at its minimum.

16. b.   The $300 will have to be paid whether the house is rented or not. It is a sunk cost and should not be considered. Any rent over $100 will allow the family to pay the $100 utilities and at least have some left over to put toward the mortgage payment.

17. c.   The decision at hand is whether to pay $2 to watch a movie you value at $5. The $3.50 paid originally is a sunk cost because the movie store will not refund it if you bring it back and say that you did not get a chance to watch it.

18. c.   The others shift it upward.

19. a.   Economic profits subtract more costs (the opportunity costs) and are thus generally lower.

20. d.   When per-unit costs fall as plant size is expanded, the LRATC curve will slope downward.

21. b.   This is a definition.

22. b.   Rules are implemented to minimize employee shirking.

23. c.   Limited liability makes investing in a corporation less risky than in other forms of business because the remainder of your assets are not held against the debts of the company.

24. c.   Accounting profit is $100,000 − $60,000, while economic profit is $100,000 − $90,000. Her eco-

nomic cost is the accounting cost of $60,000 plus the opportunity cost of her equity capital (the forgone interest of $2,000) plus her forgone wages of $28,000.

25. c. Zero economic profit means accounting profits equal opportunity costs.

26. c. In the long run, all factors of production can be changed.

27. c. Remember, MC always "pulls" ATC.

28. b. Most of the information is irrelevant. To find AFC at twenty units, we need to know TFC and then divide it by output. We know AFC is $14 when output is 10, so TFC is $140. Then $140 divided by 20 gives the answer.

29. b. This is just an application of the law of diminishing returns. Do not confuse it with the law of diminishing marginal utility which applies to consumers.

30. b. This is one of the reasons for economies of scale listed in the book.

CHAPTER NINE

TRUE OR FALSE

The following are true: 1, 2, 4, 5, 7, 8, 9, 11, 15

The following are false:

3. For a price taker, marginal revenue is equal to price.

6. A firm's short-run supply curve is its marginal cost (MC) curve above average variable cost (AVC).

10. They always produce where MC = MR but only produce where ATC is at its minimum in the long run.

12. Zero *economic* profit means that the firm is earning an accounting profit that is typical of the profit it could earn elsewhere in other industries. There is no reason for the firm to leave or for firms from other industries to enter.

13. In a constant cost industry, long-run supply is horizontal and market price will return to its original level. It would rise for an increasing cost industry.

14. Fixed costs remain present when a firm shuts down in the short run.

PROBLEMS AND PROJECTS

1. a. Total Revenue: $0, 25, 50, 75, 100, 125, 150
   b. Marginal Revenue: $25, 25, 25, 25, 25, 25; equal to price
   c. Marginal Cost: $10, 5, 10, 20, 30, 40
   d. Profit: $–20, –5, +15, +30, +35, +30, +15
   e. Produce all units up to where marginal cost equals price (MC = P)
   f. Yes; it falls when the unit is produced.
   g. 4; 4; yes
   h. 6
   i. No change; profit equals $105 for both.

2. a. Total Cost: $0, 10, 30, 60, 100, 150
   b. Marginal Cost: $10, 20, 30, 40, 50
   c. 3
   d. $60; $20; $10

e. 3 tons × $10 per unit profit equals $30; $90 total revenue minus $60 total cost equals $30; yes.

3. a. Output is 1,000 (total revenue divided by price); total cost is $8,000 (average total cost times quantity); marginal revenue is 8 (marginal revenue equals price); marginal cost is 8 (marginal cost equals marginal revenue when maximizing profits); total profit is $0 (total revenue minus total cost).
   b. Yes (zero economic profit).
   c. Stay the same.

4. a. 60 (the output level where MC = MR)
   b. $1,200 total revenue ($20 price × 60 units); $600 total cost ($10 average cost per unit × 60 units); $600 profit ($1,200 total revenue minus $600 total cost).
   c. It is the rectangle above $10 and below $20 from the price axis out to 60 units.
   d. $550; less.
   e. 200 firms (12,000 total units of output ÷ 60 units per firm)
   f. Firms would enter because there are economic profits; price would fall to minimum average total cost which is $9.

5. a. Economic profit; increase
   b. Zero economic profit; stay the same
   c. Economic loss; decrease; remain open in short run

6. a. New market price where D_2 intersects S.
   b. Profits increase; firm output increases.
   c. More firms will enter.

7. a. Price: $60, 40, 30, 50
      Rooms rented: 30, 20, 0, 25
      Profits: +, 0, –, –
   b. No; shut down during summer because price is below AVC, thus you will rent no rooms during the summer.
   c. You would see whether the profits during some seasons are enough to offset the losses during others so that you did not have losses for the entire year.

MULTIPLE CHOICE

1. c. In a price-taker market, there are a large number of small firms producing identical products. They must take the market price as given and will earn zero economic profits in the long run.

2. a. This is the definition. A price-searcher firm can set its own price, but the number of units sold will depend on the price chosen because the firm will face a downward-sloping demand curve.

3. a. For a price taker, marginal revenue equals price.

4. c. This is the rule for profit maximization. For a price-taker firm, because price equals marginal revenue, this could also be correctly stated as marginal cost equals price.

5. a. This unit adds more to revenue than it does to cost.

6. c. It is earning $4 profit on each unit, times 50 units.

7. d. These are the two important things to remember about marginal revenue for the price-taker firm.

8. c. Zero economic profit means that the firm is doing as well as it could in other alternative industries. There is no incentive for the firm to exit or for other firms to enter.

9. c. Marginal revenue is the change in total revenue, while marginal cost is the change in total cost.

10. a. This is an alternative term that you might run into in another economics class.

11. d. This is how a price-taker market reaches long-run equilibrium.

12. d. Higher demand increases price, firms expand output, and the profits attract new competition.

13. b. Short-run profits (price above average total cost) attract new firms into the industry until zero economic profit (price equal to average total cost) is restored.

14. d. All of these are true.

15. d. Lower demand reduces price, causing losses and firms to exit.

16. b. A firm's short-run supply curve is its marginal cost curve above average variable cost.

17. a. Both b and c are opposites of what is correct.

18. a. In an increasing cost industry, all firms' costs rise with the entry of new additional firms because resource prices in the industry are bid upward.

19. d. It will create losses in the short run, some firms will go out of business, and the market price will rise until the remaining firms can cover their costs (including the cost of the antipollution devices).

20. b. As long as a market is "open" and firms are free to enter and exit, the industry can earn neither abnormally high nor abnormally low profits in the long run.

21. b. Because the firm will shut down in the short run at prices lower than AVC, the short-run supply curve is only the portion of MC above AVC.

22. a. Total revenue ($400) is larger than total *variable* cost ($300), so you should remain open. If you shut down, your loss is equal to your rent and other fixed costs of $200. If you remain open, you lose only $100. Put in another way, even though you cannot cover your entire rent, you are at least making $100 from being open to put toward your rent.

23. c. It should continue to operate until the lease expires because it can cover its variable cost. This answer is similar in logic to the previous question.

24. a. In his own words he has said that he follows the marginal-cost/marginal-revenue rule and also that he is out to maximize profit. This producer is exactly what is being modeled in "fancy" economic theory.

25. d. This is how price changes in a market economy help to redirect resources when consumer tastes (or other conditions) change.

26. c. Profit is equal to $10 at an output level of three units. You can work this problem in two ways, either by computing marginal cost and producing every unit with marginal cost less than price or by computing total revenue and finding actual profit for each level of output, then selecting the level with the highest profit.

27. c. This is the level of output where MC equals MR (at point F).

28. b. It is a profit, not a loss, because P is greater than ATC. Profit is the area that represents per unit profit times quantity [(P –ATC) × q].

29. a. Positive economic profits will attract new firms into the industry.

30. d. Because price equals ATC, there is zero economic profit; the industry is in long-run equilibrium.

31. c. This is the level of output where MC equals MR (at point H). The firm would not shut down in the short run because price exceeds AVC.

32. c. It is a loss because P is lower than ATC. The loss is the area that represents per unit loss times quantity [(P – ATC) × q].

33. b. Some of the firms experiencing losses will shut down, and market price will rise until the remaining firms earn zero economic profit.

34. a. Price is less than AVC; the firm should shut down in the short run.

35. a. An upward-sloping long-run supply curve shows that it is an increasing cost industry.

CHAPTER TEN

TRUE OR FALSE

The following are true: 2, 5, 6, 7, 9, 10, 12, 14

The following are false:

1. All firms, regardless of market conditions or industry, maximize profits by producing at MR = MC.

3. Price discrimination is the practice of charging different prices to different customers for the same product.

4. For a price searcher, marginal revenue is less than price, so the marginal revenue curve lies below the demand curve for the firm.

8. The entry of new firms will result in a reduction in demand for existing firms in the market.

11. A contestable market is one in which the barriers to entry are low, in other words, the cost of entry and exit is low.

13. Price will be greater than marginal cost. The firm will equate marginal cost and marginal revenue, but for a price-searcher firm marginal revenue is less than price. Thus, marginal cost is also less than price.

15. Marginal revenue is the change in total revenue. Three units at a price of $5 yields total revenue of $15, while four units at a price of $4 yields total revenue of $16. Thus, the marginal revenue from the sale of the fourth unit is $1 (the difference, $16 − $15). Note that this is less than the price at which the fourth unit is sold.

PROBLEMS AND PROJECTS

1. a. Total Revenue: $0, 60, 110, 150, 180, 200, 210
      Marginal Revenue: $60, 50, 40, 30, 20, 10
      Marginal Cost: $50, 20, 25, 29, 40, 50
      Profit: $−40, −30, 0, 15, 16, −4, −44
   b. To maximize profit, charge a price of $45 and produce a total of 4 units. You can find this either by finding the row in the table with the highest total profit or by using the marginal-cost/marginal-revenue rule.
   c. Price of $45 is greater than marginal cost of $29.

d. The demand curve for your firm would drop as other firms entered the business, drawing away some of your customers. This would continue to occur until all firms earned only zero economic profit.

2. a. The firm is a price searcher because it faces a downward-sloping demand curve.
   b. The output is where MR = MC; the price is the price on the demand curve associated with the profit-maximizing output.
   c. The firm is making a profit because its price is greater than its ATC.
   d. The positive economic profits will attract competitors to the industry. As new firms enter the market, the demand curve for this firm will decrease (shift downward and to the left) until it is exactly tangent to the ATC curve.

3. a. The output is where MR = MC; the price is the price on the demand curve associated with the profit-maximizing output.
   b. The firm is making a loss because its price is less than its ATC. It will remain open in the short run because price is still above AVC.
   c. The economic losses will cause some firms to exit the industry until the demand curves for the remaining firms increase enough to restore zero economic profit. This will happen when this firm's demand curve shifts upward and to the right until it is exactly tangent to the ATC curve.

4. a. 1, students have more limited budgets and more substitute activities available to them.
   b. 2, they have more options available (different possible dates of travel, different possible transportation such as a car or bus, etc.)
   c. 1, these people have the option of continuing to drive their current car.
   d. 1, the poor will have more limited budgets and will be more sensitive to price.

MULTIPLE CHOICE

1. d. Differentiability of goods and services is an important reason why competitive price searchers experience downward-sloping demand curves, unlike the horizontal demand curve confronting price takers.

2. d.   All of these conditions will be met.

3. d.   To maximize profit, all decisions should be made with this rule.

4. a.   The money lost on the earlier units (for which price was lowered) is why producing an additional unit adds less to revenue than the price at which it is sold.

5. c.   A price searcher is different because they face a downward-sloping demand curve. The demand curve for a price taker is a horizontal line at the market price.

6. a.   These are the conditions that define a competitive price-searcher market. Note that answer d contains the conditions for an open price-taker market.

7. a.   This is the difference in total revenue. Four units at a price of $6 yields total revenue of $24, while five units at a price of $5 yields total revenue of $25. By producing and selling this additional unit, revenue increases by $1.

8. b.   This is how the market will return to zero economic profit in the long run.

9. d.   Answer c is incorrect because P > MC for the price searcher.

10. d.   This is the definition of a contestable market. It has low barriers to entry.

11. c.   This is the main result both markets share in common.

12. d.   Answer c is incorrect because a price searcher does not maximize profits at this point, see the next question.

13. c.   This is a potential source of inefficiency in price-searcher markets.

14. b.   The standard model of competitive price searchers does not account for the benefits consumers derive from product differentiation. As a specific example, the model simply shows that if all brands of beer were exactly identical, beer could be produced at a lower per-unit cost and sold at a lower price to consumers.

15. c.   Since entry barriers are low, economic profits will attract new entrants. Existing firms will experience a drop in the demand for their product, and prices will fall until zero economic profits are restored.

16. b.   Firms charge those groups with the more elastic (or less inelastic) demand lower prices, and those groups with the more inelastic (or less elastic) demand higher prices. The result is generally a larger output and an improvement in allocative efficiency.

17. a.   This is a basic similarity between price-taker and competitive price-searcher industries. This condition is true for any contestable market (any market in which the cost of entry and exit is low).

18. a.   Quantity (E) is where MR = MC, and the demand curve gives the price firms are able to charge for that quantity (A).

19. a.   Profit = TR – TC = (P $\times$ q) – (ATC $\times$ q) = q $\times$ (P – ATC), or in words, profit is equal to per-unit profit (P – ATC) times the quantity sold (q). Per-unit profit is equal to the height KG and the quantity is equal to the width of CK. This is a profit, not a loss because price exceeds ATC.

20. b.   Profits attract new competitors into the industry who will draw away some of this firm's customers, reducing demand.

21. b.   Quantity I is where MR = MC, and the *demand curve* gives the price firms are able to charge for that quantity C.

22. d.   This is a loss because price is less than ATC. Per-unit loss is equal to the height EF and the quantity is equal to the width of CF. The entire area is the total loss.

23. b.   Some firms will exit due to the losses, and the demand for the remaining firms will increase.

24. b.   Total profit is $12 at this price and output, higher than at the other levels. You can find this answer either by finding the row in the table with the highest total profit or by using the marginal-cost/marginal-revenue rule.

CHAPTER ELEVEN

TRUE OR FALSE

The following are true: 1, 5, 7, 8, 9, 11, 12, 13, 14

2. High barriers preventing the entry of new competitors make it possible for monopolies to earn economic profits in the long run.

3. To maximize profits, all firms produce the output level where MR = MC.

4. Inefficient production means higher costs that lead to lower profits, so the monopolist still has some incentive to produce efficiently.

6. A market dominated by a monopoly will have a higher price and a lower level of output than if it were competitive.

10. Market power refers to the ability of the firm to earn abnormally high profits. A firm facing heavy competition has the least market power.

PROBLEMS AND PROJECTS

1. a. Since the LRATC curve decreases over the range of quantities that are demanded, a single firm would be the lowest-cost producer. This is a situation of natural monopoly.
    b. The firm will produce the Q where MR = MC.
    c. The firm will charge the price from the demand curve associated with the quantity in part b.
    d. It is the area between the demand curve and ATC out to the profit-maximizing level of output.

2. a. TR: 6,400, 7,000, 7,800, 8,400, 8,800, 9,000, 9,000
    MR: 600, 800, 600, 400, 200, 0
    MC: 400, 400, 500, 700, 1,000, 1,200
    b. $1.20
    c. Yes; $1,100 per month
    d. $1.00
    e. Approximately $13,200 ($1,100 per month times 12 months) or the present value of the expected economic profit; the university would then reap the monopoly benefits.

3. a. P_4, Q_1, the area with height of P_2 to P_4 and width out to Q_1
    b. Q_2, P_3 (where MC intersects D)

4. a. P_1, Q_2
    b. P_2, Q_1

5. a. 50,000 units of output
    b. 30 cents.
    c. It will increase to 40 cents.
    d. no; 3 (150 ÷ 50); 6 (300 ÷ 50)

6. a. Upper left: Tom's $6,000; Bob's $6,000
       Upper right: Tom's $2,000; Bob's $9,000
       Lower right: Tom's $8,000; Bob's $8,000
    b. $30 (yields $6,000, which is larger than the profit of $2,000 at a price of $40)
    c. $30 (yields $9,000, which is larger than the profit of $8,000 at a price of $40)
    d. No, set price at $30 is best strategy in both cases.
    e. $30; no
    f. Both earn $6,000; yes, both would earn $8,000.
    g. No, both have an incentive to cheat (lower price to $30) to increase profits.

7. a. P_3 and Q_1 (at point A); yes
    b. P_2 and Q_2 (at point B); zero
    c. P_1; an economic loss; the monopolist would shut down, so output in the long run would be zero

MULTIPLE CHOICE

1. b. This is the definition of a monopoly market.

2. b. The others violate at least one of the market conditions necessary to be a monopoly.

3. c. The elasticity of demand has nothing to do with how easy it is for new firms to enter the market. The only other barrier not listed is economies of scale.

4. a. Economies of scale are present if per-unit costs fall as a firm increases its size in the long run. If present, one large firm will have lower costs than several smaller firms.

5. d. They "restrict" output to increase price. Alternatively, you may remember that monopo-

lies charge higher prices and thus sell fewer units of output.

6. d. It results in higher prices and positive economic profit opportunity while the barrier to entry is in place.

7. d. A monopolist can lose money if costs exceed the price consumers are willing to pay, it will charge the price that maximizes their profit, and will make higher profits the more it can reduce costs.

8. d. All of these conditions are true.

9. b. At a price of $5 and an output of 3 units, the monopolist earns a profit of $5 (toal revenue of $15 minus total cost of $10), higher than for any other level of output in the exhibit.

10. d. This is the major difference between the markets that arises due to the barriers to entry under monopoly.

11. d. Produce the level of output where MC = MR, and set price up along the demand curve.

12. c. Produce the level of output where MC = MR, set price up along the demand curve, profit is equal to the difference between price and ATC (which is per-unit profit) times the number of units sold.

13. a. This is the definition of an oligopoly market.

14. b. OPEC is an example of a specific cartel. They attempt to act like a single monopoly and maximize joint profit.

15. a. A higher market price for oil, for example, will only come about if less oil is produced.

16. c. Cartels restrict output and raise price, in any industry.

17. a. The first major antitrust law was the Sherman Act.

18. c. The others would make successful collusion less likely.

19. d. This is why collusive agreements are so unstable. The prisoners' dilemma is one frequently used tool to demonstrate these incentives.

20. a. Cartels result in higher prices and lower output. Don't forget the law of demand; as funeral prices rise, some people will be cremated, while others might be buried in other nearby towns. There is no such thing as a perfectly inelastic demand curve.

21. d. More often than not, regulatory agencies end up using their power to help the established firms in the industry at the expense of consumers.

22. a. The only way you can earn positive economic profits in the long run is to prevent new firms from entering and offering your customers cheaper prices. This can only be done by legal restrictions on the ability of new firms to enter.

23. d. While regulation "ideally" could improve the situation, the real-world problems are generally very large in implementing the ideal outcomes.

24. c. Without a profit motive, government agencies have no incentive to conserve on resources to cut costs.

CHAPTER TWELVE

TRUE OR FALSE

The following are true: 2, 3, 5, 7, 11, 12, 13, 14.

The following are false:

1. Machines can be substituted for workers and vice versa.

4. When the demand for a final product increases, the demand for resources used to produce the good will increase as well.

6. This is true for a price-taker firm, not a price-searcher firm. For a price-searcher firm, marginal revenue (MR) is less than price (P), so MRP is less than VMP.

8. They will stop hiring before that point because they will hire only until marginal revenue product falls to equal the market wage rate.

9. The correct formula is marginal product (MP) divided by price (P), not MRP divided by price.

10. With more time to adjust, the long-run supply will be more elastic, not more inelastic.

PROBLEMS AND PROJECTS

1. a. MP: 5, 4, 3, 2, 1
        TR: 500, 900, 1200, 1400, 1500
        MRP: 500, 400, 300, 200, 100
    b. three
    c. two
    d. New TR: 750, 1350, 1800, 2100, 2250
        New MRP: 750, 600, 450, 300, 150
        New employment level = 4, so she hires one more worker relative to part b.

2. a. MP: 5, 7, 6, 3.5, 2.5, 1
        TR: 500, 1200, 1800, 2150, 2400, 2500
        MRP: 500, 700, 600, 350, 250, 100
    b. five
    c. four

3. a. 0, −, +, −
    b. +, 0, +, +
    c. 0, +, −, +
    d. −, 0, −, −
    e. +, 0, +, +

4. a. No, MP of Vitacorn/P of Vitacorn = 200/800 < 400/1200 = MP of Cornpower/P of Cornpower.
    b. The farmer could produce the same output for $400 less.
    c. Yes, the decrease in the MP of Cornpower as its usage increases will cause the ratio of the MP of Cornpower to its price to decrease, eventually fulfilling the condition for cost minimization: MP of Vitacorn/P of Vitacorn = MP of Cornpower/P of Cornpower.

5. a. For U.S. workers, MP/P = 60/10 = 6. For Mexican workers, MP/P = 30/6 = 5. This means the firm is getting six units of output per dollar spent on U.S. labor, while it would get only five units of output per dollar spent on Mexican labor.
    b. Because MP/P is lower in Mexico, costs would be higher. As an easy example, to produce sixty units would require one U.S. worker at a cost of $10, while it would take two Mexican workers (with MP of thirty each) to produce sixty units at a cost of $12 total (two workers at $6).
    c. MP/P would become equal at a Mexican wage rate of $5. So at any wage rate below $5, it would be profitable to move to Mexico to lower costs.

MULTIPLE CHOICE

1. c. There will be many workers with these skills (many close substitutes).

2. a. The demand for resources is *derived from* the demand for the product.

3. a. A small change in resource price raises product cost and reduces sales greatly. Again, the demand for resources is *derived from* the demand for the product.

4. b. Additional employment would *add* more to revenue than it would *add* to cost.

5. a. We say it is *derived from* the demand for the product.

6. b. In the long run, it is easier to change production methods to use more or less substitute resources.

7. c. Since P = MR, MRP = VMP.

8. d. This would equate MP/P for skilled and unskilled labor.

9. a. This is the condition for a firm to minimize its costs (or maximize its profits)

10. d. All of these are listed in the text as shifting the demand curve for a resource.

11. b. Currently MP/P for labor is 40 ÷ 20 = 2, while MP/P for capital is 10 ÷ 10 = 1, so the firm is not minimizing its costs. It should substitute into the one with the higher ratio (labor) and away from the one with the lower ratio (capital).

12. d. The aid would attract more students, increasing the supply of college graduates and lowering their wages.

13. b. In competitive labor markets, wages equal workers marginal revenue products. If college graduates did not have higher MP, their wages would not be higher.

14. b. Human capital is the skills and knowledge of a person. Investing in human capital is when a person spends money or other resources to increase their human capital.

15. b. Higher worker wages will mean a higher price for the final product. If the demand for the final product is very elastic, then sales of the final product will fall substantially, meaning fewer workers will be needed to produce the steel.

16. b. MRP equals MP times price. MP of the fifth worker is the change in total output that the fifth worker causes, which is 20 – 18 = 2. So MP times price is 2 × $2 = $4.

17. b. The firm should hire only those workers for which MRP is greater than the wage of $5.

18. a. The firm should hire only those workers for which MRP is greater than the wage of $7.

19. c. The tenth workers marginal product is 20 – 17 = 3. So MP times price is 3 × $200 = $600.

20. d. Hire only if the additional revenue (MRP) exceeds the additional cost.

21. d. It is the change in units of output multiplied by the price they can be sold for, so this is the same as the change in the firm's revenue.

22. b. This is why they are the same for a price-taker firm because P = MR.

23. d. Higher demand raises price and creates an incentive to supply more of the resource.

24. b. Or alternatively, you might say it is more inelastic in the short run.

25. b. Never employ a resource that costs more to hire than its value to the firm.

CHAPTER THIRTEEN

TRUE OR FALSE

The following are true: 2, 3, 6, 7, 9, 10, 11, 12, 13

The following are false:

1. This is not sufficient. Workers would have to have identical preferences, jobs would all have to be equally attractive, and labor would have to be perfectly mobile.

4. There is a strong positive relationship. More education leads to higher earnings.

5. The top performer gets a wage greater than MRP, the others get wages less than MRP.

8. It will have a higher wage to compensate the worker for taking on the higher level of risk.

14. Automation can increase employment in the industries that it affects. In addition, consumers will save money on goods and services that are cheaper due to automation, they will use that saved money to demand other goods and services.

15. There has been a "great productivity slowdown" and the rate of productivity growth is now very low compared to the past.

PROBLEMS AND PROJECTS

1. a. –
   b. +
   c. +
   d. –
   e. +
   f. –

2. a. Jane earns more in the form of money earnings.
   b. Both have identical total compensation (they are in identical jobs). The compensation is just given differently at the two companies.
   c. Yes, Bob would gain more value from the benefits to make it worthwhile to give up $5,000 in money earnings to get these benefits.

d. Jane would have to decide whether these benefits were worth $5,000 to her. For example, she might be able to buy a private health-insurance plan outside her employer for $2,000 and get her own child care locally for $2,000, in which case it would not make sense to pay the employer $5,000 to provide these for her.

3. a. Q = 3,000; P = $300
   b. Q = 4,000; P = $200
   c. Originally the industry employed 50 workers for every thousand calculators produced, or a total of 150 (50 × 3) workers when it produced 3,000 calculators. Now it employs 40 workers for every thousand produced, or a total of 160 (40 × 4). Employment has risen by 10 workers due to the increased output afforded by the automation lowering the price to consumers.
   d. See the "Myths of Economics" box in this chapter for a good refutation of this statement.

4. a. A1
   b. B1
   c. B2
   d. B3

MULTIPLE CHOICE

1. a. A college education increases your productivity on the job.

2. a. Security of income attracts more workers (increases supply) and lowers wages in secure professions relative to insecure ones.

3. d. All of these make the job more attractive, increasing the supply of labor into the occupation and lowering the wage rate.

4. a. Worker preferences, like other differences across people, create earnings differences.

5. a. Tournament pay is a theory to describe situations where the "winner" receives a very high reward, while those just underneath the winner receive substantially less.

6. d. All of these are possible sources of earnings differences.

7. b. The market punishes discriminatory firms by lowering their profits when the discrimination is rooted in the employer (not the customers). To be more selective, the firm's costs will have to rise.

8. d. These factors should serve to lower the differential between male and female average wages.

9. d. Employees pay for fringe benefits in the form of lower money wages.

10. c. Employers will either cut other fringe benefits or lower money wages.

11. c. Growth of the physical capital stock through investment increases labor productivity and is a major driving force for real wage growth.

12. a. Services of more productive workers are worth more; undesirable jobs would pay more.

13. c. Both are reasons for the differential.

14. c. True, although automation can harm *specific* individuals or groups.

15. b. Higher supply of labor into the occupation would lower wages.

16. b. Customers will be willing to pay higher prices or buy more from the discriminating firm.

17. d. The benefit of tournament pay systems is that it increases effort among all workers.

18. d. This is an example of a situation where a firm may discriminate in its hiring based upon customer preferences.

CHAPTER FOURTEEN

TRUE OR FALSE

The following are true: 1, 2, 3, 4, 6, 7, 10, 12

The following are false:

5. It will rise if the interest rate falls.

8. The real rate of interest represents the true cost.

9. More risk increases the interest rate.

11. Stock prices adjust rapidly to reflect any changes in how the market perceives the profitability of a given corporation.

PROBLEMS AND PROJECTS

1. a. A (because A has the higher inflation premium)
    b. C (because C has higher demand for borrowing loanable funds)
    c. F (because F has the lower supply of loanable funds)
    d. G (because G has the higher risk premium)

2. a. At a price of $2 per board foot, the extra ten thousand board feet is equal to $20,000 in future revenue received thirty years from now. Discounted to present value, this is equal to $4,627.55 (found as $20,000 \div [1 + 0.05]^{30}$) when the interest rate is 5 percent, so it is a worthwhile investment because it costs less than this amount. At 10 percent, the present value is $1,146.17 (found as $20,000 \div [1 + 0.1]^{30}$), still enough to make the investment worthwhile, but at 15 percent the value falls to $302.06 (found as $20,000 \div [1 + 0.15]^{30}$), below the cost of $500, so it is no longer worthwhile.
    b. At a price of $1 per board foot, the extra ten thousand board feet is equal to $1,000 in future revenue received thirty years from now. Discounted to present value, this is equal to $151.03, less than the $500 cost of the investment. At a price of $2, the present value becomes $302.06 still below the cost, but at a price of $4, the present value is $604.12, so it becomes worthwhile.

3. a. The present value of receiving $1,000 per year forever at an interest rate of 8 percent (found as $1,000 \div 0.08$) is $12,500. This is a fairly close approximation to the true value of $12,234.
    b. $4,761,900 (found as $333,333 \div 0.07$), which is a fairly close approximation to the true value of $4,136,329
    c. $15,000 (found as $150,000 \times 0.10$), which is a fairly close approximation to the true value of $15,912 (Note that an approximate monthly payment could be found by dividing these annual amounts by 12.)

4. a. $150,000
    b. $50 million
    c. $46.15
    d. $12,434.26
    e. $36,000

MULTIPLE CHOICE

1. d. More resources devoted toward investment requires less resources be devoted toward current consumption.

2. a. A positive rate of time preference means sooner is preferred to later. Different people may have different *rates* of time preference, some might prefer to have $75 now rather than $100 later, while others would prefer waiting and receiving the $100 rather than having $75 now. But everyone should prefer having $100 now rather than $100 later.

3. a. Present value is inversely related to the interest rate. (Note that the interest rate is in the denominator of the present value equation.)

4. a. The answer is found as $100 \div (1 + 0.06)^1 = $100 \div 1.06$.

5. a. The answer is found as $100 \div (1 + 0.06)^2 = $100 \div 1.1236$.

6. c. This is the sum of the answers to questions 4 and 5.

7. d. When the payments are to be received each year forever, use the asset formula given in the text ($100 \div 0.06$).

8. c. It would fall with the interest rate, it would fall if further into the future, and would only be worth $90.91 if the interest rate was 10 percent.

9. b. It also applies to investing in your education (human capital) in the same manner as for an investment in physical capital.

10. d. A government law holding the interest rate below equilibrium would reduce the quantity of savings and increase the quantity of loans demanded. There would be a shortage of money available for loan.

11. c. The value of an asset is the discounted present value of future profits. This present value falls immediately.

12. c. Growth requires high investment (and thus high savings), but it also requires that the money is invested in the most beneficial and productive activities (the function of a capital market).

13. a. These are listed in the book as the items leading to economic profit.

14. d. All of these would lower present value (lower interest rate, fewer years of repayment, and less increase in earnings).

15. a. We prefer shorter time until acquisition of an item.

16. b. Answer c refers to pure interest yield, a slightly different concept.

17. a. the difference between 10 percent and 7 percent

18. b. Pure interest is the nonrisk component.

19. b. The present value of these three payments added together is approximately $8,170 (found as $[\$3,000 \div (1 + 0.05)^1] + [\$3,000 \div (1 + 0.05)^2] + [\$3,000 \div (1 + 0.05)^3]$).

20. d. The resulting present value is greater than the project's current cost for any interest rate less than 5.4 percent. (Hint: There is no simple way of working this, you must try several different values to find the answer.)

21. c. At an interest rate of 10 percent, the value of an asset generating $15,000 per year is $15,000 ÷ 0.10 = $150,000.

CHAPTER FIFTEEN

TRUE OR FALSE

The following are true: 1, 2, 4, 5, 6, 7, 9, 12, 14

The following are false:

3. Only one in five millionaires in the United States inherited their fortunes.

8. Means-tested income transfer programs are the only programs for which eligibility is dependent upon having a low income status. Less than one-fourth of government income transfers are means-tested.

10. While cash benefits are counted as income, in-kind benefits are not.

11. It is just the opposite. Transfer payments to the poor reduce the cost of choices that lead to poverty.

13. Despite a rather large growth in transfer payments, income inequality and poverty among the nonelderly have risen.

PROBLEMS AND PROJECTS

1. a. $7,568; $7,448; $9,229
    b. $5,509; will fall by $120 (from $7,568 to $7,448)
    c. Less. The $2,000 cost of transportation and child care exceeds the increase in disposable income of $1,661 ($9,229 − $7,568).
    d. $120 less in 1984 ($7,448 − $7,568); $2,109 more in 1994 ($9,657 − $7,548).
    e. $1,661 more in 1984 ($9,229 − $7,568); $3,389 more in 1994 ($10,937 − $7,548).
    f. Increased her incentive to work.

2. a. B
    b. C
    c. F
    d. H
    e. They would be the same. While most people would think country I should be considered to have more inequality, this is a drawback of traditional income distribution statistics based upon annual income data.

3. a. 6.7 percent; more likely to fall than remain (42 percent remained, so 58 percent fell).
    b. 46 percent; 2.7 percent; more likely to rise than remain (46 percent remained, so 54 percent rose).
    c. 20.2 percent; 44.4 percent (18.2 + 26.2); 35.4 percent (21.8 + 13.6).
    d. 12.3 percent (2.7 + 9.6); 15.9 percent (6.7 + 9.2).
    e. 43.4 percent (10.8 + 6.7 + 16.7 + 9.2); 35.3 percent (9.6 + 14.3 + 2.7 + 8.7).

MULTIPLE CHOICE

1. a. There has been steadily rising income inequality since the 1970s.

2. b. Lifetime income is distributed much more equally than annual income.

3. d. Only money income is counted.

4. d. All of these have contributed to the rise in income inequality.

5. c. Income is determined by resources supplied. This income is created by the individuals who supply the resources.

6. a. These are the reasons why large transfer programs can actually lead to more poverty.

7. c. The others would be the same given the statement in the question. Even if we all earned the same identical amount at each age, it would not be the case that different people who are different ages would earn the same amount.

8. b. Only money income is counted.

9. a. The poverty threshold for this family would be $16,400. It is adjusted for family size and inflation.

10. c. This is a major shortcoming of income distribution statistics based upon annual incomes at any one point in time.

11. d. All of these are true.

12. b. When more persons in a family work, that family will have higher income.

13. b.   It fell from the 1950s to the 1970s but has risen ever since.

14. a.   In net, taxes and transfers raise the disposable income of the poor and lower the disposable income of the nonpoor.

15. b.   Some data on this is given in the book.

16. b.   Because of substantial income mobility, lifetime income is more equally distributed than annual income.

17. c.   They both are true. The data is given in the book.

18. b.   It reduces the incentive to work and earn just like having high marginal income tax rates.

19. c.   Because they have lost one-half of their income in the form of reduced benefits.

20. a.   This is the definition of the Samaritan's dilemma.

21. d.   There is a more unequal distribution of income, a higher poverty rate among the nonelderly and more single-parent families.

CHAPTER SIXTEEN

TRUE OR FALSE

The following are true: 3, 4, 5, 6, 8, 11, 12, 13

The following are false:

1. Both countries benefit from free trade.

2. Specific domestic producers of goods that are imported may "lose," and domestic consumers of goods that are exported may "lose," but in both cases the gains of the "winners" outweigh the losses to the "losers."

7. Even countries with an absolute advantage in all goods can gain by trading for goods in which they have a comparative disadvantage.

9. Jobs would be lost in the industries that were protected by the tariffs, but they would be more than offset by gains in other industries.

10. NAFTA has resulted in trade expansions that have benefited all three countries involved.

PROBLEMS AND PROJECTS

1. a. For Lebos, a line from 160 food and zero clothing (point E) in the upper left to zero food and 160 clothing (point A) in the lower right. For Egap, a line from 40 food and zero clothing (point E) in the upper left to zero food and 120 clothing (point A) in the lower right.
    b. D; 40 food; 40 clothing; 40F = 40C
    c. 10 food; 30 clothing; 10F = 30C
    d. Lebos: 1F = 1C; Egap: 1F = 3C; Lebos gives up the least clothing to produce one food and thus has a comparative advantage in food. In terms of one clothing, Lebos: 1C = 1F, Egap: 1C = 1/3F, so Egap has the lowest opportunity cost of producing clothing.
    e. 40 clothing (point D) for Lebos; zero clothing (point E) for Egap
    f. 160; 40; 80
    g. Compared with part e, Lebos has the same amount of food (120) but has more clothing (80 versus 40). Lebos is better off.

    h. From part g, Egap has sent Lebos 80 clothing in exchange for 40 food. So, Egap now has 40 clothing left (it produced 120 and traded away 80) and 40 food. Compared with e, Egap has the same amount of food (40) but more clothing (40 versus zero). Egap is better off.

2. a. $1,500 and 8,000 (where Arcadia's quantity demanded equals Arcadia's quantity supplied)
    b. Total quantity demanded: 6,000; 8,000; 10,000; 12,000; 14,000; 16,000. New equilibrium $2,000 and 10,000 (where total quantity demanded equals Arcadia's quantity supplied).
    c. Price has risen from $1,500 to $2,000; quantity produced has risen from 8,000 to 10,000; quantity of other goods must have fallen (moved along production possibilities curve).
    d. At the new price of $2,000, Arcadians demand only 7,000 compared with 8,000 prior to trade and the higher price. With trade, Arcadia exports 3,000 computers (it produces 10,000 and domestic consumers buy 7,000 of them leaving 3,000 for exports).
    e. hurts domestic citizens (higher price and lower consumption) and helps domestic producers (higher price and higher sales)

3. a. $700; 70; 70
    b. $500 is the new price; 90 is the quantity demanded (consumed); 90 is the total quantity supplied; 50 is supplied by domestic suppliers (found along the domestic supply curve); 40 is imported (the difference between total supply of 90 and domestic supply of 50).
    c. Price rises to $600; quantity demanded (and consumed) falls to 80; domestic production expands to 60; amount imported falls to 20.
    d. Everything would be identical with a 20-unit quota as it is with the tariff.

4. a. U.S.; U.S.; South Korea; U.S.
    b. South Korea
    c. U.S. production: −8; +80
        U.S. trade: +10; −50
        U.S. consumption: +2; +30
        S. Korea production: +16; −32
        S. Korea trade: −10; +50
        S. Korea consumption: +6; +18

MULTIPLE CHOICE

1. d. Restrictions on imports create benefits only to domestic producers in the import competing industries. Consumers and producers in export industries are made worse off. The losses outweigh the gains and the country is worse off.

2. c. Buy goods abroad when they are cheaper than alternative domestic products.

3. b. It will fall by 4 units from a total of 8 to a total of 4.

4. c. From above 2 food equals 4 clothing. Dividing both sides by 2 gives 1 food equals 2 clothing.

5. b. Slavia has the comparative advantage in food, Italia in clothing. Remember that low opportunity cost producer and comparative advantage mean the same thing.

6. d. Slavia specializes in food, Italia in clothing, and they trade.

7. b. With free trade, all nations that are involved benefit.

8. a. This is a restatement of the law of comparative advantage.

9. d. They are both levied on imports. A tariff is a tax, while a quota is a limit on the quantity.

10. a. With less foreign competition, the price to domestic consumers will rise, which allows the relatively inefficient U.S. firms to stay in business with their higher costs.

11. a. There is a link between a nation's imports and its exports. Imports give foreign countries the money to buy domestic exports. Lower imports mean lower exports.

12. b. They are harmful by wasting our resources in areas where we are relatively unproductive, thus lowering our standard of living. Consumers pay higher prices for goods (and thus cannot afford as many goods to consume), and only domestic producers in the specific industries gain (producers in export industries suffer).

13. c. Many tariffs originally put in place to protect infant industries remain in place forever. It is always politically costly to remove the tariff because of the special interest groups involved.

14. b. The evidence shows that these bad economic policies lead to lower levels of income and economic growth in the long run.

15. b. Consumers will benefit from lower prices; our resources will be redirected to more efficient uses.

16. a. Increased competition lowers price; increased imports generate higher exports.

17. d. Domestic producers would want to stop this action even though domestic consumers would gain substantially. Dumping is selling goods at prices below cost.

18. c. Foreign competition lowers price, which lowers domestic quantity supplied.

19. b. Higher demand raises price, lowering domestic consumption but increasing domestic production (the difference is exported).

20. c. This is the *basic* lesson of comparative advantage.

21. c. The other three are listed in the textbook as "partially valid" reasons for adopting trade restrictions. Their validity is hotly debated.

22. a. Use a horizontal line at P_W to find the answers. Domestic supply is where this line crosses the domestic supply curve, while domestic consumption is where the horizontal line crosses domestic demand. The difference between these values $(100 - 30 = 70)$ is the value of imports.

23. d. All are correct. Use a horizontal line at $P_W + t$ to find these values as is described in the answer for question 22.

24. d. All are correct. A + B + C + D represents the loss in consumer surplus, C the revenue to the government, and A the gain in producer surplus (domestic).

25. a. A quota equal to the new level of imports with the tariff (30 units) would produce the same price and level of imports.

CHAPTER SEVENTEEN

TRUE OR FALSE

The following are true: 1, 2, 8, 10, 11, 12

The following are false:

3. A balance-of-payments equilibrium is automatic under purely *flexible* exchange rates. With fixed exchange rates, central banks must buy and sell foreign currency to maintain balance.

4. The exchange rate will move to ensure a balance-of-payments equilibrium.

5. The foreign exchange market is ruled by supply and demand as is any other market.

6. Black markets in foreign currency arise when the official exchange rate differs substantially from the exchange rate that would be set by the market.

7. When a country's balance of trade is in deficit, its current account is nearly always in deficit as well. However, the balance of payments must always balance to zero so this implies a capital account surplus.

9. When the U.S. imports more than it exports, Americans are able to consume more than they otherwise would. The long-term desirability of a trade deficit depends on the underlying causes of the trade deficit.

13. The IMF is an international banking organization. It does not control the world supply of money, however, it does hold currency reserves for member nations and makes currency loans to national central banks.

PROBLEMS AND PROJECTS

1. a. 38,018 German Marks [$20,000 × 1.9009 or $20,000 ÷ 0.52607]
   b. 23.529 U.S. dollars [150 × 0.15686 or 150 ÷ 6.3753]
   c. 132,103.19 French francs [2,500,000 ÷ 120.65 × 6.3753]
   d. 18.9246 [120.65 ÷ 6.3753] yen per franc, or 0.05284 francs per yen, which is exactly what the

true exchange rate was between these two currencies on this date.
   e. The Mark has depreciated, the yen has appreciated, and the pound depreciated.

2. b. 0, −, depreciate
   c. −, +, appreciate
   d. +, −, depreciate
   e. −, +, appreciate
   f. +, +, indeterminate (could either appreciate or depreciate)
   g. 0, 0, no change

3. a. (1) –25.3; (2) 36.1; (3) 3.7; (4) 4.5; (5) 8.2
   b. The official reserve account must run a deficit of 8.2.
   c. There has been a rising current account deficit and a rising capital account surplus to offset it. The causes are discussed in the text, but likely the combination of restrictive monetary policy and expansionary fiscal policy (large budget deficits) has caused this change.

MULTIPLE CHOICE

1. d. One dollar now buys more yen, and one yen now buys fewer dollars.

2. b. Capital would leave the U.S. and flow toward England, thus an increase in the supply of dollars and an increase in the demand for the pound. The others would cause an appreciation of the dollar.

3. b. Every dollar traded results in obtaining 6 Marks, so 20,000 U.S. dollars would exchange for 120,000 Marks.

4. d. All would either reduce the supply of dollars or increase the demand for dollars, leading to an appreciation of the dollar.

5. b. If the dollar depreciates, it exchanges for fewer units of foreign currency. Foreign goods become more expensive to U.S. citizens, and U.S. goods become less expensive to foreigners.

6. b. The expansion in the supply of dollars will cause a depreciation, making exports less expensive and imports more expensive.

7. d. Flexible exchange rates make the balance-of-payments accounts automatically balance.

8. c. A trade deficit is when imports exceed exports.

9. a. The others would supply the foreign currency and create a demand for dollars.

10. d. This combination appreciates the dollar and draws a capital inflow, see the discussion in the book for more detail.

11. b. The trade deficit is not an obligation or a government account. It is simply an aggregate number, such as the number of people who migrated out of (or into) your state this year. The balance of payments must balance, so a current account deficit means a capital account surplus.

12. c. Otherwise, the free market value will differ substantially from the official value causing major balance of payments and official reserve problems.

13. b. Cheaper foreign currency means cheaper foreign goods and services.

14. d. Demand for foreign currency will rise and the supply of foreign currency will fall as investors in all countries shift investment to foreign countries. The domestic currency depreciates as a result.

15. a. An increase in supply (of anything) tends to decrease price (cause depreciation).

16. b. Depreciation makes foreign goods more expensive and domestic goods cheaper.

17. b. Increased exports of U.S. wine and fewer imports of French wine would reduce the trade deficit and thus also reduce the current account deficit.

18. a. Higher real interest rates lead to an increased demand for U.S. assets and an increased demand for U.S. dollars in order to buy those assets.

19. b. Higher prices raise demand for foreign exchange (imports) and lower supply (exports).

20. c. Higher prices and output cause depreciation, while higher interest rates cause appreciation, but all induce a deficit in the current account.

APPLICATION ONE

TRUE OR FALSE

The following are true: 1, 3, 4, 6, 7, 8, 10, 11

The following are false:

2. Their economies have not been in recessions, and their rates of inflation have been low and steady. These are not causing the difference in unemployment rates.

5. They make labor markets less flexible and cause higher rates of unemployment.

9. Higher benefits encourage longer spells of unemployment and thus raise the unemployment rate.

PROBLEMS AND PROJECTS

1. a. +
   b. −
   c. −

2. a. Japan, United States
   b. Japan, United States
   c. Japan, United States
   d. Japan, United States
   e. They are the same. The countries with the lowest unemployment rates (Japan and the United States) also have the lowest unemployment benefits, the lowest collective bargaining, and the least restrictive government policies on dismissal.
   f. Spain, France
   g. France, Germany
   h. Italy, Spain
   i. France, Spain
   j. The countries with the two highest unemployment rates (Spain and France) also tend to have high values for these other variables; high unemployment benefits seem to be the most highly correlated.

MULTIPLE CHOICE

1. c. The United States had the lowest unemployment rate of the countries listed.

2. d. The difference is not the result of these factors but is rather due to structural factors in the labor markets differing.

3. d. All of them had higher unemployment rates.

4. d. Almost the entire labor force has wages set by collective bargaining.

5. d. The United States just slightly beats out Japan as having the lowest percent.

6. a. France has the highest, with a replacement rate of 38 percent.

7. c. Smaller countries have less adverse effects, but in general, higher degrees of centralized wage setting raise unemployment rates.

8. a. It raises the cost of replacing long-time workers with new workers.

9. d. Higher levels of these factors tend to raise unemployment rates.

10. c. The replacement rate is the percent of previous income that is replaced by the unemployment benefits ($600 ÷ $1,000 = 60 percent).

11. d. Higher levels of these factors tend to raise unemployment rates. The United States and Japan have much lower unemployment rates.

12. a. The lowering of benefits has reduced the unemployment rate.

APPLICATION TWO

TRUE OR FALSE

The following are true: 2, 3, 6, 7, 8, 9, 11, 13.

The following are false:

1. The system takes the current tax revenue and pays it out to current retirees. Only recently has Social Security began to save a fraction of current revenue in anticipation of the retirement of the baby boom generation.

4. Current workers will fare much worse than those before them.

5. A worker aged thirty-five can expect a rate of return of about 2 percent, about one-fourth that of an average stock market return.

10. Ninety percent of workers switched and now have retirement funds 50 to 70 percent larger than they would have if they would have remained in the government system.

12. In the middle income ranges, a worker's benefits rise by only 15 percent of their additional average annual earnings. So if worker A's average annual earnings are $10,000 greater than worker B's, worker A will receive only $1,500 more in annual benefits than worker B.

PROBLEMS AND PROJECTS

1. a. Taxes of $1,000 per worker would support a benefit level of $15,000 per retiree in the 1950s.
   b. Taxes of $5,000 per worker would support a benefit level of $15,000 per retiree in 1998.
   c. Taxes of $7,500 per worker would support a benefit level of $15,000 per retiree in 2025.
   d. Benefits would have to be cut from $15,000 to $10,000 per retiree.

2. a. Yes, technically you have savings of $5,000, and your spouse has a debt of $5,000.
   b. Your spouse would have to run a "surplus" (spend less than he or she earns) to repay the money.
   c. It is the same. The Social Security trust fund holds U.S. Treasury bonds, which will have to be repaid by the federal government (either through higher taxes or spending cuts in other areas) when Social Security needs to use the money in the trust fund. In essence, it is no different that if the surplus had never been saved.

3. a. At 1.8 percent, the money would have doubled once by age sixty-five, so you would have only $40,000 instead of $320,000. While this is an oversimplified problem, the amount is similar to the real difference, which amounts to about $200,000 for the average baby boomer.
   b. At 3.6 percent, the money would double every twenty years. So $20,000 invested at age twenty-five would grow to $40,000 at age forty-five and to $80,000 at age sixty-five. This is double the amount that would be present at a 1.8 percent return ($80,000 versus $40,000).
   c. The economy would be double its current size.
   d. $160,000; $240,000; $20,000; $40,000

MULTIPLE CHOICE

1. c. This is what is meant by a pay-as-you-go system.

2. d. The ratio was sixteen workers per retiree in the 1950s, three workers per retiree in 1998, and will fall to two workers per retiree by 2025.

3. c. By using the trust fund to purchase bonds, the money was available for the government to spend on other current programs. When these bonds come due, the federal government will have to repay this money it has borrowed from the Social Security trust fund.

4. b.. This is when Social Security will begin to draw down the trust fund.

5. b. This is when the trust fund money will have been completely used.

6. d. A young worker today is expected to earn a negative real rate of return on their contributions, meaning that the real value of the benefits received will be less than the real value of the taxes paid.

7. a. These are essentially IOUs from the federal government that will have to be repaid in the future.

8. b.   To repay the bonds, the government will have to either raise taxes or cut spending.

9. d.   These are the only options available besides substantial reform.

10. c.   Above this level of income, total annual Social Security taxes remain constant.

11. b.   Between average annual income levels of $32,000 and $65,000, a worker's benefits rise by approximately 15 percent of additional annual earnings.

12. c.   A spouse can collect benefits based upon either their own average annual salary, or 50 percent of their spouse's average annual salary. A married woman who does not work will receive the same benefits as if she had worked and earned an average annual salary equal to 50 percent of her husband's.

13. d.   These are fears that the political pressures present in government decision making will interfere with the soundness of the investments.

14. a.   All of the other countries have taken steps toward privatization.

15. c.   The vast majority of workers left the government system and can now expect much higher retirement benefits as a result.

APPLICATION THREE

TRUE OR FALSE

The following are true: 2, 3, 4, 6, 9, 10

The following are false:

1. Real returns have averaged 11.7 percent, far greater than the 7 percent long-term average.

5. These will generally lead to good performance of the stock market.

7. The highest returns with the least risk are made by holding a diversified portfolio of stocks over a long period of time.

8. This is a subject of debate, but no solid economic evidence supports this view.

11. They are buying ownership rights in the assets of a corporation.

PROBLEMS AND PROJECTS

1. a. decrease
   b. increase
   c. increase

2. a. $173.55 = (\$100 \div (1.10)^1) + (\$100 \div (1.10)^2)$
   b. $185.94 = (\$100 \div (1.05)^1) + (\$100 \div (1.05)^2)$
   c. $177.69 = (\$150 \div (1.10)^1) + (\$50 \div (1.10)^2)$
   d. $260.33 = (\$100 \div (1.10)^1) + (\$150 \div (1.10)^2)$
   e. $214.88 = (\$150 \div (1.10)^1) + (\$150 \div (1.10)^2)$

MULTIPLE CHOICE

1. a. Answers b and c would increase risk.

2. c. Both will lower risk.

3. c. This is even true compared to investing in U.S. Treasury bonds.

4. c. Both are true.

5. b. The recent good performance of the stock market has been partially due to the opposite case.

6. b. The others are the opposite of what is true.

7. b. Answers a and c are opposite of what is true.

8. d. The random walk theory is consistent with all of the statements.

9. d. The others are the opposite of what is true.

10. b. Real returns have averaged 11.7 percent, far greater than the 7 percent long-term average.

APPLICATION FOUR

TRUE OR FALSE

The following are true: 2, 7, 8, 11.

The following are false:

1. Traditional economic regulation began in the late 1800s.

3. Regulations tend to be very inflexible, causing problems when they become outdated by changing market conditions.

4. Just the opposite. With time, they tend to come to reflect the interest of the business firms in the industry they regulate at the expense of consumers.

5. Higher production costs will reduce supply, causing the price to rise to consumers.

6. The cost for private parties (such as business firms, consumers, and individuals) to comply with the regulations far exceeds the budgets of these agencies. This expense is not compensated by government.

9. The recent emphasis has been on health and safety regulation and away from traditional economic regulation.

10. Cars are approximately five hundred pounds lighter, thus resulting in more fatalities in automobile accidents.

PROBLEMS AND PROJECTS

1. a. 330 [$7,600,000 ÷ $23,000]
    b. toward the FAA or some of the other agencies with very low cost per life year saved
    c. They should all be equal.

2. a. +
    b. +
    c. +
    d. +
    e. ? (New cars don't pollute, but they would be so expensive most people would continue to keep driving their old cars much longer than they otherwise would have. Without the regulation, many of these people would have bought newer cars that would still have polluted but would have polluted less than their old cars.)

MULTIPLE CHOICE

1. d. Unlike health and safety regulation, traditional economic regulation does not directly regulate the production process.

2. c. The added production cost acts similarly to a tax imposed on the industry.

3. c. These are both shortcomings of regulation through the political process.

4. d. Both *a* and *c* would benefit the natural gas industry, but *b* would not.

5. b. This is how it is modeled in a supply and demand diagram.

6. b. It is difficult to estimate how the benefits created compare to the costs.

7. a. With fewer homes available in the area (and also the lure of a home in a less crowded area), the price of the existing homes would rise.

8. d. All of these are true statements.

9. d. These are all shortcomings of regulation through the political process.

10. b. The deaths created when a defective product is released too soon will be very visible, while the deaths created by delaying the release of a beneficial product are generally not as visible.

11. a. This is how it is modeled in a supply and demand diagram.

12. b. This is a result produced from the standard competitive model. The industry will return to zero economic profit in the long run.

13. a. The average weight fell by five hundred pounds, making cars less safe when they were in accidents.

14. d. Compared to other agencies, the EPA has very large costs relative to the benefits created. These same resources could save more lives in other areas.

APPLICATION FIVE

TRUE OR FALSE

The following are true: 1, 2, 4, 5, 8, 9, 10.

The following are false:

3. It has risen substantially from 14.9 percent in 1970 to 19.2 percent in 1997.

6. When they remain out of the workforce, their skills depreciate making them less employable.

7. Welfare caseloads fell by 37 percent between 1993 and 1998.

PROBLEMS AND PROJECTS

1. a. Change in Earned Income: $2,000; $2,000; $2,000; $2,000
    Change in Net Transfer Benefits: −$1,633; −$1,633; −$1,701; −$1,019
    Implicit Marginal Tax Rate: 81.7 percent; 81.7 percent; 85.1 percent; 51.0 percent
   b. $6,000 to $8,000; $299 ($9,956 − $9,657)
   c. $3,389 ($10,937 − $7,548); child-care expenses for her two children and transportation costs to and from work combined might exceed this amount. After all, $3,389 per year is only $65 per week.
   d. Yes. She would have $11,048 ($3,500 + $7,548) of disposable income instead of $10,937.

2. Case 2: 50 percent; 30 percent; 20 percent
   Case 3: 45 percent; 30 percent; 25 percent
   Case 4: 55 percent; 30 percent; 15 percent
   a. Case 4 is the most unequal; Case 3 is the most equal.
   b. same; all have more money income
   c. more equal; all have less money income
   d. less equal; all have more money income
   e. All would prefer case 4 as all have the highest money income in that case.
   f. No, distributions reflect percentages of income, and not the true level of income. It is possible for all incomes to rise, or for all incomes to fall, when the distribution becomes either more or less unequal. There is no clear relationship.

3. a. The rich in State A would move to State B. The poor from State B would move to State A. So State A will have a higher proportion of poor, and State B a higher proportion of rich.
   b. State A will not raise as much revenue and will not be able to afford as high a level of benefits.
   c. In the extreme, all the richer people are in one state and all of the poorer people are in the other. So each state will have a more equal distribution of income.
   d. It will lower it, just as in the case where the rich move to the other state.

MULTIPLE CHOICE

1. b. Transfer spending has doubled, the overall poverty rate is virtually unchanged. However, the poverty rate among certain groups, such as children, has changed significantly.

2. c. It was 13.3 percent.

3. d. In real terms, average income per person rose from $14,936 in 1965 to $27,138 in 1997.

4. a. These are two of the negative side effects caused by transfer programs.

5. c. The poverty rate of children has risen.

6. d. Only a and b are part of the legislation.

7. d. Welfare caseloads fell by 37 percent between 1993 and 1998, with a 2 million reduction in the initial year after the federal reform in 1996. Many states, however, had begun their policies earlier.

8. d. Recipients of transfers or subsidies will devote resources to obtaining the money that lowers their net gain.

9. a. When a subsidy is tied to an asset, the value of the asset will rise to fully reflect the value of the subsidy.

10. d. These have all been proposed, but opponents think each of these will instead harm the lower-income individuals whom the policy is trying to help.

11. d. Opponents stress that a fair process is more important than the outcome produced and that high tax and transfer rates reduce the total economic pie.

APPLICATION SIX

TRUE OR FALSE

The following are true: 2, 3, 4, 5, 8.

The following are false:

1. Union membership has continuously declined over this period.

6. A much higher proportion of male workers are union members.

7. It is one of the least unionized.

9. The southern states tend to have the lowest rates of union membership.

10. While unions increase the wages of their members, they probably end up decreasing the wages of nonunion workers because of the expanded supply of workers in the nonunion sector.

PROBLEMS AND PROJECTS

1. a. +
    b. −
    c. +
    d. −
    e. Higher wages increase tuition, lowering enrollment, and thus the university needs fewer professors. In addition, the university will substitute away from labor to other factors of production (say building new buildings with larger classrooms), which will further reduce the number of professors needed by the university.

2. a. 3, +
    b. 1, −
    c. 3, +
    d. 2, −
    e. 3, +
    f. 1, −

MULTIPLE CHOICE

1. b. The others are all opposites of what is true.

2. d. There has been a decrease in the desire of workers to form unions.

3. c. The others are the three listed in the book. A union wage increase makes a firm less competitive because it must raise price to cover the added cost of labor.

4. b. Right-to-work laws forbid union shop contracts.

5. a. When only one firm raises prices, their sales fall substantially as consumers switch to substitute products. When all firms in an industry raise price, consumers cannot as easily avoid the higher prices caused by union wage increases.

6. b. When union labor becomes more expensive, firms will use less union labor and more of substitute inputs such as machines and nonunion labor.

7. b. But the percentage differs substantially between industries and occupations.

8. a. Since the 1950s, it has fallen in half.

9. b. Consumers do not like to pay high prices. Whenever competition is present, consumers will switch to nonunion products, limiting the ability of the union to increase wages.

10. c. The evidence shows no linkage between unionization and the share of national income going to labor.

11. a. When there are no good substitutes, it will be hard for the firm to switch to other inputs to avoid paying the higher wages.

12. c. This is known as the union wage premium.

APPLICATION SEVEN

TRUE OR FALSE

The following are true: 1, 2, 7, 8, 9, 10.

The following are false:

3. Market incentives and private ownership improve conservation. One study cited in the book found that market economies use less than half as much energy per unit of output produced.

4. Opportunity costs are equally important in decisions involving natural resources and energy.

5. The evidence suggests that resource scarcity has fallen over the past century, and as a result, most real resource prices are much lower than in the past.

6. The "crisis" originally began when OPEC (the oil cartel) greatly restricted the supply of oil; it was made into a real crisis by government price controls and regulations that worsened the situation.

PROBLEMS AND PROJECTS

1. a. 30.9 years worth of supply "remained" (185.6 ÷ 6.0). So we "should" have run out of natural gas in about 1981!
   b. Proved reserves are only the amount that is known to exist and can be extracted at current (here 1950) prices and technology. New finds, better technology, and higher prices increased proved reserves.
   c. While total proved reserves are falling, they are not falling by nearly as much as they would have if no new proved reserves were found. Because consumption was about 100 trillion, while reserves fell by only 4 trillion, approximately 96 trillion of new reserves were found during this five-year period. The rate of increase in proved reserves has been just slightly less than the rate of consumption.
   d. The price of natural gas more than tripled, and consumption fell as a result. Because demand is more elastic in the long run, consumption continued to decline past the change in the price.

e. Price fell and consumption rose between 1990 and 1995. Overall since 1970, the real price has fallen suggesting that natural gas is relatively less scarce than it was in 1970.
   f. The correct answer is never, even though the data "tell" us that there is only a 7.6 year's supply remaining!

2. a. They correspond very well to the price data. There was a large price jump between 1970 and 1980, and this is when usage fell the most. The price almost was the same in 1960 and 1970, and usage of homes built in these periods was almost the same as well.
   b. The higher prices have provided an incentive for new homes to be built using more electric power instead of natural gas. In addition, they have provided an incentive to spend more on making the home more energy efficient (insulation, thicker windows, etc.), reducing overall energy consumption by homes.
   c. This is almost entirely due to the incentives created by market prices. When homeowners began receiving very high fuel bills for using natural gas, they wanted to switch to electric to save their own money, not in an effort to "save" the remaining supply of natural gas!
   d. Yes, except for prior to the 1960s. The recent changes correspond fairly well.

3. a. A movement from point A to B caused price to rise from P_1 to P_2 and quantity to fall from Q_1 to Q_2 in the short run.
   b. A movement from point A to C caused price to rise from P_1 to P_3 and quantity to fall from Q_1 to Q_3 in the long run. Relative to the short run, the price in the long run falls from P_2 to P_3, and quantity falls further from Q_2 to Q_3.
   c. There is a greater reduction in quantity used in the long run. Demand is always more elastic in the long run because it takes time for people to fully adjust to a change.

4. a. –
   b. –
   c. +
   d. +

MULTIPLE CHOICE

1. c. Both producers and consumers have more time to adjust and find substitutes in the long run.

2. c. They ignore the increased finding and extraction of reserves and the reduction in consumption, which results from the higher prices that occur as a resource is depleted.

3. a. Market incentives and private ownership improve conservation. One study cited in the book found that market economies use less than half as much energy per unit of output produced.

4. d. All of these affect how much energy a person consumes.

5. b. This is simply the idea that demand becomes more elastic with time because a larger number of substitutes become available (more time to adjust).

6. b. Because anyone can buy or sell them (regardless of whether they want to use the resource or conserve it), everyone can alter resource consumption patterns.

7. d. These are a few of the beneficial incentives created by private ownership listed in the book.

8. b. Establishing private property rights is an extremely effective way to protect resources.

9. c. These are the poor incentives created by the act discussed in the book.

10. d. This is a definition and is the reason why doomsday predictions using this data are wrong.

11. a. For example, in 1926 the U.S. government informed people that the supply of oil would last only another seven years. These types of predictions happen very frequently but have never come true.

12. d. Market prices provide the proper incentives to find more and use less of the resource when its price rises due to an increase in relative scarcity.

13. a. The real prices of most resources continue to decline, suggesting that supply is growing faster than demand. These resources are thus becoming relatively less scarce.

14. c. The act changed the incentives people faced and caused harmful, unintended, secondary effects.

APPLICATION EIGHT

TRUE OR FALSE

The following are true: 3, 4, 6, 10.

The following are false:

1. The rising incomes and better technology associated with economic growth increase some problems but lower others. In sum the net effect is that environmental quality generally rises as economic growth happens.

2. Private ownership in England had lead to much higher quality than in the United States.

5. Value is subjective. You might be willing to pay $50 to have a cleaner river, but this does not mean that everyone else is willing to pay the same amount.

7. The debate over global warming is far from being settled. There is debate not only over whether it will happen or not, but also over the effects it would bring if it does ever happen.

8. The *lack* of private ownership is the major problem.

9. Government regulation often has unintended secondary effects and cannot respond to changing market conditions. It is thus inferior to establishing private property rights in most cases.

PROBLEMS AND PROJECTS

1. a. Column 2 only.
    b. Column 1 only.
    c. Yes, the animals that are going extinct are the ones that the government has forbid private ownership of.
    d. Cows, pigs, and chicken are slaughtered at rates hundreds of times greater than any other animals, but are the ones that are the least subject to extinction. Indeed it is their value to humans for consumption that provides the incentive to breed them and keep massive numbers of them alive.
    e. The ranchers who own and kill cattle for beef are identical to those who would kill elephants for ivory. The only difference is in the ownership. If

ivory poachers could own the elephants, they would breed them so that they do not go extinct. After all, if the elephants go extinct, the poachers are out of income, just like if a cattle rancher killed all of his cattle.

2. a. The Audubon Society does this to generate more revenue with which to buy additional lands to preserve. Yes, both parties are better off.
    b. They only allow drilling during certain times of the year, and also only if it will create very little (or no) lasting damage to the environment.
    c. No. Because the cost of the road exceeded the value of the timber, it would not have been profitable to do so.
    d. Yes. Yes. It is $5 million cheaper for the environmental group, and $5 million more profitable for the oil company.

3. a. decrease
    b. increase; decrease
    c. increase

MULTIPLE CHOICE

1. b. This is why growth leads to more spending on environmental protection.

2. c. This would increase their profitability for years to come and would raise the value of the corporation.

3. d. These are a few of the key points in this application chapter.

4. b. Market institutions (private property rights and market determined prices) and better technology are both beneficial to the environment.

5. a. Poor countries' main worries are about food and clothing and other necessities. They have little money left to spend on luxury items such as environmental quality.

6. a. See the opening quote for this application chapter in the book.

7. c. A private owner would be able to sue others for damages to their property.

8. b. When possible, establishing private property rights is a better solution than the others.

9. d. Environmental quality is a good like any other.

10. d. All of this is under debate and is far from being settled conclusively.